# SNOWSHOE ROUTES

## Colorado's Front Range

# SNOWSHOE ROUTES
## Colorado's Front Range

ALAN APT

THE
MOUNTAINEERS
BOOKS

Published by
The Mountaineers Books
1001 SW Klickitat Way, Suite 201
Seattle, WA 98134

First edition, 2001

Published simultaneously in Great Britain by Cordee, 3a DeMontfort Street, Leicester, England, LE1 7HD

Manufactured in the United States of America

Project Editor: Julie Van Pelt
Editor: Kris Fulsaas
Cover and Book Design: The Mountaineers Books
Layout Artist: Kristy L. Welch
Mapmaker: Jennifer LaRock Shontz
Photographer: Alan Apt unless otherwise noted

Cover photograph: *Man out snowshoeing, Quandery Peak, CO* © Todd Powell/Index Stock Imagery
Frontispiece: *Enjoying a light snow in Rocky Mountain National Park*
Page 39: *Medicine Bow Mountains*
Page 119: *From Glacier Basin Campground near Sprague Lake*
Page 157: *From Camp Dick Campground along Middle Saint Vrain Creek*
Page 185: *Saint Marys Glacier*
Page 195: *South Park from Kenosha Pass*

*Library of Congress Cataloging-in-Publication Data*
Apt, Alan, 1948-
  Snowshoe routes : Colorado's Front Range / by Alan Apt.— 1st ed.
     p. cm.
Includes bibliographical references.
  ISBN 0-89886-832-7 (pbk.)
  1.  Snowshoes and snowshoeing—Colorado—Guidebooks. 2.
Trails—Colorado—Guidebooks. 3.  Colorado—Guidebooks. I. Title.
  GV853 .A68 2001
  917.88'60434—dc21
                            2001004263

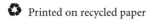

# Contents

*Preface* • *10*
*Acknowledgements* • *11*
*Introduction: The Snowshoe Revolution* • *13*

**NORTHERN COLORADO**
*Chapter 1. Red Feather Lakes Area*
   1. Mount Margaret • 41
   2. Beaver Meadows Resort Trails and Trappers Pass • 44
   3. Deadman Road and North Lone Pine Trail • 48

*Chapter 2. Poudre Canyon*
   4. Mineral Spring Gulch • 52
   5. Crown Point Road • 53
   6. Little Beaver Creek Trail • 55
   7. Signal Mountain • 57
   8. Stormy Peaks Trail • 59
   9. Cirque Meadows and Emmaline Lake • 62
  10. Big South Trail • 64
  11. Green Ridge Road • 65
  12. Blue Lake • 68
  13. Sawmill Creek • 70
  14. Long Draw Road • 72
  15. Trap Park • 75
  16. Zimmerman Lake and Meadows Trail • 76
  17. Montgomery Pass • 79
  18. Cameron Connection • 81

*Chapter 3. Colorado State Forest*
  19. Michigan Ditch, American Lakes, and Thunder Pass Trails • 85
  20. Lake Agnes • 88

21. Seven Utes Mountain and Mount Mahler  •  89
22. Ranger Lakes and Silver Creek  •  93
23. Grass Creek Yurt Trails  •  94

*Chapter 4. Steamboat Springs Area*
*Rabbit Ears Pass*
24. Hogan Park Trail  •  98
25. Walton Creek Loop 3A and North Walton Peak Trail 3C  •  100
26. Fox Curve Loop 2B  •  104
27. West Summit Loop 1B  •  106
28. West Summit Loop 1A  •  107
*Dunckley Pass*
29. Spronks Creek and Chapman/Bench Trails  •  109

*Chapter 5. Glen Haven Area*
30. Crosier Mountain  •  114
31. North Fork Trail  •  115

## MAP KEY

| | | | |
|---|---|---|---|
| ———————— | paved road | (P) | trailhead parking |
| –·–·–·– | unpaved road | ▲ | campground/campsites |
| - - - - - - - | main trail | ⊼ | picnic area |
| ·········· | side trail | ■ | building/site of interest |
| – – – – | boundary (park or wilderness area) | ▲ | mountain/peak |
| (84) | interstate highway | ★ | trailhead |
| (101) | U.S. highway | ✕ | mine |
| (1) (530) | state highway | — | gate |
| [3060] | Forest Service road | ·········· | powerline |
| [26] | county road | | river and lake |
| ● | city or town | | glacier |
| ⚲ | ranger station | ⓬ | route number and name |

# ROCKY MOUNTAIN NATIONAL PARK

*Chapter 6. Beaver Meadows Entrance*

32. Deer Mountain  •  121
33. Cub Lake  •  123
34. Fern Lake  •  125
35. Hollowell Park and Mill Creek Basin  •  126
36. Sprague Lake Trails  •  127

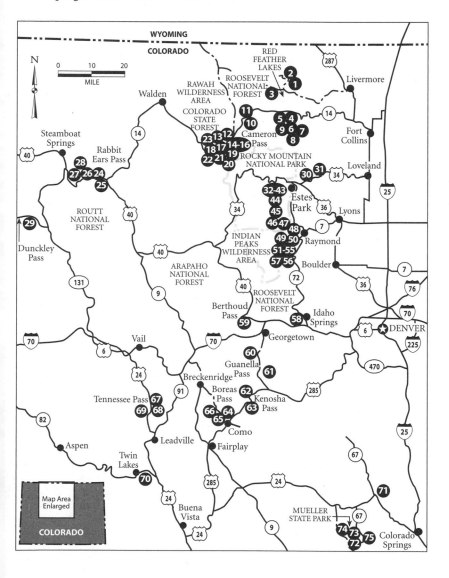

37. Alberta Falls and The Loch  ·  130
38. North Longs Peak Trail  ·  132
39. Mills Lake, Jewel Lake, and Black Lake  ·  134
40. Bear Lake Loop  ·  136
41. Nymph Lake, Dream Lake, and Emerald Lake  ·  138
42. Flattop Mountain  ·  140
43. Odessa Lake  ·  143

*Chapter 7. Longs Peak Trailhead*
44. Estes Cone  ·  147
45. Chasm Lake  ·  148

*Chapter 8. Wild Basin Entrance*
46. Copeland Falls, Calypso Cascades, and Ouzel Falls  ·  152
47. Allenspark Trail and Finch Lake  ·  155

## INDIAN PEAKS AREA
*Chapter 9. Peaceful Valley Area*
48. Buchanan Pass Trail and Middle Saint Vrain Creek  ·  159
49. Coney Flats Trail  ·  161
50. North Sourdough Trail  ·  162

*Chapter 10. Brainard Lake Recreation Area*
51. South Sourdough Trail  ·  166
52. Niwot Mountain and Ridge  ·  169
53. Red Rock Lake and Brainard Lake  ·  171
54. Mitchell Lake and Blue Lake  ·  176
55. Long Lake and Lake Isabelle  ·  178

*Chapter 11. Arapaho Peaks Area*
56. Rainbow Lakes  ·  181
57. Arapaho Glacier Trail  ·  182

## CENTRAL COLORADO
*Chapter 12. I-70 Corridor*
58. Saint Marys Glacier and James Peak  ·  186
59. Jones Pass Trail  ·  188

*Chapter 13. Guanella Pass Area*
60. Silver Dollar Lake  ·  191
61. Mount Bierstadt  ·  192

# SOUTHERN COLORADO

## *Chapter 14. Como Area*
62. Kenosha Pass and Colorado Trail West  •  197
63. North Twin Cone Peak  •  199
64. Boreas Pass Road and Halfway Gulch  •  200
65. Gold Dust Trail South  •  202
66. Gold Dust Trail North  •  203

## *Chapter 15. Leadville Area*
67. Vances Hut  •  206
68. Taylor Hill  •  208
69. Mitchell Creek Loop  •  210
70. Twin Lakes  •  212

## *Chapter 16. Colorado Springs Area*
71. Rampart Reservoir  •  215
72. School Pond and Preachers Hollow Loops  •  217
73. Peak View, Elk Meadow, Livery, and Revenuers Ridge Trails  •  219
74. Homestead and Black Bear Loop  •  220
75. The Crags  •  221

*Appendix: Who to Call*  •  *225*
*Bibliography*  •  *231*
*Index*  •  *233*

# Preface

*We aren't inheriting the Earth from our fathers, we are stealing it from our children.*

David Brower, *Let the Mountains Talk, Let the Rivers Run* (2000)

I have a confession to make. As an outdoor enthusiast who much preferred cross-country skiing, I was a late convert to snowshoeing. A trek in the woods near Durango, engineered by my daughter, Kate, introduced all of our family to the new technology of easier-to-use, better-designed snowshoes. With that introduction came an adventure that featured less downhill (and uphill) angst than that experienced on skis.

When traveling downhill on snowshoes, what you give up in speed, you gain in complete control of your destiny—and destination. If you aren't an expert cross-country or downhill skier, you probably have experienced having to either execute a "face plant" or grab a tree to stop or slow down while "gliding" downhill. With snowshoes, you can run and float through deep powder. Snowshoes allow you to walk straight uphill without having to wax your skis just right or grunt furiously beneath a set of poles as your skis slide out from under you. A good day on snowshoes feels like the synchronized kick and glide you get when cross-country skiing or the airborne feelings of a downhill run on skis. Needless to say, snowshoeing does take some getting used to, but it requires far less technical skill than do most other winter sports.

The most surprising thing about snowshoeing is how similar it is to hiking, and yet how different. If the snow is fresh and not too compacted, you will fairly float on its surface. Your body doesn't absorb the pounding it gets from hiking over rocks or hard-packed trails. Hiking trails in the winter are transformed by deep snow, ice crystals in the air, and trees draped in white.

What snowshoes give us is another way to safely access the magic of winter in the mountains.

# Acknowledgments

First and foremost, I thank my wife, Ginna, for her unflagging support for this and my many other outdoor activities. I'd also like to thank the rest of my family—Amy, Kate, Laura, and Ryan—for their enthusiasm.

I appreciate the following people who accompanied me on my field research and/or gave me advice and information: Kate and Ginna, Bill Bertschy, Dan "Buddy" Bowers, David Bye, Larry Caswell, Joel Claypool, Jeff Eishmy, Phil Freidman, John Gascoyne, Amy Johnston, Rodney Ley, Ward Luthi, Ellen Montague, Jay Stagnone, Alan Stark, and Jim Welch.

In addition, John Gascoyne made marvelous suggestions; Ellen Montague created the map scrap and did a terrific job carefully checking all of the trails. My daughter, Kate, also read parts of the manuscript and made valuable suggestions.

I thank Ben Faranda Photography for taking the superb snowshoe photos, and the snowshoe companies who loaned us their equipment.

Thanks to the Colorado State Forest, U.S. Forest Service, and Rocky Mountain National Park employees who answered countless questions and provided excellent information: Maribeth Higgins, Vicki McClure, Diana Barney, Becky Kelly, Patti Turecek, Dick Putney, and Jeff Maugans. I especially thank Kristi Wumkres of the Canyon Lakes Ranger District for the Poudre Canyon Nordic Ranger photos she provided.

Thanks to the Mountain Shop in Fort Collins for loaning us the topo maps we used to create the map scrap, and to Maptrails for providing map support.

I also thank the staff at The Mountaineers Books for giving me this opportunity, especially my patient editors, Margaret Sullivan and Julie Van Pelt, who gave me practical and invaluable advice, and Kris Fulsaas for her superb copyedit. Mountaineers Books former director of marketing, and my climbing partner, Alan Stark, was instrumental, as was former editor-in-chief Margaret Foster.

Our natural heritage and resources are fragile and limited. I will contribute 20 percent of the proceeds from this book to environmental organizations to help preserve our wild places.

# Introduction: The Snowshoe Revolution

Though estimates vary, snowshoes have been around for many thousands of years. They first evolved in Asia and likely came to North America when ancient peoples migrated, at least 12,000 years ago, across the Bering Land Bridge. According to Gene Prater and Dave Felkley, in their authoritative book *Snowshoeing* (Mountaineers Books, 4th ed. 1997), snowshoes were perfected by North American natives in Canada and Alaska. The craftsmanship demonstrated in these shoes was remarkable, but use of these early models was daunting to all but the hardiest outdoor recreationists, because they were so long and unwieldy.

Snowshoeing is rapidly growing in popularity today largely because of the less intimidating design of snowshoes. Gone are the 4-foot-long bamboo wicker baskets of an earlier time. Snowshoes are shorter, lighter, and easier to use than ever before. Now even a large person can use a much shorter snowshoe to float on top of all but the deepest powder.

Outdoor enthusiasts have discovered that if they can hike, they can snowshoe. With a minimal amount of equipment, they can strap on their snowshoes and explore the closest snow-covered terrain.

## WHAT TO TAKE

### Snowshoes

Before you purchase snowshoes, you will probably benefit by renting a few different types, brands, and sizes. It's a good idea to rent snowshoes from a local snowshoe store that also sells them. The staff will be more knowledgeable because they likely deal with more than one brand. Make sure the sales clerk you are dealing with has firsthand experience. The more your salesperson knows,

*Silver Dollar Lake*

*Snowshoes come in a variety of effective designs.*

the more likely it is you'll get the snowshoe that's right for you. Sometimes stores are willing to apply part of or the entire rental fee toward the purchase of snowshoes.

Most models of snowshoes are very much alike. They feature underfoot claws, webbing, or a solid piece of plastic to walk on, and straps to hold your boots in place. Snowshoe manufacturers have buyers guidelines for the different models they sell. Some of these are available online at the manufacturers' websites. Ask your local outdoor store about buyers guides you can read or websites you can investigate. Pick the shoes that seem easiest to get in and out of, that aren't too big for your needs, and that are comfortable to walk in.

**Tip:** Ask the sales clerk whether your snowshoes have a right and left foot, and if so, to show you how to determine one from the other if they aren't clearly marked.

### Design and Function

Snowshoe designs vary according to the type of use anticipated. Some snowshoes are better than others for climbing steep slopes and maneuvering on tricky traverses. Some snowshoes are solid rather than made of webbed material. These can perform well in the outback and can be lighter and less expensive than webbed models. Some of the solid snowshoes have extra cleats along the sides that make climbing steep slopes easier.

A somewhat longer backcountry shoe is suitable when you carry a heavy backpack, which can

*Snowshoes can be webbed nylon or solid plastic.*

increase your weight significantly; a shorter, lighter model is suitable for day trips. If you are planning to be out in the light, fluffy powder of December and January, you will find that flotation isn't as good as it is on more consolidated or heavier, wetter, late-season snow. Some snowshoes come with extensions or "tails" that can be added on, or removed, depending on snow conditions.

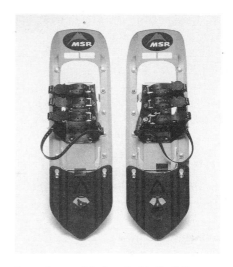

### Size

Appropriate size is determined by the size and weight of the snowshoer, as well as the type of snow expected. What you are looking for

*Snowshoes with detachable "tails"*

is the ability to stay on top of, or float, on the snow. Originally, it was true that the longer the snowshoe, the better the flotation. While more length still tends to mean more flotation, there are now other considerations. With advances in technology and snowshoe design, shorter snowshoes can provide good flotation in many instances. Flotation varies from model to model, and, with the right snowshoes on, even larger, heavier people can use smaller shoes and not sink deeply into the snow.

Use common sense when selecting snowshoes. A larger, taller person can better handle a larger, wider snowshoe. A shorter, smaller person is more comfortable propelling a shorter, narrower snowshoe. When you try on snowshoes, walk in them and see if the width widens your stride too much, or if the length makes them very awkward to propel and control.

Here are some general guidelines, but keep in mind where you fall in the weight/size range: If you are at the high end of the range (heavier), then opt for the longer or wider snowshoe, especially if you are expecting deep powder as the norm. If the snowshoes are primarily going to be for day trips and likely to be on heavily used, firmly packed trails, the low end or middle of the range is a good choice. If you will be carrying a backpack, add its weight to yours when figuring which weight range is appropriate for you.

*Shorties (for carrying 100–140 pounds):* The smallest, shortest snowshoes are those used for running, racing, or fast-paced fitness outings on firm snow. They are usually 21 inches in length and no more than 8 inches in width. A length of 21 to 25 inches and width of 8 inches will work for a variety of uses. For someone at the lower end of the weight range, a snowshoe this size can work even in deeper, less firm snow. You might sink down as much as 6 inches, but in powder that isn't unusual with snowshoes of any length. The convenience of a shorter, lighter snowshoe is worth the little bit of extra work caused by a little less flotation.

*Midsize (for carrying 140–250 pounds):* These are good on firm snow, or for lighter people in deep powder. They measure from 27 to 33 inches in length and are 8 to 9 inches in width. They could be used with a backpack. If you are at the top end of this weight range, the longer, wider snowshoes are advisable.

*Large (for carrying 160–270 pounds):* Larger snowshoes should be used for deep powder and rolling terrain, especially if the snowshoer is a larger individual. Larger snowshoes are 8 to 10 inches wide and measure 30 to 36 inches long. If you are very tall or have short legs, you might not want to use the longest snowshoes in this range, even for carrying heavier weight. The wider snowshoes might make your gait very uncomfortable, and powering long, wide shoes might be more difficult than sinking in a bit more with shorter shoes.

*Jumbo (for carrying more than 200 pounds):* If you weigh more than 200 pounds and will be carrying a heavy backpack and traveling in deep, unconsolidated snow, opting for the longer, wider snowshoes is the safer choice. These shoes are 10 to 11 inches wide and 37 to 42 inches long. Here again, you won't want the longest snowshoes unless you are planning a serious backcountry expedition in deep snow and you're tall and strong enough to power them up significant grade changes.

## Strap Systems

The fastening devices for getting the snowshoes on and off vary somewhat. Ask the outdoor-store staff to show you how they compare. The strap system used to hold your foot to the snowshoe can be crucial, especially in cold, icy

conditions. A simpler lacing and tightening system is generally better. Be certain that you know how to tighten and loosen the straps. You want to be darn sure you know how to make them fit comfortably and can get them on and off, especially in deep snow or in freezing temperatures with ice coating the straps. This is especially desirable if you you party will include children of any age.

*Straps should be easy to use.*

*Lightweight solid plastic snowshoe*

*Webbed snowshoe with larger forefoot claw—good for running*

If you cannot master the strapping-in process in the store, you're even less likely to be able to do so on the trail when your hands are cold.

Does all of this mean that owning more than one pair of snowshoes is necessary in order to enjoy the sport of snowshoeing? No, not at all. If you are relatively new to the activity but want to own rather than rent, for your first season look for one style, make, and size that fits *most* of your anticipated needs. Your first purchase might be geared toward the best average snowshoe for the average conditions—snowpack, gear being carried, et cetera—that you expect to encounter. As you find yourself drawn more into this exciting winter activity, you can shop for more specific shoes for more particular needs.

### Other Equipment

#### Boots and Gaiters

In addition to a pair of well-designed snowshoes, you will need waterproof boots. If you have lightweight, high-top summer hiking boots that can be thoroughly waterproofed and you're planning a very short, close-to-the-car trek, you can probably avoid freezing feet and frostbite by wearing them. It is highly recommended, however, that you use heavier, insulated, waterproof boots with thick polypropylene (synthetic composition) liners and/or thick wool or moisture-wicking socks. You can usually rent boots along with your snowshoes if you don't have adequate winter footgear. Fleece-lined rubber boots, insulated hunting or snowboarding boots, or even snowmobiling boots should also work.

*Tip:* Do not use low-top boots or you will risk freezing feet and frostbite. Keep in mind that every pound on your foot is equivalent to 2 pounds on your back. You also want to avoid getting blisters. Bring moleskin in case your rental boots create hot spots on your heels, soles, or ankles. If you are wearing rental boots or new boots, you can apply moleskin to your heels *before* you get on the trail in order to prevent blistering. If you have the opportunity, wear your boots around a bit before wearing them to snowshoe. This will allow them to mold to your feet somewhat and can tell you where hot spots might develop out on the trail.

If you are on the move in powder, snowshoes can spray your feet or the backs of your legs with snow as you walk—the deeper the snow, the heavier the spray. A pair of gaiters works well to keep the snow out of your boots. If your boots are completely waterproof and calf high, you may get by without gaiters, but if you are wearing ankle-high boots without this protection, you will likely have some snow in your boots and possibly very wet, cold feet in a short time. Some rental shops also rent gaiters, so rent them or invest in a pair. Gaiters are inexpensive and effective foot protection for snowshoeing and cross-country skiing.

*Tip:* If you do end up snowshoeing without gaiters and get snow in your boots, you can modify your gait so that you spray less snow onto and into your boots. Try sliding your foot more across the snow rather than lifting your feet high with each step.

## Poles

Poles are optional equipment and many avid snowshoers do not use them, but they can be useful (see "Care and Use of Snowshoes" later in the introduction). Most rental shops offer poles at a slight or no additional cost. If you have cross-country ski poles, they work fine for snowshoeing, if they aren't too long. A good length allows your elbow and arm to assume a 90-degree position. The poles can be of any strong, durable material (wood, metal, graphite) but must have good baskets that will prevent them from sinking into the snow.

## Packs

On day trips, carry a day pack; you'll want it for peeling off your clothing layers so you don't overheat. You'll need a pack large enough for bulky winter clothing.

*Tip:* Pack your clothing around your water bottle to prevent your water from freezing. Start with warm water so it is less likely to freeze solid.

Be prepared! Bring hand or foot warmers (gel packets) if you tend to get cold easily. Bring an extra pair of prescription glasses if you wear contacts.

And always bring the Ten Essentials:

1. Extra fleece or wool clothing, polypro long underwear, socks, and layers of clothing for emergencies or changing weather conditions (see "Clothing" later in the introduction)
2. Extra food and water for one additional day in case of emergency (see "Food and Water" later in the introduction)
3. UV-rated sunglasses and goggles (for strong winds and subzero windchills), sunscreen of SPF 15 or greater
4. Knife
5. First-aid kit
6. Fire starter (especially important in snowy terrain)
7. Waterproof matches or lighter
8. Flashlight with spare batteries, or a headlamp
9. Map
10. Compass

Other safety gear to consider includes a Boy Scout–style whistle, a space blanket and/or tarp, and two black garbage bags for emergency shelter or sleeping bag. Good additions for steep or avalanche-prone areas include a shovel (one per person), an avalanche beacon/locator (one per person), a snow probe (one per person), and an ice ax or ski poles. Camera and extra film and a GPS locating device are optional items you might consider taking.

There is some controversy about the use of cellular phones as a safety device in the greater outdoors. If you feel better with one, that is your choice, of course. Consider that being able to talk to someone on the phone may seem comforting, but it may also provide little immediate help when you are lost or in an emergency situation. Cell phones are no substitute for being prepared. Cell phones are often not usable in high mountain valleys because there is no service to such locations.

### Clothing

Fortunately, the high fashion standards of downhill skiing have not made an impact in the world of snowshoeing. You can dress yourself for snowshoeing for warmth rather than fashion because you won't encounter "fashion police" on the trails. As for most active outdoor winter sports, dress in warm layers. When you pack, imagine warm, sunny weather followed by driving snow and subzero wind (pack for all conceivable conditions). Use water-repellent or waterproofed gear and moisture-wicking clothing: nylon, synthetics, or wool.

Begin your excursion dressed a bit lightly for the given day's conditions.

You may be somewhat cold at first, but as you walk, you'll warm up nicely. If you are dealing with extreme conditions, pay particular attention to what your body is telling you: Don't go too long before putting on warmer layers; stop and rest often rather than overheating or, especially, breaking into a sweat and creating a potential chill situation later when you stop. When you break for lunch, you'll cool off quickly and you will want to put some layers back on.

Cotton is not recommended. When cotton gets wet or damp, it does not dry out easily nor will it insulate you against the cold. On your average winter day, a pair of polypropylene (synthetic composite) long underwear is highly recommended. Don't use cotton for bottom layers; avoid cotton completely if you can. For the next layer, a wool sweater, fleece, or a lightweight down or wool jacket will work. Fleece is more effective than wool when wet. It insulates better and dries out more easily. The outer layer should be breathable and waterproof.

Headgear is especially important because you lose most of your body heat through your head. Keep it covered with a good wool or polypro hat, one that covers your ears. A ski mask or balaclava is a good idea in case it gets windy or starts to snow. Goggles are also important for an enjoyable experience in wind or snow. Mittens are generally warmer than gloves, but either should be waterproof and at least double layered with insulating material. If you don't have waterproof mittens or gloves, you will want more than one pair of non-waterproof gloves. An extra pair of dry socks is a good idea too. Remember, no cotton socks! For snowshoeing in comfort, refer to the following list before you head out.

- Long underwear tops and bottoms
- Turtleneck shirt or wool scarf to protect your neck
- Fleece or wool sweater
- Wind- and waterproof outer coat or shell
- Wool or warm synthetic socks
- Warm mittens
- Warm cap
- Face or ski mask

### Food and Water

Take the same sorts of food and drink when you go snowshoeing that you would when hiking. Be practical, however, and consider what the cold will do to your hands if you're trying to peel an orange, for instance.

Bring easy-to-access snacks such as energy bars, trail mix, et cetera. You'll burn lots of energy and calories snowshoeing, some estimate up to 1,000 calories per hour. Exercising in the cold burns far more calories than summer mountain activities; plan accordingly. Eating something with a bit of fat in it will also help to keep you warm. Arctic explorers often eat large quantities of butter, lard, or blubber; you might prefer something more palatable such as chocolate. Bring extra high-calorie food in case of an emergency, and ask your compatriots to bring enough so you won't have to feed them too.

Much has been made of the new high-protein diets and foods designed as an adjunct to exercise. Although eating something that contains protein along with carbohydrates works well, carbohydrates are still the key ingredient for energy. You don't have to overeat, however, because excess calories from either carbohydrates or protein are simply stored as fat. Exercising aerobically for longer than 40 minutes will cause your body to use fat stores as energy. If you don't want to deplete your glycogen supply (the fuel your muscles use) and want to stay as fresh as possible, stop for a small snack about once an hour. Try to exercise at an aerobic pace (without being constantly out of breath) so that you won't accumulate the lactic acid that leads to sore muscles.

Also carry water, at least two quarts if you plan a multi-hour walk, and carry it in something that will prevent it from freezing solid. Don't wait until you feel thirsty to drink some water; drink regularly as you go. Eating snow as a substitute for drinking water is a poor idea at best—you will burn calories as your body melts it and adjusts to its lower temperature, and it will chill you to the bone. This is especially true when you are cold, as you could be increasing the likelihood of hypothermia.

You can add a sports drink or fruit-juice mixture to your water. Liquids such as wine, rum, brandy, and schnapps have no place at all on your back-woods menu. Alcohol lowers your metabolic rate and actually makes you feel colder. Forget about the Saint Bernard doggy with the cask tied to its collar. Save the fun for the ski lodge after your trek.

**Mountain Water**
You need to drink plenty of water, but don't drink from mountain streams and lakes. Though they look crystal clear and inviting, they are not creature-free. Cold does not purify mountain water, and a nasty parasite called *Giardia lamblia* actually thrives in cold water. If you want to drink from streams and lakes, take along a water filtering/purification system or water-purifying tablets. Mountain water can also be boiled for 10 minutes to kill *Giardia* without tablets or a filtering system. Take along plenty of water from home or the right purifying equipment, and know how to use it. Filtering water in the winter can be a challenge. Melting fresh, clean snow is a viable option but can be very time- and fuel-consuming because snow is typically quite dry and doesn't yield much moisture.

If you ever do drink untreated water, watch for the following symptoms: diarrhea, nausea, cramping, fever, foul-smelling belching or gas (more than normal), chills, and weight loss (contracting giardiasis is not a good strategy for weight loss). These symptoms might not manifest for a week or two after you have ingested tainted water. So avoid an unnecessary and unpleasant illness by making the effort to purify mountain water.

## CARE AND USE OF SNOWSHOES

Snowshoes are tough, but they aren't indestructible. Snowshoes prefer soft, powdery snow for running or jumping. In fact they relish nice, big bites of the soft stuff without any chewy stumps or dirt. Walking or running on hard surfaces such as rocks, trees, or really thin snow over a hard, icy surface can bend or break the claws on your snowshoes. The claws on a friend's quality snowshoe bent when he ran on late-season, hard-packed snow. If you are on your own shoes, you will want them to last for many years. If you are renting them, consider the next user and the fact that you probably have a deposit riding on their being returned in good shape.

Establishing a steady, consistent rhythm is much more enjoyable, and easier on the body, than lots of sprints, stops, starts, and high stepping. Sliding your foot across the snow rather than lifting your feet high with each step is a technique that is easier to maintain on a long hike. Sometimes snow conditions don't allow this because you'll sink in too much to slide effectively; however, most of the time it does work. You can also get into a nice rhythm not unlike that of cross-country skiing or hiking.

A safe estimate for travel time on snowshoes is 1 mile per hour or slower. When considering time estimates, always remember that snow and weather conditions have a severe impact on the amount of time it takes to negotiate a trail. Deeper, freshly fallen, powdery snow is challenging regardless of equipment and physical conditioning, especially if you are breaking trail. Late-season snow that has layers of frozen and melting snow can collapse under each step, sinking you deeply regardless of the length or design of your snowshoe. This means the time to complete your hike could be double or even triple that of the same hike under friendlier conditions.

If novices are along, it is wise to shorten the day's ambitions and monitor snowshoers' conditions frequently. Old, crusty snow might be easier to walk on early in the day when it is cold, but if it is warm enough later on, it can collapse several inches with each step, thus making for a much more challenging experience on your return route. Use your watch to judge your time out and estimate your time back, and be conservative. You don't want to end up far from your car or cabin in the dark and cold of midwinter.

### The Advantages of Poling

Poles are very useful, particularly off trail in deep snow or on a steep slope. They are especially helpful when you are traversing downhill or crossing uneven hillocks of snow. When you are descending through deep powder, you can almost simulate skiing with jump turns and feel like you're floating downhill. Poles take thousands of pounds of pressure off your knees, a major asset if you are prone to knee problems. Poles also add extra stability and power to your effort. If weight loss is a goal, using poles also gets more of your body involved in the activity and provides an upper-body workout that can help to burn off unwanted pounds at a faster rate. While poles aren't essential unless you are planning to climb or descend very steep slopes, you may still want to try them once or twice.

## WINTER CAMPING

Winter camping can be magical if you remember that it requires different equipment and skills than camping in other seasons. Pick a cozy site in the trees in case the wind kicks up—and it often does—with subzero windchills. If you don't have snow-caving skills, owning or renting a good four-season tent and a good camping stove are essential for surviving in comfort, regardless of the temperature or the wind. Also make sure that you bring a cold-weather

sleeping bag. On one midwinter trip I took, the temperature was a balmy 49 degrees Fahrenheit in Boulder and a pleasant 40 degrees Fahrenheit at the trailhead, even with the 30-mile-per-hour wind gusts. That night, however, winds were clocked at 100 miles per hour and the temperature sank to minus 25 degrees Fahrenheit. Warm weather in the flatlands or even at the beginning of a trip has little or no bearing on the rapidly changing and very localized weather of the higher reaches of the Rockies. Proper equipment and preparation will ensure a safe trip.

*Snow ridges make travel challenging without poles.*

One of the best spots for snow camping, even if you are a beginner, is the American Lakes and Thunder Pass Trail (Route 19) near Cameron Pass because some of the best snow conditions in the state make it ideal for building snow caves as you reach the higher elevations of the lakes or the first mile or so beyond Michigan Ditch. The area is good for beginners because, when the sun goes down, you feel like you are in the wilderness even though you are only a couple of miles from the road, giving you a margin of safety. Needless to say, a blizzard can erase that margin in a very short period of time, so thorough preparation and enough food for a multiday stay is essential for even an overnight. Having a cell phone is a modern-day luxury that should be used even though the odds of it being usable in remote areas are slim. It is important that you let someone know exactly where you are going and when you will return.

### Rental Yurts and Cabins/Huts

*Never Summer Yurt System and Colorado State Forest Cabin/Yurt System:* These are two good, inexpensive, less-demanding alternatives for winter overnights in the high-mountain winter paradise of the Colorado State Forest north of State Highway 14. The Colorado State Park System rents several rustic cabins in the Gould area on North Michigan Lake, and Never Summer Yurts has a system of yurts available. The settings for the yurts and cabins are dramatic, with the Medicine Bow Mountains' Rawah Range forming an enormous and majestic backdrop to the east and north.

*Grass Creek Yurt*

*Ski Cooper from Vances Hut*

The Lake Agnes Nokhu Hut, a delightful, low-stress way to spend the night in the Cameron Pass area, is the latest addition to the Never Summer Yurt System. Plan well in advance to use the hut because reservations with the Never Summer Yurts are necessary, and it is a popular alternative that is often booked up for weekends. It is inexpensive but prices can change, so check the website for the latest price (see Never Summer Nordic, Inc., under "Contact Information" in the appendix). The hut includes a wood-burning cook stove that is also used for heat. Wood is included in the rental fee. Though there are beds, bring sleeping pads and warm bags because it gets quite cool when the stove goes out overnight. There are nice, easy trails in and around the huts, with views in every direction. To get to the hut, go west over Cameron Pass on State Highway 14 and watch for the turnout in about 2 miles on the left side of the road. The road to the cabin and summer parking area is closed in the winter; walk the closed road to reach the hut.

The yurts vary in size and sleep six to ten people. They are heated with wood-burning stoves and have a variety of bunks and beds. Dancing Moose and Grass Hut are 0.25 and 0.6 mile from the road, respectively; the others are farther. The website includes complete descriptions, pictures, and prices.

The North Michigan Reservoir cabins are heated by either wood-burning stoves or propane. Water is available nearby. There are vault toilets within walking distance of the cabins. Each cabin sleeps six to ten people on bunk beds. They are between 100 and 400 feet from parking places.

*Tenth Mountain Division Huts Association:* During World War II, Camp Hale near Tennessee Pass north of Leadville was the training center for the elite Tenth Mountain Division troops who fought courageously in the Alps. After the war, many of the veterans returned to Colorado to found the Aspen, Breckenridge, Vail, Steamboat, Loveland, Arapaho Basin, and Winter Park Ski Areas. They also converted the training huts they used during the war so they could be used as European-style climbing huts by backcountry skiers and snowshoers. Staying in these huts is a terrific way to explore the high country around Leadville in winter. There are more than sixteen Tenth Mountain Division huts stretching from Vail Pass on I-70 north of Leadville to Aspen in the west on State Highway 82. Getting to some of the huts is a challenging long-distance trek, but others are close to civilization and can be reached by the reasonably fit. You can find out more information by visiting the Tenth Mountain Division Huts Association website (see "Contact Information" in the appendix).

## SAFE WINTER RECREATION

### Hypothermia

Hypothermia is deadly. It is an acute traumatic event that occurs when your body's core temperature drops below 98.6 degrees. It doesn't take extremely low temperatures to get into trouble; people have died from hypothermia when air temperatures were in the 40s and 50s. Core temperature loss can easily happen if someone falls into a lake or stream and isn't able to get warm and dry right away. It can also happen if you are simply not dressed adequately and temperatures drop, the wind picks up, or it snows or rains on you.

You can avoid hypothermia by taking along the right kinds of clothing (see "Clothing" earlier in the introduction). Preventing hypothermia is much wiser than waiting until the situation becomes life threatening. Some symptoms of hypothermia are:

- uncontrollable shivering
- slurred or slow speech
- fuzzy thinking, poor memory (more than normal), incoherence
- lack of coordination, causing stumbling or vertigo
- extreme fatigue or sleepiness

If you observe any of these symptoms in yourself or another person, take immediate action to warm the individual experiencing the problem. If someone dresses inadequately or falls into a lake or stream, stop immediately and take steps to get him or her dry and warm. Stop and use your emergency supplies to make a fire and provide warm liquids, or wrap the individual in additional warm clothing and urge him or her to move around enough to warm up. A backpacking stove is ideal for heating up liquids or providing warmth. Weather in the mountains can change dramatically in a matter of minutes. Early fall or late-spring blizzards are especially sneaky.

Pay attention to weather forecasts, pack extra gear, and when the weather is in doubt, head back out! Zero-visibility snow conditions known as whiteouts have been deadly for more than one winter recreationist. If you study the histories of winter disasters, you will find that most of them could have been prevented by better preparation and by knowing when to retreat from difficult conditions.

### Avalanches

Colorado has the highest number of reported avalanches in the United States, with more than 21,000 estimated per year. The number of avalanche deaths has skyrocketed, roughly proportionate to the number of backcountry recreationists. This section cannot take the place of an avalanche safety course or in-depth avalanche guidebooks such as *Avalanche Safety for Skiers, Climbers, and Snowboarders, The Avalanche Handbook,* and *Staying Alive in Avalanche Terrain* (see the bibliography).

The climate in Colorado's Front Range tends to produce light, "dry," fluffy powder snow that skiers love, but it tends to evolve into a highly unstable and dangerous snow underlayer that propagates avalanches. When such snow first falls, it is known as *surface hoar.* When these layers of powder snow are buried beneath subsequent layers of heavier snow, they are called *depth hoar.* The water content of this hoar snow is often only one-half that of snow in other regions; even Utah has much wetter snow.

Terrain, weather, and the condition of the snowpack determine the likelihood of avalanches. Inform yourself as to the most current weather and snow conditions and then pick the safest terrain possible. Call the Colorado Avalanche Information Center (see the appendix) for avalanche hazard ratings (defined later in this section) before entering the backcountry so you know the risky areas and can plan accordingly; the reports tell which aspects of the hills are most dangerous at a given time. Call your local Forest Service office or weather bureau (see the appendix) and ask about the safety of the trail you plan to explore. Take avalanche warnings seriously. Those steep, powdery slopes can be inviting; they can also be deadly, especially to the unwary.

Don't snowshoe alone when avalanche danger is high. Even a small slide 10 feet across and 5 feet deep can bury and smother a person. Carry a shovel and avalanche beacon and know how to use them. If you have any serious question about the safety of a proposed route, turn around and follow your own route back to a known safe destination.

*Seemingly unlikely site of an avalanche death in the Jones Pass area*

### Avalanche Hazard Ratings

*Low:* On steep, snow-covered gullies and open slopes, avalanches are unlikely and snow is mostly stable except in isolated pockets. Natural and human-triggered avalanches are unlikely. Backcountry travel is generally safe.

*Moderate:* Areas of unstable snow and slabs make avalanches very possible on steep, snow-covered gullies and open slopes. Human-triggered avalanches are possible. Backcountry travelers should use caution.

*Considerable:* Unstable slabs make human-triggered avalanches probable. Naturally triggered avalanches are possible. Backcountry travelers should use extreme caution.

*High:* Mostly unstable snow on a variety of aspects and slopes makes natural and human-triggered avalanches likely. Avalanches are likely on steep, snow-covered gullies and open slopes. Backcountry travel is not recommended.

*Extreme:* Widespread areas of unstable snow on a variety of aspects and slopes make natural and human-triggered avalanches certain on steep, snow-covered gullies and open slopes. Large, destructive avalanches are possible. Backcountry travel should be avoided.

### Strategies for Avoiding Avalanches

*Stay on marked trails when danger is high.* A marked trail reduces but does not eliminate risk. Check your route with the Forest Service if it isn't familiar to you.

*Avoid walking on, or below, steep slopes.* Most avalanches occur on slopes of 30 to 45 degrees but also occur on slopes of 25 to 55 degrees. North-facing, leeward slopes are usually most dangerous in the winter months. They stabilize more slowly and are likely to have wind-drift snow. Avoid north-facing, shaded slopes in the winter, especially after recent snow- and windstorms. South-facing slopes are most dangerous in the spring because of dramatic solar heating and melting. Open slopes are more likely to slide than those with tree cover or rocks that can anchor snow. However, avalanches can occur on tree-covered slopes as well: The sparser the cover, the more likely the avalanche.

*Stay high, on ridge lines if possible, but away from cornices.* Cornices are masses of overhanging snow, blown by wind, that typically form along ridges. Don't ski or walk on cornices or under them.

*Go straight up or down the edge of the slope* if you have to descend or ascend a possible avalanche slope, and avoid the middle portion.

*Move across dangerous slopes one person at a time and as high as possible.* Generally stay far apart. This provides for less weight stress on the underlying snow and enhances the opportunity for at least one person to be available to assist in a rescue effort.

*Avoid old avalanche chutes or slide zones.* Don't walk below steep slopes that might be avalanche starting zones; these could catch you in a "run-out" area.

*If you hear a whumping sound, alert your companions and make your way to trees or the edge of the slope.* If ever it sounds as though the snow is collapsing beneath you, you are in a dangerous position and should take immediate precautions.

*Avoid areas with fracture lines in the snow.* This indicates that a slab avalanche, the largest and most destructive kind, is likely to activate in the area.

*Beware of cold temperatures, high winds, and snowstorms* with accumulations of more than 6 inches of snow or a rate of snowfall of 1 inch per hour or greater. Keep in mind that 90 percent of avalanches occur during or after snowstorms. Dry, powdery snow is more likely to avalanche than wet, heavy snow, unless the heavy snow is on top of the weak, powdery layer known as depth hoar.

*Never assume that an area is safe* simply because others have safely used it.

*Avoid holes and gullies,* not just steep slopes.

## Precautions Before Crossing a Potential Avalanche Site

*Wear an avalanche beacon.* Ensure that your companions are wearing similar models, and know how to use them. When crossing a hazardous area one at a time, the person crossing sets his or her the beacon to "transmit," and everyone else sets theirs to "receive."

*Equip everyone in the party with shovels and probes.* When crossing a hazardous area one at a time, everyone waiting to cross should have his or her probe at the ready.

*Avalanche class checking temperature and strength/stability of snow near Jones Pass by digging a snowpit*

*Loosen your bindings* if you can do so without destabilizing your snowshoe. Snowshoe bindings don't release like some ski bindings can.

*Slip your hands out of the pole straps* if you are using poles.

*Study the area* and ask yourself, "If I am caught, where will I end up?" Discuss this with your companions.

*Loosen pack straps.* Unfasten belt and chest straps and be prepared to shed the pack.

### Increasing Your Odds of Surviving an Avalanche

*Shed as much of your gear as possible* if you are caught in an avalanche. Shed large packs but retain small ones for protection when caught. Small packs can protect from debris while large packs can trap you.

*Swim to stay on top* and "fight like hell." Grab a rock or tree if possible and try to stay on top or as close to the top as possible.

*Make an air space for breathing* with your arm or hand.

*Hold one hand up* so rescuers can find you more easily.

*Remain calm;* focus on breathing fully and slowly.

### Finding an Avalanche Victim

*Don't leave to go for help;* rescue by companions is a victim's best chance for survival. After a half hour beneath the snow, the victim's chances for survival are less than 50 percent. Time is critical.

*Mark the spot* where you last saw the victim.

*Search downhill* from where you last saw the person; use beacons or probe with ski poles.

*Try to excavate the victim immediately;* the longer a person is buried, the less likely it is he or she will survive.

## Altitude

The best snow in Colorado is usually found in the mountains, at higher elevations. Most of the snowshoe routes in this book are at relatively high elevations. If you are accustomed to exerting yourself in the high country, you have little reason for concern. If you rarely venture above 5,000 feet, recognize your and your party's potential limitations at higher elevations. Keep in mind that altitude's effects are unpredictable, especially for those who are visiting from sea level.

If you or visitors have just arrived from a lower elevation, take at least 1 or 2 days to acclimate before venturing above 5,000 feet. If you live at or above 5,000 feet, less time is needed to adjust. Taking acetazolamide, 250 mg twice daily for 2 days before going to high altitude and for the first 2 days you are at altitude, can also help. Plan short, easy adventures until you determine how well everyone is acclimating.

It is risky to drink a lot of alcoholic beverages the evening before or especially during a high-country adventure. Alcohol has a greater effect at altitude. The dehydration and oxygen deprivation that alcohol consumption cause are likely to give you a headache. Alcohol slows down your metabolism and makes you feel colder, not warmer. Wait until you're back beside the fire before enjoying your favorite alcoholic beverages.

Drinking a lot of water before and during high-altitude exercise is a good, though not foolproof, preventive measure. Have at least two quarts of water with you for an all-day excursion. Take along some headache medication (aspirin substitute, because aspirin can upset the stomach) and nausea medication (some feel that antacids have ingredients that can prevent the effects of altitude), just in case.

Altitude and elevation gain can certainly slow you down. Assume that you will travel 1 mile per hour or 1,000 feet of elevation gain per hour, at most, even if you are well conditioned. Physical conditioning helps, but it doesn't prevent altitude sickness.

## Mountain Sickness

*Mild altitude illness* is the most common of this high-elevation phenomenon. Symptoms are severe headache; nausea; loss of appetite; a warm, flushed face; lethargy; and insomnia, or poor sleep with strange dreams. Mountain sickness can last a couple of days. Resting, snowshoeing at lower elevations, eating lightly, and drinking more liquids can help. Avoid taking barbiturates such as sleeping pills, because they can aggravate the illness. Some people, most often women, experience swelling of the face, hands, and feet, with a weight gain of as much as 4 to 12 pounds, when dealing with mild mountain sickness. The weight gain subsides after returning to lower elevations. The cause for this is unknown, but the condition can be treated with a low-salt diet and diuretics.

Nosebleeds are more common at higher elevations because of the very dry air. Staying hydrated and avoiding getting a cold (good luck) are the best way to avoid them. The most effective way to stop a nosebleed is to gently pinch the nose shut for 5 minutes.

*High Altitude Pulmonary Edema (HAPE)* is fluid filling the lungs. Symptoms are difficulty breathing, a severe headache with incoherence, staggering, and a persistent, hacking cough. This is a serious illness caused by altitude.

*High Altitude Cerebral Edema (HACE)* is swelling of the brain. Symptoms include persistent vomiting, severe and persistent headache, extreme fatigue, delirium or confusion, staggering, and/or coma. This is the most serious illness caused by altitude.

If you or anyone in your party experiences the symptoms of either HAPE or HACE, go to a lower altitude immediately and get to a physician as soon as possible.

### Here Comes the Sun

The sun's ray are much stronger at higher elevations. Add to this the added effect of reflection off the snow, and, even on a cloudy day, you can end up fried. The harmful effects of the sun are magnified at high altitudes, so covering up and avoiding direct sunlight is the best strategy, especially between the hours of 10 A.M. and 2 P.M.

Sunscreen is essential at high altitude. Use one that is at least SPF (sun protection factor) 15 to avoid sun damage. Sunburns can set the stage for skin cancer at a later age. Excess sun also adversely affects the immune system. Your dermatologist will tell you that there is no such thing as a healthy tan.

Sunglasses or sungoggles are also essential to avoid sun damage to the eyes. If you do not protect your eyes, you might become temporarily snowblind, which is very painful and makes travel difficult.

### *Picking your First Adventure*

Be conservative your first time out. Don't be like my friend "Buddy": He always wants to live on the edge and push himself, or his few remaining friends, beyond reasonable limits. He usually ignores weather forecasts, gets a late start, and insists on going off trail and straight uphill at a rapid pace. In fact, I've even seen "Buddy" go charging off into the winter wilderness postholing his way stubbornly up mountainsides without the benefit of snowshoes, with miserable friends in tow.

Don't be like "Buddy." Pick a short, easy round trip that will be an enjoyable half-day jaunt. That will give you a chance to see how your body reacts to snowshoes and how you react to dealing with the equipment in the cold and snow. You're much more likely to have a good time if you don't expect too much of anyone, especially yourself.

Snow conditions can vary dramatically and unpredictably at any time of the season. Snow trails that are normally relatively easy to negotiate can become very challenging in deep powder or on a crust that breaks under your feet. Deep, fluffy powder is typical in midwinter and can mean that you could sink in a foot deep, or more, with every step, regardless of the length or style of snowshoe. Spring conditions can vary greatly and can make even a short jaunt exhausting due to poor flotation.

My most recent spring trip had some of the most variable conditions I have seen, all on the same trail. The south-facing slopes were bare; north-facing slopes were covered with deep, frozen drifts that gave way with every step. The part of the loop that I faced last required the most work. Needless to say, it made for an interesting day, one that required twice the energy expenditure than I had anticipated.

### Traveling Safely

Do not snowshoe alone; go with a companion.

Let others know where you are going and when you will be coming back. Sign in on trail registries.

Watch for trail markers and be very aware of your surroundings. Route-finding, even on marked trails, is more challenging in winter.

Prevent frostbite by keeping your hands, feet, and face well protected. Tingling, numbing sensations are the early warning signs of frostbite.

Use extreme caution whenever you are crossing what appear to be frozen streams and lakes. They are often not frozen solid, especially around inlets and outlets, and falling through the ice far from your car or tent can be fatal.

## WILDERNESS ETHICS

Public land is not "government land." It is land that we, the public, own. Our national forests are valuable land that is protected and maintained for us by the government. This ownership comes not only with the opportunity for recreation, for "re-creation" of the body and soul, but also the responsibility to care for and respect the land. Many of the areas described in this book are wilderness areas that require extra precautions and work to prevent deterioration of the wilderness experience for present and future generations. We should all try to apply the "Leave No Trace" philosophy to the use of all public lands. The things that move us to go into the wilderness tell us that it is one of our most cherished national possessions.

### Plan Ahead

Know the risks and regulations of the area you are visiting.

To minimize impact, visit the backcountry in small groups. Try to avoid popular areas in times of high use.

To minimize visual impact, use naturally-hued clothing and equipment. Note that winter recreationists often wear bright-colored clothing as a safety measure; in the event of avalanche or rescue, bright colors are easy to spot.

To minimize garbage, repackage food into reusable containers that won't leak.

### Leave No Trace

*Camp at least 200 feet from trails, water sources and muddy areas, and wildlife forage or watering areas.* Animals are stressed in winter, and you could reduce their chance of survival.

*Avoid building a fire;* bring a lightweight stove and extra clothing for cooking and warmth. On overnight stays, enjoy a candle instead of a fire. Where fires are permitted, use them only for emergencies and don't scar large rocks, overhangs, or trees with the flame from your fire. Use only downed or dead wood and do not snap branches off live trees. If you burn garbage, burn only paper; remove all unburnable and unburned trash; bury ashes.

*Pack out whatever you pack in.*

*Dismantle snow structures,* and cover snow pits.

*Use backcountry toilets* whenever they are available. Get as far off the trail as possible when you have to answer nature's call—50 feet at least for a urination stop—and camouflage soiled snow. Use toilet paper or wipes sparingly and pack them out. Use bare ground for burial or pack out human waste—don't "bury" it in the snow. Dispose of solid waste at least 200 feet from trails or water sources.

*Leave your pets at home;* they will love you for it. Snow and ice often cause painful paw injuries, and dog booties rarely work properly. If you do bring a pet, control it at all times. Camouflage soiled snow from your dog's urination. Pack out dog feces.

*Leave what you find.* Do not remove trees, plants, rocks, or historical artifacts; they belong to everyone.

### Snowshoe Etiquette

It is courteous to avoid walking in ski tracks whenever possible. Skiers count on good tracks for gliding, and can get a bit annoyed when snowshoers destroy their glide tracks. It is best to have parallel tracks on every trail that is wide enough, one for snowshoers and one for skiers. Breaking trail next to ski tracks can be extra work, but you will have the satisfaction of getting extra exercise.

*Parallel snowshoe and ski tracks* (courtesy Canyon Lakes Ranger District)

### Friends of the Forest

You can help maintain our forests by volunteering time and energy with the U.S. Forest Service or the National Park Service. Check at the local Forest Service office for opportunities. The Fort Collins office sponsors a winter volunteer group known as the Nordic Rangers. (See the appendix for contact information.)

## HOW TO USE THIS BOOK

The routes in this book range from family adventures to winter mountaineering treks. Most of the easy out and backs are suitable for families with young children. Included are some trails specifically for young children or less ambitious family outings with visitors from lower elevations. There are also many trails suitable for serious winter mountaineering, including overnight stays.

Routes are grouped according to five geographic regions and further segmented into chapters covering local areas. General driving directions to each local area are given at the beginning of each chapter. Each route then begins

*Clearing fallen timber from Blue Lake Trail, Route 12* (courtesy Canyon Lakes Ranger District)

with an information summary that enables you to judge whether that trip is appropriate for you. Following the summary is an overview of the route mentioning its highlights and attractions. This is followed by more specific driving directions to the trailhead and a detailed description of the hike itself. The accompanying maps are not intended to be used for routefinding, but to assist you in visualizing the hike and to help you locate the route on a topographical map.

### Distance
The distance for each route, whether an out and back (termed "round trip"), a loop, or one way, is given in miles.

### Difficulty
For many of the routes, the difficulty rating is given as a range because you can always opt for traveling only a portion of the trail and thereby turn a moderate or challenging hike into an easier one. Many of the routes offer more than one option because even a short out and back can be a nice outdoor experience with pleasing scenery.

The difficulty ratings in this book are generally on a par with those given by the U.S. Forest Service. *Easy* routes are appropriate for beginners or novices; the number of steep sections and the overall elevation gain are limited. *Moderate* routes include several steep sections and require a longer, more sustained effort that is appropriate for intermediate snowshoers. *Challenging* routes have many steep sections and likely include a sustained climb.

These ratings assume that people using this book are reasonably fit and physically active, or have been medically cleared for physical activity at altitudes above 7,000 feet. If you have been leading a sedentary lifestyle, check with your health-care provider before engaging in strenuous outdoor activity.

### Skill Level

*Novice:* Novices have never used snowshoes or have used them only once or twice. To truly enjoy one of these treks, novices should be physically active and exercise at least two times per week for at least 20 minutes per session; they should also be able to handle an elevated heart rate and lack of oxygen at higher elevations. Novices probably won't attempt the entire route, but will cover a section of it and then turn around before they become exhausted. As a novice, decide how long you want to be out before you go, and then time your outbound trip, frequently estimating how long it will take to return to the trailhead. This way, you won't accidentally exceed your limits. Needless to say, the physically active young generally have an advantage over equally active "mature" adults.

*Intermediate:* Intermediate snowshoers have used snowshoes several times. They enjoy routes rated as moderate if they have a somewhat higher level of fitness. This doesn't mean they have to be serious athletes. It just means they are physically active and exercise at least three times per week for 20 to 40 minutes per session.

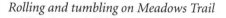

*Rolling and tumbling on Meadows Trail*

*Expert:* Expert snowshoers have been using snowshoes for a year or more and have a high level of fitness. They successfully enjoy routes rated as challenging and have the experience to survive under the possibility of rapidly changing weather and snow conditions. Experts should be challenging themselves with almost daily exercise in order to enjoy all-day, strenuous treks to the mountain tops. Experts also have very good routefinding skills, always carry a topo map and compass or GPS, and know how to use them.

### High Point and Elevation Gain

These two entries tell you the highest elevation reached on the hike, and the elevation difference between it and the trailhead. These are both given in feet.

### Avalanche Danger

The hazard rating for avalanches is given here as low, moderate, considerable, high, or extreme based on the terrain. See "Avalanche" earlier in the introduction for a description of the ratings and for specifics regarding weather and snow conditions. Call the Colorado Avalanche Information Center for up-to-date reports (see the appendix).

### Maps

The relevant topographical map or maps for the area of each route are listed here.

### Who to Contact

This entry lists the land managing agency to contact for more information; phone numbers are listed in the appendix under "Contact Information."

## A NOTE ABOUT SAFETY

Safety is an important concern in all outdoor activities. No guidebook can alert you to every hazard or anticipate the limitations of every reader. Therefore, the descriptions of roads, trails, routes, and natural features in this book are not representations that a particular place or excursion will be safe for your party. When you follow any of the routes described in this book, you assume responsibility for your own safety. Under normal conditions, such excursions require the usual attention to traffic, road and trail conditions, weather, terrain, the capabilities of your party, and other factors. Keeping informed on current conditions and exercising common sense are the keys to a safe, enjoyable outing.

*The Mountaineers Books*

# NORTHERN COLORADO

*I frequently tramped eight or ten miles through the deepest snow to keep an appointment with a beech-tree, or a yellow birch, or an old acquaintance among the pines.*
Henry David Thoreau, *Winter Visitors* (1856)

*Chapter 1*

# RED FEATHER LAKES AREA

One of the lesser-known areas for winter recreation is the Red Feather Lakes area, approximately 45 miles northwest of Fort Collins and very close to the Wyoming-Colorado border. The lakes region is a transition zone between the foothills and mountains, combining the characteristics of rolling foothills, hogbacks, and the conifer forests of the high mountains. This geographical transition zone is bordered on the northwest by the Medicine Bow Mountains that sneak into Colorado from Wyoming and then tower majestically as they stretch to the southwest. The undulating foothills and low mountains eventually flatten into wide horizons of the High Plains of southern Wyoming and northeastern Colorado.

The Red Feather Lakes area isn't as heavily used as the upper reaches of nearby Poudre Canyon because the snow isn't as reliable as it is at the higher altitudes of Cameron Pass. (Routes 4 through 18 are in Poudre Canyon.) The snow in the lakes region is usually more than adequate by mid-January; however, double-check conditions before you venture forth if the weather has been warm in the foothills or high mountains.

To reach the Red Feather Lakes area from Fort Collins, drive north on US 287 for approximately 20 miles until you reach the Red Feather Lakes Road (County Road 74E) junction known as The Forks, near Livermore (there is a restaurant at the intersection). Many maps show the intersection as Livermore. The turnoff is on the left at the bottom of a long hill where US 287 veers to the right. Turn left (west) onto paved CR 74E, which features lots of curves and climbs (speed limit is generally 45 mph). It's around 23 miles to the Dowdy Lakes area (allow at least 1 hour and 30 minutes from Fort Collins); around 29 miles to the Beaver Meadows Resort Ranch (allow about 1 hour and 45 minutes from Fort Collins); and around 49 miles to Deadman Road (allow 1 hour and 30 minutes).

--*1*--

# Mount Margaret

**Round trip:** 8 miles; 7 miles from Dowdy Lake trailhead
**Difficulty:** Easy
**Skill level:** Novice
**High point:** 7,957 feet
**Elevation gain:** 257 feet
**Avalanche danger:** None
**Map:** Trails Illustrated Red Feather Lakes, Glendevey
**Contact:** Canyon Lakes Ranger District, Roosevelt National Forest

This popular summer hiking route is often overlooked for snowshoeing or skiing because of the relatively low altitude (7,700 feet at the trailhead) and inconsistent snow conditions. By January there is often good snow and not very many people. It features nice vistas of the foothills, rock outcroppings, and peaceful mountain meadows guarded by stately conifers and of the smaller canyons and valleys of northern Larimer County. Though the round trip to the summit can be a pleasant all-day adventure (allow 5–8 hours), it is still very worthwhile to snowshoe a small part of the hike because it is scenic from start to finish; you don't have to bag the anticlimactic Mount Margaret summit to enjoy a feeling of satisfaction. The trail is generally out in the open, so warm weather can melt the snow much more readily than the tree-protected trails in Beaver Meadows (see Route 2).

**Warning:** Be prepared to hike rather than snowshow if the snow is inadequate, because this trail is at a relatively low altitude.

The Mount Margaret trailhead is on Red Feather Lakes Road a couple of miles before the Dowdy Lake turnoff. The trailhead, on the north (right) side of the road, is easy to miss if there aren't any cars in the small parking lot; look for a low wire fence—the area is used for grazing in the summer. The trail from Red Feather Lakes Road travels through beautiful open meadows.

**Tip:** There are other trailheads for Mount Margaret in the immediate area, on the north and southeast sides of Dowdy Lake. The north trailhead is about a mile closer to the Mount Margaret summit, but entails almost 4 additional miles of driving. Continue west a couple of miles on CR 74E to the Dowdy Lake turnoff on the right. Drive a little more than 0.5 mile and turn right; in another 0.25 mile turn left onto road 218 and continue another long 0.5 mile to the road end. The Dowdy Lake trailhead avoids a stream crossing that can be a bit tricky. Also, if you have a second vehicle available for a shuttle, you can do a one-way hike using this second trailhead.

From the trailhead on Red Feather Lakes Road, the trail follows a gentle hill up and then down, into the South Lone Pine Creek drainage, through rolling meadows with rock outcrops and small peaks in the distance. After about 0.5 mile, cross South Lone Pine Creek, which is generally subdued in the winter. There is a footbridge to the east (right) of the trail that isn't difficult to find but you have to hunt and peck your way through the tall willows. Crossing the footbridge in your snowshoes is a judgment call. It might be easier to take them off and walk across unless the snow is packed thick enough for your claws. Having poles is especially helpful for negotiating the narrow board.

On the other side of the stream, the trail goes gently uphill north and in 1 mile veers west for 0.25 mile then back north for 0.25 mile; at 1.5 miles it passes a connector trail to the Dowdy Lake Loop on the left—stay to the right. The trail then flattens and enters trees, traveling northeast for 0.75 mile to a five-way intersection at 2.5 miles. Go straight, past Loop A, which is to the right. In about 0.15 mile pass Loop B, which is on the left. (The loops are longer and better for biking than snowshoeing.) You'll be in trees but there are views and a nice meadow. After 0.3 mile you reach another intersection with the other end of Loop A on the right; go left/north past a pond. In 0.25 mile you pass the other end of Loop B on the left at just under 3 miles; bear right toward Mount Margaret—there is a sign.

The trail opens up completely as you go downhill and savor views of rock towers. The trail rolls, going up and down several times, before finally reaching the base of Mount Margaret. Climbing the rock summit is difficult when dry, and it's definitely not advisable when covered with snow and ice. One hundred yards past the summit, downhill to the left of the rocks, is a great view of the spectacle of canyons and valleys that surround the rocky summit.

For variety on the return, at the five-way intersection don't take Loop A hard to the left, the trail to the left that you came in on, or the trail to the right to Dowdy Lake; go straight ahead on a very visible route. In 0.75 mile you come to a gate; 100 yards before it is the connector trail on the left that takes you back to the main trail from Red Feather Lakes Road.

## OTHER TRAILS TO EXPLORE
Bellaire Lake and Molly Lake, off Manhattan Road (CR 162) about 3 miles west of the Dowdy Lakes area, are also worth exploring.

*Mount Margaret Trail*

## --2--

# Beaver Meadows Resort Trails and Trappers Pass

**Trappers/Inca/Ute loop:** 2.5 miles
**Difficulty:** Easy
**Skill level:** Novice
**High point:** 8,800 feet
**Elevation gain:** 400 feet

**Trappers/Renegade loop:** 3 miles
**Difficulty:** Moderate
**Skill level:** Novice to intermediate
**High point:** 9,200 feet
**Elevation gain:** 800 feet

**Trappers/Buckskin loop to Trappers Pass:** 4.8 miles
**Difficulty:** Moderate
**Skill level:** Novice to intermediate
**High point:** 9,200 feet
**Elevation gain:** 800 feet

**Avalanche danger:** None to low
**Map:** Beaver Meadows Resort Trail Map
**Contact:** Beaver Meadows Resort Ranch

This family-oriented resort and ski area is about 50 miles from Fort Collins, a drive of about 1 hour and 30 minutes. It is a good place for a first snowshoe adventure if you want groomed, well-marked trails and the convenience of helpful staff, a lodge, and a restaurant nearby. The lodge rents snowshoes, cross-country skis, and tubes; call ahead to determine equipment availability. There is a daily user fee ($10 for adults and $8 for children at this writing), but you can also cross-country ski and tube once you have paid the fee. The resort also offers a variety of overnight accommodations.

There are sixteen trails, several of which are open to snowshoers. The trails are compacted by snowmobiles to make snowshoeing easier for the uninitiated. If you complete all the resort's snowshoe routes, you will have a satisfying day with a wide variety of views and trails that ascend and descend through an aspen and pine forest and cross some beautiful sunny meadows. The Trappers Trail is a beauty, offering gentle climbs and descents, good views, and a nice mix of forest, outcrops, and small meadows. From the Trappers Trail you can

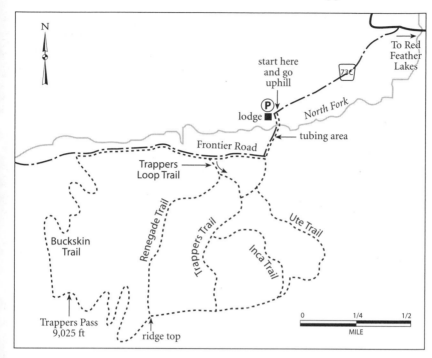

make many loops; here, three are described. The longest adventure, to Trappers Pass, features a bit more elevation gain and a panoramic view from one of the highest ridges in the resort.

The resort is about 6 miles (20 minutes) northwest of the Mount Margaret trailhead on Red Feather Lakes Road (Route 1). From the Dowdy Lake area, continue west on the Red Feather Lakes Road/CR 74E past the Pot Belly Restaurant (the local landmark, heated by a potbellied stove) and CR 162 on the left. When CR 74E ends at the fork (it becomes Deadman Road straight ahead), go right on CR 73C, a dirt road, and continue for 4.3 miles. The sign for the resort is on the left. Go under the sign and take the private road another 0.8 mile to the parking area.

To start all of the loops described here, go across the meadow south of the lodge and up the hill to the right of the tubing run. At the top of the hill you reach Frontier Road; turn right onto the road and go down the hill 0.25 mile. At the bottom of the hill, look to the left for a yellow sign marking the snowshoe trail. Go left up the hill on the Trappers Loop Trail. It climbs gradually uphill through thick trees with a rock outcropping on the right. The snow is usually surprisingly good in the trees. After you crest the first hill, follow the trail to the left; soon you break out of the trees and have a very nice view of the surrounding pine-covered mountains.

If you look carefully at the mountain across the valley, you will notice that most of the trees are smaller and about the same age, as though there was a clear-cut or fire years ago. Actually, the trees are finally obscuring traces of a fire caused by a small plane crash that obliterated the forest on that mountainside more than twenty years ago. Now it is not really noticeable unless you look closely.

Once you crest the hill, at 0.4 mile there is a trail junction that isn't well marked; the Renegade Trail is to the right (west). Whether you see it or not, continue straight on the Trappers Loop Trail. Soon, at the top of the next ridge, you intersect the well-marked Trappers Trail, marked by red flags; bear to the right (west) sharply to stay on the trail. Trappers Trail winds its way through the mixed aspen and pine forest. If it isn't snowing or blowing hard, the snowmobile track is fairly easy to follow to the meadow filled with healthy white aspen. Break into the aspen-filled meadow and, after crossing it, you'll see two more signs for the Trappers Trail. After climbing and winding your way through the very pretty forest with a nice variety of lodgepole, spruce, and aspen, you eventually intersect the Inca Trail. It takes about 30 to 40 minutes of easy walking with very frequent stops to reach this point at 0.6 mile. From here you can continue straight on Trappers Trail or turn left onto the Inca Trail.

**Trappers/Inca/Ute loop:** Turn left onto the Inca Trail, which is on a north-facing slope in a well-shaped tree tunnel that goes downhill through deeper, more powdery snow. The trail is well protected from sun and wind because of the blanket of trees. If you leave the trail, you will likely enjoy deep powder among the trees. After 0.5 mile (25 minutes) of gentle meandering downhill, the Inca Trail reaches an open valley with views of several large rock outcroppings. There is a colorful mixture of mature aspen and fairly tall lodgepole pine trees in this valley. This is a good place for a snack or lunch because it enjoys warm southern exposure, though it is also open to wind. At this point you can go left on the Ute Trail back to the base area in another 0.75 mile; the route described here goes right on the Ute Trail to rejoin Trappers Trail and complete the loop back to the lodge.

Turn right (west) on the Ute Trail and go up and down rolling terrain in and out of trees in a long, narrow meadow nicely framed by trees on both sides. Most of the trail on this back side of the area is open, with good views. Unfortunately, the warmth of the southern exposure can expose much of the trail, so you might have to take off your snowshoes and hike a bit. It can be a pleasant change of pace that is worth the warm, springlike sunshine and breezes. After less than 0.5 mile you reach the well-signed junction with the top of the Trappers Trail at about 1.4 miles. Here you can continue on the next loop by going straight; to complete this loop, turn right. The Trappers Trail takes you uphill a bit and then downhill back to the Inca-Trappers trail intersection at about

*Beaver Meadows*

1.9 miles, where you go straight on the 0.6-mile return loop to the base area.

**Trappers/Renegade loop:** At the Ute-Trappers junction at 1.4 miles, continue straight on the Trappers Trail, which in 0.25 mile intersects the top of the Renegade Trail at about 1.7 miles. Take the Renegade Trail to the right, uphill; this section has southern exposure, so the snow might be mediocre. After 0.5 mile you crest the ridge and enjoy a good view of the base valley far below. The Renegade Trail descends gradually and, because it is a north slope, usually features deeper and more powdery snow. It is a very nice forest that speaks to you with silence as you descend through the stately trees. At 2.4 miles you join back up with the Trappers Loop Trail near where you started; here go to the left back to the base area.

**Trappers/Buckskin loop:** From the intersection of Trappers Trail and the top of Renegade Trail at 1.7 miles, continue straight ahead (west) on Trappers Trail to get on top of the highest point in the area and extend a beautiful day. Go uphill on a very reasonable switchback that is not recommended for small children but is certainly doable for ambitious families. In 1.25 miles reach the top of Trappers Pass, 9,025 feet, at 3 miles.

After enjoying the view from Trappers Pass, walk along the short top of the ridge line to the Buckskin Trail to the right, which goes gradually downhill, meandering through the trees with occasional nice views of the base area and surrounding hills, through nice powder because of its northerly orientation. The powder is especially welcome after the sparse and crusty snow on the south side of the mountain. The trail loses about 400 feet of elevation back to Frontier Road in 1 mile, 4 miles from the start. Turn right and walk another 0.8 mile to return to the base facilities.

-- ϡ --

# Deadman Road and North Lone Pine Trail

**Round trip:** 8 miles from gate closure; 11 miles from end of plowed road
**Difficulty:** Moderate
**Skill Level:** Novice to intermediate
**High point:** 10,700 feet
**Elevation gain:** 300 feet from gate closure; 1,300 feet from end of plowed road
**Avalanche danger:** None on road; low on trail
**Map:** Trails Illustrated Red Feather Lakes, Glendevey
**Contact:** Canyon Lakes Ranger District, Roosevelt National Forest

In the summer, this enchanting and nonthreatening drive into the mountains and meadows on the border between Colorado and Wyoming can easily lead you to imagine roaming bands of Arapaho hunting enormous herds of buffalo. In the winter, there is no mistaking that this terrain is not to be taken lightly, but it can still be enjoyed. You'll need a four-wheel-drive vehicle to reach the gate closure; or with some extra travel on foot either with snowshoes or on skis, you can reach the gate closure 1.5 miles beyond the plowed road in spite of snowmobiles. The North Lone Pine trailhead is well marked but the trail is not, requiring good routefinding, map reading, and compass skills to navigate it successfully. Clear-cutting and forest fires have raked this part of the Roosevelt National Forest in the past, but it now enjoys thick new growth varying between 20-foot-high fir trees and 2-foot-tall pines. The topography is similar to that of Beaver Meadows (Route 2) and Mount Margaret (Route 1). The difference is that you climb to the higher summits and earn spectacular views of the High Plains and canyons as they climb steeply into the stark terrain of southern Wyoming and blend into the subtle beauty of the Medicine Bow Range. You will also enjoy a view of North Bald Mountain. Wait for the reliable, fresh snows of midwinter to avoid potentially spotty early season snow.

From the Dowdy Lake area, go straight (west) 2 miles on the Red Feather Lakes Road/CR 74E and pass the Creedmore Lakes Road/CR 73C turnoff, beyond which CR 74E turns into gravel Deadman Road/CR 162. It is about 2.5 miles west to the winter road closure gate; the road gets steeper, narrower, and less plowed as you progress. If it is snowpacked, it is not wise to attempt to negotiate it to the road closure without a four-wheel-drive vehicle. Without one, you will likely have to walk uphill an extra 1.5 miles beyond where the road is plowed (at about 8,400 feet) to reach the gate closure.

If the snow cover is good, from where the road requires four-wheel-drive

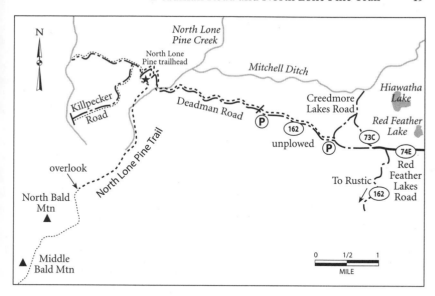

you can snowshoe approximately 1.5 miles to the gate closure. This can be pleasant because the vehicle and snowmobile traffic is light, and if you are subjected to snowmobiles and SUVs up Deadman Road, you can take side paths through the adjoining forest rather than staying on the road. You can also try to get a ride to the gate closure (elevation 8,700 feet).

From the gate closure go about 0.5 mile gradually uphill to where the road levels; you will be treated to the first overlook to the north and west. You can see the summit of the heavily forested back side of the mountains that cradle the Beaver Meadows Resort ski area (Route 2) west of Red Feather Lakes. On a clear day you can also enjoy a view of the High Plains of Wyoming in the distance. From the first overlook the road goes downhill and back into the trees for 1.5 miles before resuming the climb up the mountainside. In another 0.5 mile of climbing on the road, or through the adjoining trees, reach the trailhead on the south (left) side of the road (elevation 9,400 feet) and the picnic area on the right (north) side of the road, 2 miles from the gate closure (3.5 miles from the end of the plowed road). You are fairly high up on the mountain here. The very well-marked trailhead is an ideal place for photos, lunch, or a snack break before entering the trail, weather and wind permitting.

From the trailhead picnic area, you can take on some routefinding on the unmarked North Lone Pine Trail. The beginning of the trail is fairly obvious from the trail marker and information board, but is unmarked after that. You can tell where the trail goes by the small tree tunnel that it forms. The trail climbs steadily and roller-coasters a bit as it meanders through the thick tree

*Beaver Meadows*

cover. As you travel to the higher reaches of the trail, there are some tree breaks that offer views. After 1.5 miles (approximately 40 to 60 minutes) on the trail, you cross an old logging road. You cross it again in 0.25 mile (about 20 minutes later), though the map doesn't show this.

The trail levels somewhat and you get a view to the left of one of the Bald Mountains. Stay up high on the ridge. At 2 miles from the trailhead (4 miles from the gate closure; 5.5 miles from the end of the plowed road) there's a rock outcropping on your left. Leave the trail and climb the rock carefully to see the best view of the two mountains. It takes at least 2 hours from the gate closure to reach the North Bald Mountain overlook. Though the trail does continue from there to eventually dead-end at the Elkhorn-Baldy four-wheel-drive road (not accessible in winter), it's wiser to turn around and find your way back to the trailhead and then your car.

*Chapter 2*

# POUDRE CANYON

The Poudre Canyon is one of the Front Range's real treasures. One of the longest and most spectacular canyons in the state, it offers some of the state's best snowshoeing. Its upper reaches around Cameron Pass are among the most reliable for early and late-season snow.

Pingree Park (Routes 4 through 9), a branch summer campus of Colorado State University, is in the lower reaches of Poudre Canyon. It is surrounded by Roosevelt National Forest and features the majestic mountain backdrops of the Cache la Poudre Wilderness, Comanche Wilderness, and Rocky Mountain National Park. It is generally less heavily used than the Cameron Pass area and some of the closer trails are a real treat. But some start at low elevations (8,000 feet) and usually aren't reliable until midseason unless it is an early snow year. While most of the trails are closed to snowmobiles, the closed roads are not and snowmobile traffic on the closed roads is variable.

Cameron Pass (Routes 10 through 18) is the summit of State Highway 14, at 10,200 feet, and one of the most popular destinations for snowshoers and cross-country skiers. You might also encounter some overlap with snowmobilers approaching from the Lake Agnes area. Most of the trails in this area start at an elevation of at least 9,000 feet. This generally means snow conditions are great but wind chills are potentially dangerous, so bring lots of warm clothing layers. Fortunately these trails are generally well protected by stately pine trees that act as windbreaks, and there are a lot of relatively warm, sunny, calm days. The pass is bordered on the south by Rocky Mountain National Park's aptly named Never Summer Mountains, crowned by the jagged Nokhu Crags, and on the north by the Medicine Bow Range. To the west is the Colorado State Forest and the stark beauty of North Park, offering additional access to the Rawah Wilderness.

To reach the Poudre Canyon, take US 287 north from Fort Collins about 10 miles and exit west onto State Highway 14 at Ted's Place. This Scenic Byway

51

winds through the Poudre Canyon alongside the largely unfettered Poudre River. The Pingree Park Road/CR 63E turnoff is on the left (south) side of State Highway 14 approximately 27.5 miles west of the entrance to the canyon at Ted's Place. Pingree Park Road is a well-maintained dirt road that is plowed all winter, but it might not be plowed immediately after a snowstorm. The Cameron Pass trailheads are just off of State Highway 14 starting at about 48 miles from the canyon entrance to the pass area at around 65 miles from the canyon entrance. The best trails are a drive of at least 1 hour and 30 minutes from Fort Collins.

--*4*--

# Mineral Spring Gulch

**Round trip:** 4 miles
**Difficulty:** Easy to moderate
**Skill level:** Novice
**High point:** 9,800 feet
**Elevation gain:** 500 feet
**Avalanche danger:** None on lower road, low on higher road unless several feet of new snow
**Map:** Trails Illustrated Poudre River, Cameron Pass
**Contact:** Canyon Lakes Ranger District, Roosevelt National Forest

This is a short, midwinter excursion that goes up a Forest Service road into a pretty woodland meadow/park area with a pleasing mixture of aspen and pine trees. From the top of Prospect Mountain, there are nice views of the Poudre Canyon and the distant Rawahs or Medicine Bow Mountains.

From State Highway 14, take the Pingree Park Road south for 4 miles. At a sign for Crown Point Road, turn right (west) onto it. After the two turnoffs on the right for Salt Cabin Park, in approximately 4 miles from Pingree Park Road, Mineral Spring Road is on the right (north). You might need a four-wheel-drive vehicle to get to this point.

Begin walking uphill on the closed road (Mineral Spring Road); in less than 0.25 mile, at the first side road with a locked gate, stay left. Eventually crest the hill at about 0.75 mile. The road then goes downhill and enters the trees. At a trail junction in 0.25 mile, go left (west), winding your way to the bottom of a nice high mountain park with a pretty meadow where you can see the ultimate goal, the top of Prospect Mountain. Look for a faint road or trail on the left at 1.5 miles, which makes its way to the top of the mountain.

You are in thick trees at the outset of this climb, but will break out into nice southern exposure for a possibly sunny trek to the top. If it is early or late season, some of the road might be snow free, but you should be able to navigate around in the trees to find snow to walk on. As you near the top, there are great views of the plains to the east and the top of the Poudre Canyon to the north. You might have to shed your snowshoes before reaching the top because of sunny or windblown conditions. The top affords views of the Rawah and Mummy Ranges to the west. The wind and temperature will likely determine the length of your stay on top. If you can find shelter and it isn't too cold or breezy, it is a nice place for a snack break. Otherwise, there are warmer, sunnier spots back down in the trees or in the gulch.

## --5--
# Crown Point Road

**Round trip:** 3 miles to spur road; 7 miles to FR 142; 12 miles to Browns Lake trailhead
**Difficulty:** Moderate
**Skill level:** Novice
**High point:** 10,500 feet (Browns Lake trailhead)
**Elevation gain:** Up to 1,100 feet
**Avalanche danger:** None
**Map:** Trails Illustrated Poudre River, Cameron Pass
**Contact:** Canyon Lakes Ranger District, Roosevelt National Forest

This is an easy route along a wide, unplowed road with a gradual incline. You can take worthwhile shorter trips to a spur road or FR 142 or a longer trek to the Browns Lake trailhead. In any case, you will have nice views of Poudre Canyon country and the plains from the higher reaches. Crown Point Road is not plowed, so how far you can drive depends on the depth of the snow and the clearance of your four-wheel-drive vehicle. If you are not driving a four-wheel-drive vehicle, you can still have a reasonable trip starting at about 1 mile from Pingree Park Road. It will be more fun if you can drive another 4.5 miles up the road; that is where the very best scenery starts. You can of course turn around at any point and choose the distance and hiking time that best suit you given your starting point.

From State Highway 14, take Pingree Park Road south for 4 miles. At a sign for Crown Point Road, turn right (west). After heavy snowfall, Crown

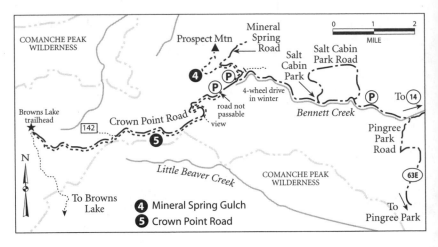

Point Road closes approximately 5.5 miles or less from Pingree Park Road, and offers snowshoeing or skiing from that point.

Starting 5.5 miles from the intersection with Pingree Park Road, there are good views in the first mile. There are some sunny lunch or snack spots in the trees on the right in the first mile or so. Just beyond the initial road switchbacks, you can see a good view area from the main road before you enter a tunnel of trees. Once you exit the switchbacks there are a couple of side trails on the left. The first one, a spur road at 1.5 miles, is a short dead-end route for firewood gathering that offers nice panoramic views into the Comanche Peak Wilderness. It is a nice out-and-back side excursion if you aren't planning to try the entire route to the Browns Lake trailhead.

After that, the main route becomes a tall lodgepole-pine tree tunnel for a couple of miles. You are on the north side of the mountain, and if it is midwinter, your exposure to the sun will be limited until you break from the trees at 3 miles. In approximately 3.5 miles, you reach FR 142 on the right. This intersection is a good place for a break and snack.

From there Crown Point Road swings more westerly, catches a lot of late-afternoon sun, and affords more views. If you aren't too tired and have plenty of time to make the return downhill trek, continue 2.5 miles to the Browns Lake trailhead. It is the best scenery on the route. (If you are really ambitious and exceptionally fit, you could go partway or all the way down to Browns Lake, but this is only advisable under ideal conditions. If you take along some skis for your return, it would be considerably faster.)

On the return, most of the way down you have striking views of the top of the Poudre Canyon and the plains far below. You should be able to make much better time because you are descending 1,000 feet back to your car.

--*6*--

# Little Beaver Creek Trail

**Round trip:** 2 miles to Fish Creek Trail; 10 miles to Beaver Park
**Difficulty:** Moderate
**Skill level:** Novice with good routefinding skills
**High point:** 9,500 feet to Beaver Park
**Elevation gain:** 1,500 feet
**Avalanche danger:** None to low
**Map:** Trails Illustrated Poudre River, Cameron Pass
**Contact:** Canyon Lakes Ranger District, Roosevelt National Forest

This double trailhead is at a little under 8,000 feet, so it is best if it has been a very good early snow season that has blanketed the lower reaches of the Poudre Canyon. The trail intersects Fish Creek Trail; both go into the Comanche Peak Wilderness Area. Little Beaver Creek Trail features an almost nonstop view of the peaks in the Comanche Peak Wilderness Area, including its namesake. After a steep start, the trail makes a gradual ascent. It is not marked for winter activities but is a fairly obvious ridge-line route that then follows the creek to Beaver Park, where it intersects with the Flowers Trail.

From State Highway 14, take Pingree Park Road south. Pass Crown Point Road (see Routes 4 and 5) and the Jack Gulch Campground, both on the right.

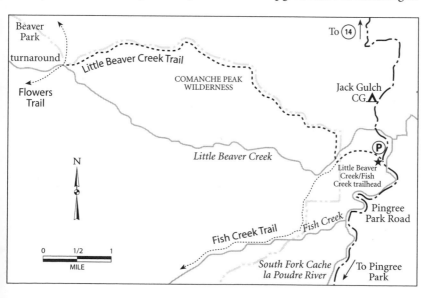

*View of Comanche Peak from Little Beaver Creek Trail*

In 8 miles reach the lower Little Beaver Creek/Fish Creek trailhead on the right (west). Go through the cattle guard and park near the largest trailhead sign. Make sure you don't block the cattle-guard gate. The trailhead is well marked, though the trail's exact starting point isn't completely obvious when covered with snow if you are the first to break trail. To get to the trailhead, walk back through the cattle guard and look for a mileage marker sign to the right of the fence. The trail goes up the hill to the left at a sharp angle.

At first, the trail goes steeply uphill. It travels west and then switchbacks toward the top of the ridge, winding through the pine trees. After 0.5 mile it emerges from the trees and there is a great view of Fall Mountain, Comanche Peak, and other mountains in the Mummy Range. The trail is not well marked for snowshoeing, except with occasional tree "blazes," so keep the drainage and peaks on your left as you hike west and stay on top of the ridge line. The trail eventually levels at around 8,600 feet and follows the ridge line in a much more gradual climb eventually topping out at around 9,500 feet in a little under 2 miles. At the sign marking the wilderness boundary at about 0.75 mile, the trail takes a sharp turn to the left (south), descending slightly, before heading back to the west. If you don't see the sign or lose the trail, climb uphill to the northwest, and then west. The ridge narrows considerably, making the route more obvious. Stay on top of the ridge in a lodgepole pine and spruce forest. You won't be able to see the peaks to the southwest.

After less than another 0.5 mile there is (ironically, since you are in a wilderness area) a power pole and telephone line for Pingree Park. You will be treated to a nice panorama of Comanche Peak and the Mummies to the west. This is a good spot for a break because the trail begins to head downhill, back into the trees, and it won't be quite as sunny and warm once you reach the bottom of the hill. The trail goes downhill about 0.25 mile to the intersection with the Flowers Trail in a little over 1 mile. For a nice, short excursion, you can turn around here. Except for reclimbing the last hill, it is downhill back to the trailhead.

To go farther, stay right on the Little Beaver Creek Trail, or left on the Flowers Trail, which soon crosses Little Beaver Creek. The Flowers Trail continues to have good views of Comanche as it heads southwest along the creek, gradually climbing.

--7--

# Signal Mountain

**Round trip:** 5 miles to beaver ponds; 10.5 miles to Signal Mountain
**Difficulty:** Easy to challenging
**Skill level:** Novice to intermediate
**High point:** 9,000 feet at beaver ponds; 11,200 feet near Signal Mountain
**Elevation gain:** 450 feet to beaver ponds; 2,700 feet to Signal Mountain
**Avalanche danger:** None to low, except on final slope to summit
**Map:** Trails Illustrated Poudre River, Cameron Pass
**Contact:** Canyon Lakes Ranger District, Roosevelt National Forest

This little-used trail offers protection from winter winds and a tour of a magical river arroyo. The trail is down at stream level, along Pennock Creek, and is fairly level for the first few miles, with nice views across the stream. The trail climbs gently before it steepens and pushes you to a final challenging assault of Signal Mountain. It offers a walk through a beautiful riparian area that features a mixed old-growth forest of aspen, pine, fir, and spruce and striking rock outcrops. It makes a nice out-and-back trip of any length, although climbing Signal Mountain is a serious all-day adventure. There is also a south access to this trail near Glen Haven.

From State Highway 14, take Pingree Park Road south approximately 10 miles, about 0.5 mile beyond the turnoff for Pennock Pass. The trailhead is on the left (east) side of the road 2 miles before the Pingree Park Campus. Park alongside the road.

The trail drops down from the road to a stream and then climbs up the other side of the drainage, winding its way through the thick forest. It drops again to reach Pennock Creek at 0.5 mile. When the trail meets an old road, bear right. At approximately 1 mile cross Pennock Creek on a footbridge that goes left (east) across the creek and might require removing your snowshoes. If it has been very cold and the stream is solidly frozen, you might be able to just walk across the stream, but don't take any chances.

The trail then begins to climb, gaining about 300 feet up and over a small

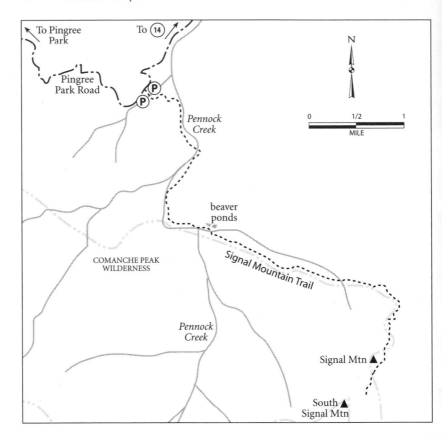

ridge at 8,800 feet at about 1.5 miles. It climbs steadily and gains another 200 feet, rising to 9,000 feet, in the next 0.5 mile or so as you parallel the stream on your right. The beaver ponds at about 2.5 miles mark the halfway point; here the trail leaves the main Pennock Creek drainage, crosses a smaller stream, and begins to climb more steeply as it leaves the streambed. There is a striking rock spire that can be a lunch or turnaround point, depending on your ambitions. The trail continues to climb, crossing the stream again at about 3.75 miles. At about 10,400 feet and 4.5 miles it reaches a bit of a saddle that is still obscured by trees, where you might see an old road. Look to the right to pick up the faint trail.

Continue to climb toward tree line. This section is difficult to follow because of the good snow cover. At tree line you might encounter some windswept tundra. The summit of Signal Mountain is up to the right at a little less than 5.25 miles; South Signal Mountain (14 feet lower) is a 0.5-mile ridge walk farther. The view from the summit ridge is superb, with a great panorama of the canyons, foothills, and plains below. You can also see Longs Peak in the distance.

--8--

# Stormy Peaks Trail

**Round trip:** 3 miles to wilderness boundary; 6 miles to RMNP boundary; 10 miles to pass
**Difficulty:** Easy to challenging
**Skill level:** Novice to intermediate
**High point:** 9,600 feet to wilderness boundary; 10,400 to RMNP boundary; 11,700 feet to pass
**Elevation gain:** 572 feet to wilderness boundary; 1,372 feet to RMNP boundary; 2,672 feet to pass
**Avalanche danger:** None to low
**Map:** Trails Illustrated Poudre River, Cameron Pass
**Contact:** Canyon Lakes Ranger District, Roosevelt National Forest

The Stormy Peaks Trail starts at the end of Pingree Park Road, featuring almost nonstop views of the impressive mountain backdrop as you climb out of the valley and gradually make your way above tree line. You might not be able to wear your snowshoes all of the time initially, but because the trail is on a north-facing slope at a high elevation, you will be using them. The trail travels through the stark beauty of a burn area and eventually climbs into a forest that is primarily lodgepole pine but also includes fir and spruce trees. The trail climbs into Comanche Peak Wilderness and then Rocky Mountain National Park; dogs are not allowed in the park.

From State Highway 14, drive Pingree Park Road south 18 miles to the end of the road at Pingree Park Campus and park in the last parking area on the left.

The trail starts off through a fairly rocky area that was burned during a fire; it might be exposed if there hasn't been a recent snowfall. It quickly goes into tree cover and takes a short set of switchbacks toward the top of the low ridge line. You will soon enjoy a very nice view of the campus and most of the Pingree Park area. You can see the cirque that frames Emmaline Lake above the valley to the northwest. The trail isn't always easy to follow, so it is important to watch for tree blazes; stay on the west side of the ridge when in doubt. You soon reenter the area that was burned, and the stark contrast of the burned trees against the white snow is dramatic. The trail parallels Pingree Park; as you travel southwest, there are ever-changing, magnificent views of the Comanche Peak massif. After a mile or so you enter a tree tunnel that lasts for more than 0.5 mile until you reach the Comanche Peak Wilderness boundary

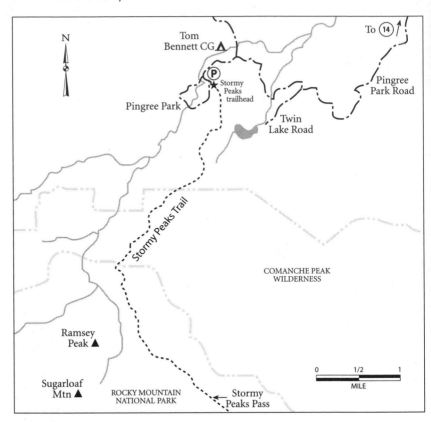

at approximately 1.5 miles. As the trees thin, you have your best view yet of Comanche Peak, Emmaline Lake, Mummy Pass, and Wyoming off to the north. This is a good place for a snack, water, and photos before you start climbing again—or a good place to turn around.

Once you enter the wilderness area, good routefinding skills are necessary. Look for tree blazes and keep in mind that wilderness trails are not well marked. The trail gets considerably steeper on a series of steep switchbacks; several rocky sections and stream crossings might require you to remove your snowshoes. Most of the rocks and all of the streams should be under a thick blanket of snow unless you are attempting an early season trek. It is well worth the minor aggravation of having to put on and take off your snowshoes because in about 0.25 mile you have a superb view of the U-shaped, glacier-carved "park" of Pingree that is in the canyon below Ramsey Peak (11,582 feet) and Sugarloaf Mountain (12,101 feet). You pay for this view by gaining another 200 feet of elevation. In the next scant mile the trail gains 600 feet, and at just under 3 miles you reach the Rocky Mountain National Park boundary.

Enjoy more views of the glacier-carved box canyon below and get a good view of the Stormy Peaks above for the first time. This is another good break or turnaround spot.

From here the trail veers due south; it is very poorly marked. Stay parallel to the Stormy Peaks drainage; frequently check the landscape so you can orient your direction. After 0.25 mile there is a sign for the Rocky Mountain National Park Stormy Peaks campsite. Just when you think you'll never reach tree line, at 4 miles you emerge into a wonderland of high mountain snow, windswept meadows, and dramatic rock outcroppings at about 11,000 feet. It is worth the additional effort to walk another mile and mount the pass (or even climb the Stormy Peaks, 12,148 feet). The only avalanche danger is the final approach to the peaks; the pass is fairly low angle.

*Pingree Park burn area along the Stormy Peaks Trail*

## --*9*--

# Cirque Meadows and Emmaline Lake

**Round trip:** 6.5 miles to meadows; 10.6 miles to lake
**Difficulty:** Easy to challenging
**Skill level:** Novice to intermediate
**High point:** 9,800 feet at meadows; 11,000 feet at lake
**Elevation gain:** 900 feet to meadows; 2,100 feet to lake
**Avalanche danger:** None except near lake (can be avoided)
**Map:** Trails Illustrated Poudre River, Cameron Pass
**Contact:** Canyon Lakes Ranger District, Roosevelt National Forest

This trail offers nice views of Pingree Park, the Stormy Peaks, and the dramatic backdrop of Fall Mountain and the Comanche Peak Wilderness framing the high mountain lake. The first mile of the trail makes a nice family out and back; going all the way to Emmaline Lake makes for a challenging day for an experienced snowshoer. Cirque Meadows is a nice intermediary stop along the way. This trail is rewarding regardless of the distance traveled.

From State Highway 14, drive Pingree Park Road south about 17.5 miles to the turnoff for Tom Bennett Campground. The unnamed trailhead is just

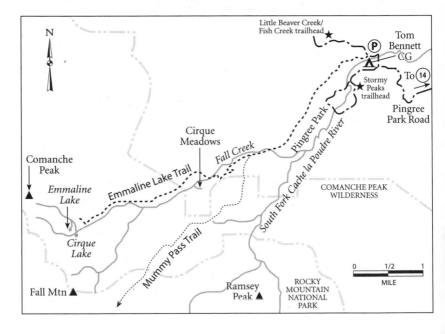

up the road from the campground, before you reach the Little Beaver Creek/ Fish Creek trailhead.

The first 1.5 miles of the trail are out in the open on an old logging road that travels through an old burn area. It is exposed to sun and wind and might not have sufficient snow cover for snowshoes. Don't be discouraged if you have to carry your shoes, because you are likely to encounter excellent snow when you reach the trees. At a little over 2 miles the trail crosses Fall Creek. At about 2.4 miles, reach the intersection with the Mummy Pass Trail to the left; stay to the right.

Just past the trail intersection you enter the trees, and that should provide good snow conditions and cooler temperatures. The trees also offer good protection from the wind on a breezy day. The trail winds, rolls, and switchbacks through a long tree tunnel with occasional glimpses of the valley below. Pass a backcountry campsite; the trail then climbs steeply until you break into the open to recross the creek at Cirque Meadows at just past 3 miles. This is a superb setting, with the backdrop of the Comanche Peak glacier-carved cirque and the vibrant rust colors of the vegetation poking through the snow around the meadow.

After the meadows you reenter the trees and climb another mile, up above the creek. At about 4.4 miles the trail climbs steeply to once again closely follow the creek a scant mile to the wintertime magic of Emmaline Lake and its surroundings.

## OTHER TRAILS TO EXPLORE

Mummy Pass Trail and a cross-country route up Comanche Peak are a couple of other moderate to challenging gems.

*Cirque Meadows along Emmaline Lake Trail*

## --*10*--

# Big South Trail

**Round trip:** 6 miles to viewpoint; 13.5 miles to Flowers Trail
**Difficulty:** Easy to moderate
**Skill level:** Novice
**High point:** 9,000 feet at viewpoint; 9,400 feet at Flowers Trail
**Elevation gain:** 560 feet to viewpoint; 960 feet to Flowers Trail
**Avalanche danger:** None to low
**Map:** Trails Illustrated Poudre River, Cameron Pass
**Contact:** Canyon Lakes Ranger District, Roosevelt National Forest

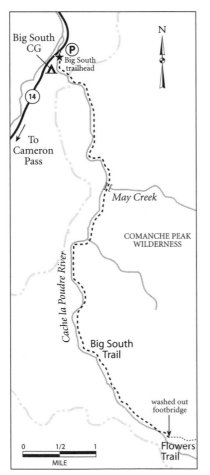

As you near the upper reaches of the Poudre Canyon and Cameron Pass, this is the first trail you encounter that has reasonably good snow cover. Big South Trail is located just past Poudre Falls, which can be dramatic in early winter as the waterfall freezes into unpredictable shapes and the sun glistens on combinations of ice and water. The Big South Trail offers similar winter ice sculptures in its first 0.5 mile. This trail is best used in midseason conditions because the elevation is lower (8,440 feet) and snow can be sketchy early in the winter. The Big South Trail follows the south fork of the Poudre River (called the Cache la Poudre River) as it descends from its origins in the high western reaches of Rocky Mountain National Park and the Comanche Peak Wilderness. With the exception of spring runoff and June rise, when the Poudre swells to a roiling river, this section is a fairly narrow stream. Most of the trail is in the Comanche Peak Wilderness, where wilderness rules apply.

From US 287 at Ted's Place, drive west and then south on State Highway 14 for approximately 48 miles. The parking lot is on the left (east) side of the road 1 mile past the turnout for Poudre Falls.

The beginning of the trail is very rocky because it is a compact canyon of frozen waterfalls, beautifully contorted ice, and snow-crested trees and boulders. The first part of the trail climbs slowly through the trees and over the rocky shore. After the first 0.5 mile you enter the wilderness. The trail stays on the east side of the river, rolling, climbing, and dropping through the scenic small arroyo created by the river. It then climbs more steeply over a section of rocks that can be tricky early or late in the season if the snow cover is thin. This is the point, at about 1 mile, where you find out if there is enough snow to make the trek. If you are able to surmount this section, which features a bit of climbing and a need for care if you have children in the party, you will be able to continue. The trail travels through more rocky sections and breaks out of the trees for some nice views. When you reach approximately 2.4 miles, you cross a bridge over May Creek. In a long 0.5 mile, you have a nice overlook of this branch canyon and the surrounding ridge lines at 3 miles. This viewpoint is a good place for a snack break and photos; turn around here for a nice shorter outing.

The trail then descends back into the arroyo and crosses another drainage, meandering through the trees and becoming much flatter. The trail climbs and descends for the next mile, with occasional vistas. Some wide sections of the river can be used for travel if it's frozen solid in midwinter. At 5 miles the canyon opens up and offers 360-degree views of rock outcrops, meadowlands, and a stately, pristine old-growth forest. It's another 1.75 miles to the junction with the Flowers Trail and a washed-out footbridge across the river.

## --*11*--
# Green Ridge Road

**Round trip:** 3 miles to Lost Lake; 5 miles to Laramie Lake; 8.2 miles to North Twin Lake
**Difficulty:** Moderate
**Skill level:** Novice to intermediate
**High point:** 9,300 feet at Lost and Laramie Lakes; 9,490 feet at North Twin Lake
**Elevation gain:** 307 feet to Lost and Laramie Lakes; 497 feet to North Twin Lake
**Avalanche danger:** None
**Map:** Trails Illustrated Poudre River, Cameron Pass
**Contact:** Canyon Lakes Ranger District, Roosevelt National Forest

This trail, which requires only a minimal elevation gain, is a good sojourn through the rolling forest that offers up nice views of and from several frozen

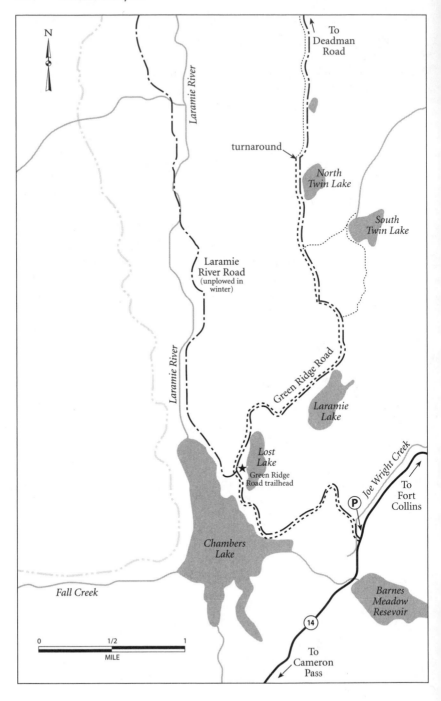

N

To
Deadman
Road

Laramie River

turnaround

North
Twin Lake

South
Twin Lake

Laramie
River Road
(unplowed in
winter)

Laramie River

Green Ridge Road

Laramie
Lake

Lost
Lake

Green Ridge
Road trailhead

Joe Wright Creek

(P)

To
Fort
Collins

Chambers
Lake

Fall Creek

Barnes
Meadow
Resevoir

14

To
Cameron
Pass

0        1/2        1
MILE

lakes. It is used by snowmobiles. Green Ridge Road is found off Laramie River Road. It is possible to cover the trail's entire 38.5 miles to Deadman Road at Red Feather Lakes (see Route 3) if you want to make a very long, multiday backpack trip of it; you will need a car shuttle plus excellent routefinding and winter mountaineering skills to make that trip. But even novice snowshoers can do as much of the trail as they want as an out and back; just watch the time and turn around when you have plenty of energy to make it back to your car.

Take State Highway 14 approximately 57 miles west from Fort Collins to the turnoff for Laramie River Road on the right (west) side of the road. It is well marked but doesn't have any facilities. The road, which in winter is closed and not plowed, crosses Joe Wright Creek at the point where it joins the canyon road (State Highway 14); parking is available on the wide shoulder.

Follow Laramie River Road north as it crests the hill and in 0.5 mile turns sharply south along the ridge above Chambers Lake. At 1 mile the road turns north again. At 1.5 miles reach the Lost Lake summer parking lot; the Green Ridge Road trailhead is on the right (east) side of the road. The trail is marked with orange Forest Service diamonds that indicate it can also be used by snowmobiles.

Make your way along the west side of the lake as the trail meanders through thick lodgepole pine and fir forest until you reach open meadows and lakeshore

*Nordic Rangers at Cameron Pass* (courtesy Canyon Lakes Ranger District)

in another 0.25 mile. It is high enough, when you break into the clear, to give you nice views of the Rawah Wilderness to the west. The trail rolls gently while steadily climbing; at 2 miles it turns northeast. At about 2.5 miles you reach the shore of Laramie Lake with additional photo opportunities.

The trail turns north at the north end of Laramie Lake. At a little past 3 miles you reach the lower side road to South Twin Lake; this is an easy 1-mile side loop, more if you circumnavigate the lake. The upper end of the South Twin Lake side road rejoins the trail at 3.75 miles. At a little past 4 miles you reach North Twin Lake. These lakes are a good turnaround point because beyond them you reenter thick trees, losing good views. The lakes are usually frozen solid in midwinter, but be very cautious about walking or sliding on them.

## --*12*--
# Blue Lake

**Round trip:** 4 miles to Fall Creek; 9.5 miles to Blue Lake
**Difficulty:** Easy to challenging
**Skill level:** Novice to intermediate
**High point:** 9,600 feet at Fall Creek; 10,800 feet at Blue Lake
**Elevation gain:** 100 feet to Fall Creek; 1,300 feet to Blue Lake
**Avalanche danger:** Low to moderate above lake (easily avoided)
**Map:** Trails Illustrated Poudre River, Cameron Pass
**Contact:** Canyon Lakes Ranger District, Roosevelt National Forest

One of the most popular Poudre Canyon trails offers easy, short round-trip excursions or a moderate to challenging all-day adventure, depending on snow conditions and how far you go—it's 4.75 miles one way to the pristine mountain lake surrounded by towering mountains. Unfortunately the first couple of miles of this trail are the least interesting because of the thick lodgepole pine tree cover and flat trail. However, the lodgepole pine forest offers good protection from the wind, so this is a good trail for days with heavy windchill. Don't hike all the way to the lake if heavy snow is predicted, unless you are prepared to spend the night. Blue Lake, a popular overnight destination for winter (or summer) backpackers, is in a magnificent setting among some of the highest peaks of the Medicine Bow Range, including its monarch, 12,951-foot Clark Peak, and 12,127-foot Cameron Peak.

Take State Highway 14 west from Fort Collins 60 miles to the Blue Lake trailhead parking area on the right (west) side of the road. It is well marked but doesn't have any facilities. If you reach Long Draw Road or Zimmerman Lake trailhead, you missed it!

The trail starts at the edge of the parking lot, traveling right (north) across Sawmill Creek and alongside Joe Wright Creek, then veering gradually northwest. You can see Chambers Lake in the distance through the trees. The trail gradually climbs about 300 feet in the first mile. It then levels out to a steady roll through the trees for the next mile and as you enter the Fall Creek drainage it opens up. The trail rolls quite a bit for most of the trip but climbs steadily farther on. These first 2 miles are under the thick cover of lodgepole pines, then you cross Fall Creek and reach a nice meadow area. This is a good spot to turn around for a shorter trip.

After this you start the steady climb to almost 11,000 feet. At about 2.75 miles, cross the Rawah Wilderness boundary; the trail is unmarked after this

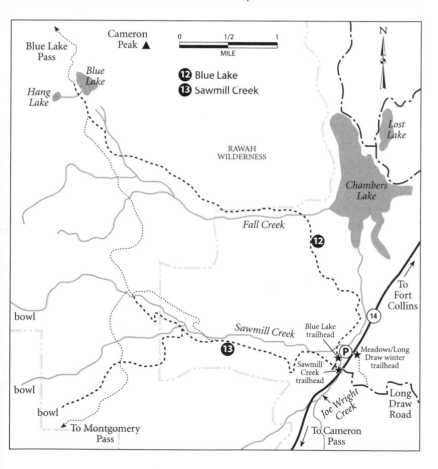

*Nordic Rangers at Cameron Pass* (courtesy Canyon Lakes Ranger District)

but the beauty of the scenery increases dramatically. It is heavily used so routefinding likely won't be a problem unless you are first on the trail. It winds its way northwest through a relatively thick forest, but there are also some nice meadows and streams at a little under 4 miles. In another long 0.75 mile you reach Blue Lake. The surrounding summits aren't visible from the lake because they are obscured by their steep, heavily forested shoulders that embrace the frozen lake, but the views as you descend to the lake are superb.

## --*13*--

# Sawmill Creek

**Round trip:** 3 miles to trail fork; 4 miles to creek fork; 7 miles to bowls
**Difficulty:** Moderate
**Skill level:** Novice to expert
**High point:** 10,000 feet to trail fork; 10,200 feet to creek fork; 11,160 feet to bowls
**Elevation gain:** 500 feet to trail fork; 700 feet to creek fork; 1,660 feet to bowls
**Avalanche danger:** None to high in bowls (can be avoided)
**Map:** Trails Illustrated Poudre River, Cameron Pass
**Contact:** Canyon Lakes Ranger District, Roosevelt National Forest

This relatively lightly used trail offers access to a high mountain panorama of snow-covered peaks in the Rawah Range. It is also an access trail for above-tree line bowls used for telemark skiing. On out-and-back trips of any length, you will enjoy nice views. The trail follows a steep old logging road for the first 2 miles, eventually leveling off and offering great views without additional steep climbs. The trail ends up in the Rawah Wilderness Area.

Take State Highway 14 west from Fort Collins approximately 60 miles to the Blue Lake trailhead parking lot on the right (west); the Sawmill Creek trailhead is just beyond the Blue Lake parking lot. It is very easy to miss because it is marked by only a road and closed gate. From the Blue Lake parking lot, walk 200 yards west on the highway shoulder to the trailhead on the right. Do not park on the road because of almost daily work by snowplows. You could be ticketed, towed, or buried by a snowplow.

The Sawmill Creek Trail starts off in the trees on a gradual and then steep uphill. It follows the old logging road; you can see blue diamond markers up fairly high on the trees directing you away from dead-ends and incorrect old logging roads. After 0.5 mile or so traveling northwest, the trail turns to the left (southwest) sharply and goes up a steep switchback. This is a very sunny section of trail and you will warm up considerably. There are nice views back to the southeast of the mountains and cliffs above Zimmerman Lake. In 0.25 mile the trail turns back toward the Sawmill Creek drainage and travels primarily west-northwest. At 1 mile the trail levels somewhat and then goes slightly downhill 0.5 mile to reach a trail intersection at about 1.5 miles. This is a nice viewpoint for photos and a good place for a snack or lunch break. At this point the nonstop views are quite spectacular, and the wind can become a factor.

To continue the journey beyond this point, you should have good bushwhacking and routefinding skills. No matter which way you choose, you will encounter steep powder sections and multiple, sometimes confusing trails. In 0.5 mile reach another trail junction at 2 miles; you can choose between the north or south route to travel another mile or so on trails. The north route to Blue Lake is a serious winter mountaineering adventure requiring expert skills.

**North:** The trail to the right follows a tributary of Sawmill Creek northwest across avalanche terrain; at about 2.75 miles you reach a creek crossing and trail junction (straight ahead eventually reaches the Blue Lake Trail, Route 12, near the lake; to the left is a trail back to Sawmill Creek).

**South:** The trail to the left climbs above Sawmill Creek, at a little over 3 miles connecting with the other end of the trail that goes either north to intersect the north route or south all the way to Montgomery Pass. If you keep traveling straight ahead, upslope to the southwest through the tall trees, in another 0.5 mile you break through the trees for a terrific sight. It is worth the extra effort to see the base of the Medicine Bows, the high bowls, and peaks even if you don't plan to ski the high mountain cirques. Be sure you carefully note the way back so you don't get lost; use a compass.

*Sawmill Creek Trail*

Avalanche hazard in the cirques can be high. If you plan to use the glacier-carved bowls, proceed very cautiously; it is wise to check for potential avalanche conditions and to know how to dig a snowpit. Also call ahead for avalanche danger levels. The trail itself is generally quite safe; going off trail always increases risk.

## --*14*--

# Long Draw Road

**Round trip:** 6 miles to Trap Lake; 14 miles to Corral Park; 20 miles to Long Draw Reservoir
**Difficulty:** Moderate to challenging
**Skill level:** Novice to intermediate
**High point:** 9,975 feet at Trap Lake; 10,200 feet at Corral Park and reservoir
**Elevation gain:** 453 feet to Trap Lake; 606 feet to Corral Park and reservoir
**Avalanche Danger:** None to low
**Map:** Trails Illustrated Poudre River, Cameron Pass
**Contact:** Canyon Lakes Ranger District, Roosevelt National Forest

Long Draw Road rolls along, climbing short hills at times, but is generally fairly flat in a tree tunnel for most of its 10-plus miles. Long Draw Reservoir is in a very dramatic setting among the Never Summer Mountains on the northern edge of Rocky Mountain National Park. Though Long Draw Road is heavily used by snowmobiles, it offers good access to some nonmotorized routes through some exquisite old-growth forest of snow-draped, stately fir and spruce trees. This road can be used for a winter backpack trip to the Long Draw Reservoir area, or, for other great options, access to the Meadows Trail (Route 16) or Trap Park (Route 15). Unfortunately, on weekends you are likely to encounter heavy snowmobile traffic. There are side trails off the road that can be used to avoid the snowmobiles if you are good at routefinding and using a compass and map or GPS unit. (See map for shortcut trails that parallel the road.) But Long Draw Road is indeed a long road in a vast area, so the odds of being subject to constant snowmobile traffic are slim.

Take State Highway 14 west from Fort Collins 60 miles to the Blue Lake parking area on the right (west) side of the highway. Less than 0.25 mile before the parking lot, just beyond the bulletin board, look for the Meadows/Long Draw winter trailhead parking lot; Long Draw Road itself is on the west side of the highway opposite the Blue Lake parking lot. You can park at the Blue Lake parking area, the Meadows/Long Draw winter trailhead, or at Long Draw Road.

Use the Meadows/Long Draw winter trailhead if you want to access the Meadows Trail or avoid snowmobiles on the lower section of the road. From the well-marked trailhead you cross a pretty meadow wetlands area with a lot of willows and then enter the trees. The trail meanders uphill through the trees and then intersects Long Draw Road in 0.5 mile. (To continue on the Meadows Trail, turn left—east—on the road and watch for the marked trail on the right in about 200 yards.)

*View from Sawmill Creek*

Whether you begin on the road or the trail, in 0.5 mile the two paths converge. Follow Long Draw Road east, then south alongside Trap Creek's box canyon, with Bald Mountain looming above. At approximately 2.5 miles, you will see the shortcut trail to Trap Park. When you reach the Trap Park Trail turnoff at just under 3 miles, stay left; in a short 0.25 you reach Trap Lake. This is a good turnaround spot for a short trip.

Just past 3.5 miles is the Peterson Lake Road; stay to the right. After this, Long Draw Road switchbacks and winds south and east; at about 5.25 miles is a shortcut trail on the right. At 6 miles the road turns sharply south to parallel

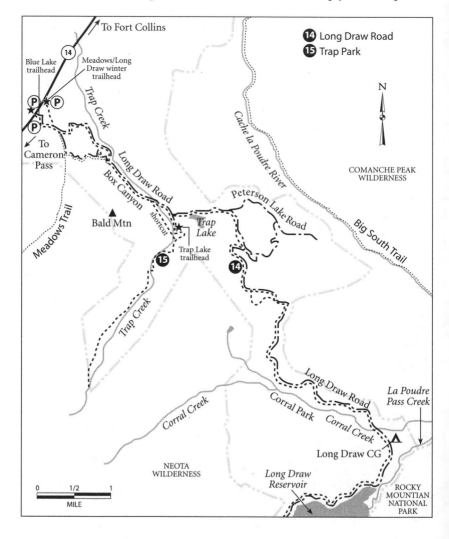

the Comanche Peak Wilderness boundary. At about 6.5 miles reach a gated spur road into Corral Park; in another 0.5 mile or so you reach the park itself, which makes a good turnaround point for a moderate trip.

Now Long Draw Road meanders between Corral Creek and the wilderness boundary for 2 miles. At 9 miles reach the campground and trailhead area. If you've made it this far, it's only another mile until at last you approach the edge of Long Draw Reservoir.

## --*15*--

# Trap Park

**Round trip:** 11.5 miles
**Difficulty:** Moderate
**Skill level:** Novice to intermediate
**High point:** 10,500 feet
**Elevation gain:** 978 feet
**Avalanche danger:** Considerable; potential avalanche run-out zones in Trap Park (can be avoided)
**Map:** Trails Illustrated Poudre River, Cameron Pass
**Contact:** Canyon Lakes Ranger District, Roosevelt National Forest

Trap Park, a draw or small canyon, that offers varied scenery and a rolling trail that is virtually flat, is worth a trip of its own. The trail rolls through a beautiful riparian area following the Trap Creek drainage for 2 miles or so, ending at the boundary of the Neota Wilderness. Avoid avalanche run-out zones at times of high avalanche danger.

Drive to the Long Draw Road parking area (see Route14).

Follow Long Draw Road approximately 2.5 miles (see Route 14) to the shortcut trail on the right to Trap Park (it is marked on the map). You can also continue on the road another 0.3 mile to the turnoff to Trap Lake trailhead; if you reach Trap Lake on Long Draw Road, you have gone too far. Trap Park begins in a small draw with very steep sides. The trail climbs over rocks and up onto a small ridge that provides an overlook. The shortcut trail joins from the right at just under 3.5 miles. The main trail then descends to the creek and crosses it at 4 miles. The branch canyon opens up and the trail levels. At 4.75 miles a side trail climbs onto the north-facing ridge and offers another overlook. The main trail continues south another mile along the creek.

## --*16*--

# Zimmerman Lake and Meadows Trail

**Round trip to lake:** 2.2 miles
**Difficulty:** Easy
**Skill level:** Novice to intermediate
**High point:** 10,495 feet
**Elevation gain:** 476 feet

**One way to Meadows/Long Draw winter trailhead:** 4.25 miles
**Difficulty:** Moderate
**Skill level:** Intermediate to expert
**High point:** 10,495 feet
**Elevation loss:** 1,000 feet

**Avalanche danger:** None to low
**Map:** Trails Illustrated Poudre River, Cameron Pass
**Contact:** Canyon Lakes Ranger District, Roosevelt National Forest

Zimmerman Lake is one of the more popular winter destinations for snowshoers and skiers. A simple round trip to the lake is a nice half-day (or less) activity that can easily be extended by taking the Meadow Trail north from the lake. Don't be discouraged if the parking lot is nearly full and the trail to the lake crowded. Once you get to the lake, people scatter and you can achieve off-trail solitude. The short and fairly gentle trail has nice views of the surrounding mountains in the Rawah Wilderness and Never Summer Mountains that form the northwest border of Rocky Mountain National Park. If you want an all-day adventure, add the Meadows Trail, which is best done one way with a car shuttle at the Meadows/Long Draw winter trailhead (see Route 14); it is downhill starting from Zimmerman Lake. Allow a long day for a round trip. The Meadows Trail round trip is only realistic during the short days of winter if you are fast, fit, and have excellent wilderness routefinding skills. Just doing a portion of the Meadows Trail is also a nice out-and-back trip from either trailhead. The Meadows Trail enters the Neota Wilderness near Zimmerman Lake, from where the trail is unmarked. It can only be used in the winter because it travels through wetlands.

Take State Highway 14 west from Fort Collins about 63 miles to the Zimmerman Lake trailhead on the left (east) side of the road a few miles before Cameron Pass. There are chemical toilets but no running water.

**Tip:** Although State Highway 14 generally travels east-west when you first enter the Poudre Canyon, it dips dramatically to the southwest at Kinikinik. By the time you reach the Zimmerman Lake trailhead, the road is actually more north-south than east-west.

The trail to Zimmerman Lake goes to the right (southeast) out of the

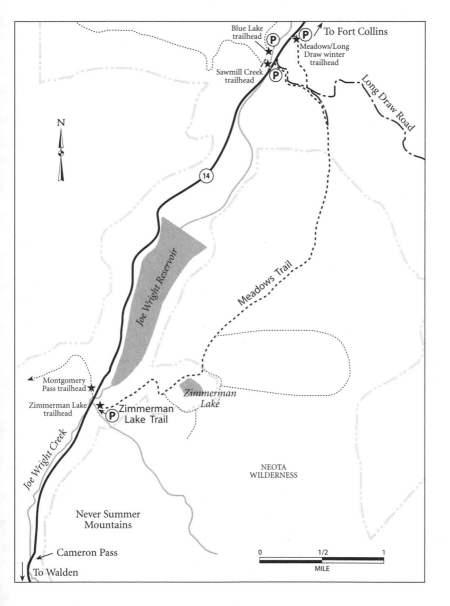

parking lot and then immediately left (east) into the tall pine trees. It climbs gently for about 200 yards and then gradually steepens and narrows into a few switchbacks. At times it is a bit of a challenge not to walk in the cross-country ski tracks because of the narrowness of the trail. The trail climbs almost 400 feet over the next 0.75 mile before exiting the trees and leveling out slightly into a tree-rimmed meadow. The trail widens on the right edge of the meadow. There is a view of the Medicine Bow Range from the top of the meadow. The trail continues to climb, then levels out as it goes left (north) back into the trees. In another 0.25 mile you reach the west edge of the lake.

At the lake you have several options. You can climb a short hill to the right up to the surface of the lake. If there is enough snow, you can snowshoe around the lake in either direction. The walk to the left (northeast) is on a terra firma–supported trail; the walk to the right (southwest) requires walking on the lake surface, which is not recommended unless it has been very cold and there are no broken or wet surfaces visible. Do not attempt it in warm early or late-season conditions or you might go for a dangerous swim. Of course, you can simply survey the great scenery, have a snack, and reverse course. You can also stay on the trail to reach the northeast edge of the lake. Continue north on the trail and at 1.1 miles reach a fork. The almost-flat right (easterly) fork takes you to the north end of the lake for more loop trails; the Meadows Trail is straight/left (north). Once you reach the northeast corner of the lake, you can bushwhack your way onto the hills above the lake. This is a fun place to practice rolling or running downhill if the snow is deep enough and there aren't any visible tree stumps.

At the trail fork at 1.1 miles is the start of the Meadows Trail, which goes straight/left (north). Look for red wooden arrows at the beginning of the trail—the Forest Service's concession for the high volume of less-experienced users—that run counter to the wilderness philosophy of minimal or no human markers

*Zimmerman Lake*

or visible intrusions. There are no markers after the start of the Meadows Trail. The delightful Meadows Trail travels through part of the Neota Wilderness in open meadows, going over ridge lines that offer great views of the Medicine Bows, and winding through a superb old-growth forest of tall, stately fir and spruce trees. It is a rolling trail with some small climbs and descents, but is generally downhill from Zimmerman Lake. It traverses and descends gently along the ridge line for 1.5 miles, affording nice views of Montgomery Pass and the Medicine Bow Range across the valley. Your best photo opportunity and a good place for lunch break is at about 2.5 miles, before you descend the ridge. At about 3 miles, the trail descends more steeply through the beautiful old-growth forest that eventually gives way to an old clear-cut area. You enter a small meadow and at approximately 3.75 miles cross Long Draw Road; in another 0.5 mile you reach the Meadows/Long Draw winter trailhead.

## --17--
# Montgomery Pass

**Round trip:** 3.5 miles
**Difficulty:** Challenging
**Skill level:** Intermediate to advanced
**High point:** 11,000 feet
**Elevation gain:** 1,000 feet
**Avalanche danger:** Moderate to high near pass (can be avoided)
**Map:** Trails Illustrated Poudre River, Cameron Pass
**Contact:** Canyon Lakes Ranger District, Roosevelt National Forest

This is one of the most rewarding and spectacular but demanding destinations in the Cameron Pass area that will take you high above tree line. It is a very popular area for telemark skiing and snowboarding because of the nice powder bowls. The view from the pass is a panorama that includes the Nokhu Crags, Diamond Peaks, and the northern reaches of Rocky Mountain National Park. It is not recommended in times of high avalanche danger, though the trail to tree line is fairly safe. This route to Montgomery Pass is much safer than the Diamond Peaks route that comes from Cameron Pass. There have been three avalanche deaths on Diamond Peaks.

The Montgomery Pass trailhead is across State Highway 14 and slightly to the right (north) of the Zimmerman Lake trailhead (see Route 16). It is well marked but not easily visible from the road and can be spotted in the trees down the road from the Zimmerman Lake parking lot.

From the road, the trail climbs north and immediately steepens, following the Montgomery Creek drainage through trees. After about 0.5 mile, it veers to the left (slightly southwest). After 0.25 mile it flattens out somewhat for another 0.25 mile so you can catch your breath. It then steepens again (get the picture?). Overall it climbs west steadily at the rate of about 200 feet per 0.25 mile, with alternating relatively flat and steep stretches. It isn't extreme but is not for the fainthearted or poorly conditioned, either, considering the elevation.

At about 10,800 feet at 1.25 miles the trail starts to switchback steeply and opens up so you can see a meadow off to the left (south). After crossing two small streams, the next 0.5 mile to the top of the pass takes you out of the trees to spectacular views in all directions. Zimmerman Lake and Joe Wright Reservoir are to the east and north; the Medicine Bow Mountains and its monarch, Clark Peak, lie to the northwest; and the Nokhu Crags of Routt National Forest and Rocky Mountain National Park's Never Summer Mountains are to the southwest. It is often fairly breezy on top, but at least you don't have to worry about the afternoon thunderstorms of the summer climbing season. The worst you can face is a horizontal hurricane-force snow squall or whiteout; fortunately, the latter is not a frequent occurrence. Depending on the weather, have a snack and then return down the trail, or climb to the ridge top if avalanche danger is low.

From the top of the pass you can climb south to the top of the ridge line at 11,400 feet, continuing all the way to Cameron Pass, or continue west down the other side on a very steep trail toward the Michigan River in the Colorado State Forest.

**Tip:** It's fun to enjoy running and floating through the deep powder in the nearby bowls above the pass or off trail on the way down in the trees; an alternate route down is in the Montgomery Creek drainage. You can switchback as you would on skis or run slowly through the powder and "float" on top. This isn't advisable early in the season or if fallen timber and tree stumps are not well covered. Don't attempt this if you are alone or there are any avalanche warnings. Fortunately, there are many periods of stable snow so you can enjoy this area.

*The view south from Montgomery Pass*

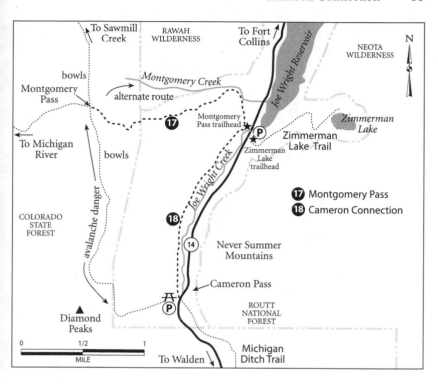

-- *28* --

# Cameron Connection

**Round trip:** 3.4 miles
**Difficulty:** Easy
**Skill level:** Novice
**High point:** 10,200 feet
**Elevation gain:** 200 feet
**Avalanche danger:** None to low (one run-out zone)
**Map:** Trails Illustrated Poudre River, Cameron Pass
**Contact:** Canyon Lakes Ranger District, Roosevelt National Forest

This short, very scenic trail through an old-growth forest of spruce and fir that shares its trailhead with the Montgomery Pass Trail (Route 17) is often overlooked. It offers excellent shelter from prevailing winter windchill, and, though it parallels the highway, is far enough from it to be completely buffered from

its sound or sight. You can also start from the Cameron Pass summit parking lot, or use two vehicles to make this a one-way trip. This trail is usable only in the winter because it crosses many streams and wetlands.

The Montgomery Pass trailhead is across State Highway 14 and slightly to the right (north) of the Zimmerman Lake trailhead (see Route 16). It is well marked but not easily visible from the road, but it can be spotted in the trees down the road from the Zimmerman Lake parking lot. The Cameron Pass parking area is 1.5 miles west on the right (west/north) side of the road. Blue diamonds mark the trail on the east/north side of the Cameron Pass parking area.

From the Montgomery Pass trailhead, turn left (west/south) and proceed parallel to State Highway 14. The Cameron Connection climbs slowly and rolls gently southwest, gaining 200 feet in about a mile, making it a good beginner's trail. The trail above Joe Wright Creek features beautiful spruce and fir trees, which shelter you most of the way on windy days. At a little over a mile the trail nears the creek, following it more closely through three nice meadows with views of the Neota Wilderness near the pass. Reach the summit of Cameron Pass at about 1.7 miles. If you start at the Cameron Pass parking lot, the trail goes downhill at the start and uphill for the finish.

*Cameron Connection* (courtesy Canyon Lakes Ranger District)

*Chapter 3*

# COLORADO STATE FOREST

The Colorado State Forest is made up of state trust lands that are, in this case, part of the Colorado State Park system. The state forest lies north of State Highway 14 between Routt and Roosevelt National Forests, with the majestic backdrops of the Medicine Bow Mountains on its northern and eastern borders and the Never Summer Mountains of Rocky Mountain National Park on its southeastern border. Within the state forest are nonmotorized and motorized trails. The Never Summer Yurt system and Michigan Reservoir cabins are available for rustic overnight "luxury" (see "Winter Camping" in the introduction).

Just driving west over Cameron Pass into Colorado State Forest is a treat because you get to enjoy several peaks on the northern border of Rocky Mountain National Park. First you are greeted by the rugged splendor of the Nokhu Crags, with their roostertop rocks and sparkling avalanche chutes. You can see Mount Richtofen peering over the Crags' shoulder, daring you to come back another day. Then you see the tail end of the Never Summer Mountains: Static Peak, Teepee Mountain, and, finally, Seven Utes. You also get to glimpse the edge of North Park and sample a piece of the one of the least-developed recreational areas in the state, the Colorado State Forest.

## --*19*--

# Michigan Ditch, American Lakes, and Thunder Pass Trails

**Round trip to American Lakes:** 6.8 miles (5 miles to trail junction)
**Difficulty:** Easy
**Skill level:** Novice to intermediate
**High point:** 10,640 feet
**Elevation gain:** 364 feet
**Avalanche danger:** None

**Round trip to Thunder Pass:** 9 miles (5 miles to trail junction)
**Difficulty:** Challenging
**Skill level:** Intermediate to expert
**High point:** 11,200 feet at American Lakes; 11,360 feet at Thunder Pass
**Elevation gain:** 924 feet to American Lakes; 1,084 feet to Thunder Pass
**Avalanche danger:** Low (American Lakes Trail), moderate to high (Thunder Pass)

**Map:** Trails Illustrated Rocky Mountain National Park
**Contact:** Colorado State Forest

Because it has something for everyone, this is one of the most popular trails in the Cameron Pass area. The almost-level trail is an excellent entrance to Thunder Pass and the Never Summer Mountains of Rocky Mountain National Park. It offers spectacular views of the Never Summer Mountains and Nokhu Crags across the Michigan River drainage, Diamond Peaks to the northwest, and North Park off in the distance to the southwest. It also features a gentle incline and very reliable snow. It can be savored by beginners or backcountry adventurers who want to spend the night or surmount the pass. The trail is actually a jeep road that is used to maintain the Michigan Ditch, which is part of the transmountain/trans–Continental Divide water storage system that funnels water from the western slope of the Continental Divide to the thirsty eastern-slope cities.

Take State Highway 14 west from Fort Collins 65 miles to the top of Cameron Pass. Parking and toilet facilities are on the right (west) side of the highway. The well-marked, gated trail is on the left (east) side of State Highway 14.

The almost flat Michigan Ditch Trail follows the road and Joe Wright Creek at first. If you are on a novice or family expedition, you can turn around in about 1 mile at some cabins. If you want more adventure and scenery,

*Michigan Ditch bulletin board just after installation* (courtesy Canyon Lakes Ranger District)

continue on the winding road. At about 1.25 miles the highway turns west while the trail continues southeast. In another 0.75 mile at a trail junction, continue straight. Reach the intersection with the trail to American Lakes and Thunder Pass in another 0.5 mile, at 2.5 miles.

From this junction you can go to the right to continue following the Michigan Ditch Trail west around the bottom of the ridge line of Nokhu Crags. This is an easy and short trek on a flat trail. You'll cross to the south side of the drainage, stopping in less than a mile before reaching avalanche chutes north of Nokhu Crags.

Or, at the junction you can go to the left on the American Lakes Trail, which climbs steadily toward the rocky panorama above tree line at 11,000 feet. This is a longer, more challenging route on a constantly climbing, rolling trail. There are some very steep stretches, but also some moderate to easy sections. You can essentially go as far and as high as you desire. Keep an eye on the time and allow enough daylight for your return. From the junction it is a little less than 2 miles to American Lakes. You reach the first lake at just under 4 miles, and a short distance later is the trail on the left to Thunder Pass. The trail straight ahead continues about 0.25 mile to the middle and upper lakes. The upper reaches of this trail offer very impressive views of the northern edge of the Never Summer Mountains, including the summit of Mount Richthofen.

The trail to Thunder Pass reaches it in another long 0.5 mile, at about 4.5 miles. If you make it to the top of Thunder Pass, you can see all the way down into the Colorado River drainage of Rocky Mountain National Park. Reaching the summit of Thunder Pass should only be attempted as an all-day adventure for the very fit and well prepared. You should have winter mountaineering gear with you. It is by no means dangerous, but is definitely a long, challenging day in high-altitude snow and cold.

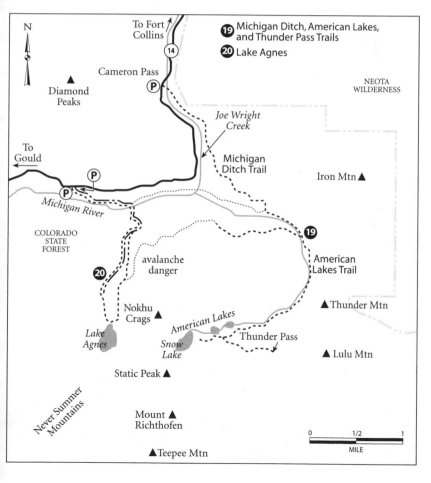

# --20--

# Lake Agnes

**Round trip:** 5 miles
**Difficulty:** Moderate to challenging
**Skill level:** Novice to intermediate
**High point:** 11,000 feet
**Elevation gain:** 1,000 feet
**Avalanche danger:** None to low
**Map:** Trails Illustrated Rocky Mountain National Park
**Contact:** Colorado State Forest

This is a steep, popular, and very scenic trail. The first mile is shared with snowmobiles, but the last 1.5 miles are for snowshoers and skiers only.

Take State Highway 14 west from Fort Collins 65 miles to Cameron Pass and continue 2.5 miles west of the pass. The trailhead is on the left (south) side of State Highway 14 . You are likely to see several vehicles parked in the driveway and along the road.

*Nokhu Crags from Lake Agnes Trail*

The trail follows the campground road downhill into an open area where you have nice panoramic views of the Nokhu Crags and the west side of Cameron Pass. At the bottom of the road in about 0.75 mile is an outhouse. Go right, staying to the left of the outhouse, and take the trail/road uphill into the trees. The trail is very steep in this section. Once you crest the hill at about 1 mile, the trail flattens out and comes out of the trees so you can enjoy the panoramic view of the Never Summer Mountains.

At about 1.25 miles there is a junction; both trails, to the right and left, take you to the lake. They are essentially equal in distance—a little over 1 mile—and difficulty. The route to the right wanders through some stunted pines; the left branch is in an almost treeless gully. You could take one up and the other down for variety. Both trails parallel the lake's outlet stream along the western foot of the Nokhu Crags. Reach Lake Agnes in a little under 2.5 miles. The lake is in a beautiful setting with a stunning ridge line of the Never Summer Mountains as a backdrop.

# --21--

# Seven Utes Mountain and Mount Mahler

**Round trip to Seven Utes Mountain:** 6.5 miles (2.75 miles to viewpoint)
**Difficulty:** Moderate to challenging
**Skill level:** Novice to expert
**High point:** 11,453 feet
**Elevation gain:** 2,000 feet

**Round trip to Mount Mahler:** 8 miles (2.75 miles to viewpoint)
**Difficulty:** Moderate to challenging
**Skill level:** Novice to expert
**High point:** 12,480 feet
**Elevation gain:** 3,000 feet

**Avalanche danger:** Low to high (upper portion can be avoided)
**Map:** Trails Illustrated Rocky Mountain National Park
**Contact:** Colorado State Forest

These little-known mountains are nestled in Colorado State Forest at the edge of the Never Summer range of Rocky Mountain National Park. They offer challenging trails with panoramic views of Mount Richthofen and the Diamond

Peaks from the top of Seven Utes, and the Never Summer, Medicine Bow/ Rawah, and Zirkel ranges from the top of Mahler. Climbing these mountains in the winter is an adventure—with avalanche risks—that should be attempted only by very experienced snowshoers who are prepared for any eventuality. Knowing how to dig a snowpit and evaluate conditions is a recommended skill for these summits. Neither of these peaks should be attempted during times of high avalanche danger. Even beginners can have a very nice, satisfying shorter out-and-back trip that affords great views of the Diamond Peaks. If you can venture just a mile or two uphill on this gradually steepening trail, you will enjoy superb views of the Medicine Bow Range. And the closer you get to Seven Utes, the more impressive it is. The trailhead begins at the former site of a failed cross-country ski lodge that has since been torn down; there are no signs or markers for it. The trail is graced with tall, stately pine trees, snow draped as on a Christmas card.

Take State Highway 14 west from Fort Collins 65 miles to Cameron Pass and continue west approximately 3.8 miles past the pass. Almost at the bottom of the hill, on the left (south) side of the road, is a partially plowed drive angling to the southeast with a green gate. This is the former Seven Utes Lodge entrance. (If you reach the Ranger Lakes Campground, you have gone about 2 miles too far west.) Park in the driveway, or go down about another 0.25 mile to a turnout on the same side (south) and park there, then snowshoe back on the road on the other side of the fence. The snow is likely to be deep enough for you to be able to step over the fence.

**Tip:** If you have trouble finding the trailhead, you can get directions at the State Forest Moose Visitors Center, 2 miles west of the trailhead on State Highway 14. It doesn't open until 9:00 A.M., however, so if you're planning an early start, they won't be able to help you.

Take a look at your topo map and the drainage you want to be in before starting; routefinding can be a bit tricky once you are in the trees and encountering lots of logging roads. The trail is just beyond the green gate, which is usually open. Go through the gate and take either of the next two trails you see on the right. (They intersect after 200 yards.) At first you go downhill for a short stretch, and gradually and then steeply uphill east and southeast on an old logging road. Ignore a trail going left (east) near the crossing of the Michigan River, before the road steepens. There are no markers such as blue diamonds, but the trail is distinct even if you are the first one to use it.

Right after the trail gets significantly steeper, at about 0.75 mile, you intersect another wide, old logging road that is used by snowmobiles. Go to the left (east) uphill on the road; you will see the continuing trail on the left as you round the very first hard right turn. It might not be well marked, so look carefully for it. Remember which drainage you want to be in, the one just east of Seven Utes Mountain, and the route will be more obvious. When you turn off the road, you will be on a narrow trail rather than an old road, with a 30- to 40-foot drop-off on your left. This continues for about 0.25 mile; there is a spectacular view of the Diamond Peaks behind you to the northeast. This 1-mile point is a good spot for a photo and snack break. This is also a good turnaround point for the inexperienced.

After approximately 200 yards, the trail crosses to the other side of the drainage, crossing the stream that is out of sight under the snow unless your trip is too early in the season. It then goes east and south uphill and back into the trees, steepening considerably at a couple of big hairpins that straighten out at about 2 miles. It wanders over, under, and around trees as you steadily make your way to tree line next to the drainage. You will see another ridge and peak to the right (west); that is Seven Utes. At intersecting trails, if you're wondering which way to go, bear to the right. When you emerge from the trees at about 2.75 miles, you can see Seven Utes to the right (southwest) and Mount Mahler to the left (southeast). From this point, you can choose to climb either Seven Utes or Mahler.

The shorter, easier, and somewhat safer choice is Seven Utes. There is a trail going to the right (west) across the top of the drainage cirque; that is your route

*Seven Utes from Ranger Lakes*

over to Seven Utes. Once you cross the top of the drainage, pick the least steep route up to the saddle at about 3 miles and avoid areas that look like starting zones or run outs for avalanches. There are definitely avalanche hazards on this route, but you can avoid them. From the summit at 3.25 miles, you have a 360-degree panoramic view of the northern edge of the Never Summer Mountains and the southern tip of the Medicine Bow Mountains in the Rawah Wilderness.

Mahler is a much higher summit that can be climbed from the same drainage as Seven Utes. There are many avalanche hazards on Mahler but it can be safely climbed if you stay on the southern shoulder of the mountain, pick your route carefully, and confirm reasonable snow stability with a snowpit. When you emerge from the trees at about 2.75 miles, where you can see Seven Utes to the right (west) and Mount Mahler to the left (east), bear left (southeast). Continue uphill bearing straight for a little more than 3 miles south, and then go left, making your way away from the obvious avalanche zones and toward the right (south) side of the mountain.

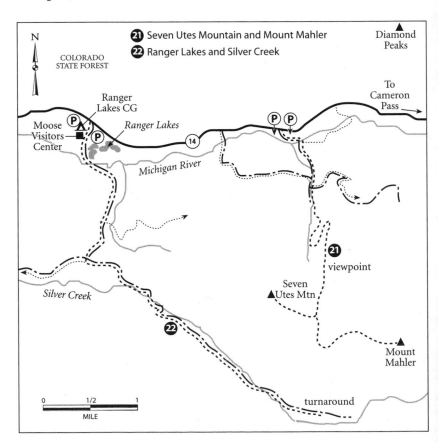

Avoid the dangerous potential avalanche zones dead ahead on the west-facing slopes. Make your way around to the south side of the mountain, safely away from these chutes. The south ridge is not without some avalanche danger—check with the State Forest for conditions—but it is much less steep and avalanche prone. Make your way to the south flank of the mountain; then carefully pick your way up to the top of the ridge saddle in a little more than a mile and then right (south and east) to the summit at 4 miles.

This is one of the more beautiful views you will enjoy on this planet, with the Nokhu Crags to the northeast, Richthofen a bit farther southeast, and the Never Summer Mountains and Zirkel Range visible to the south and west. If you carried some skis up on your back, you are in for some superb telemark turns. If you haven't, you will enjoy some great downhill running and jumping on your snowshoes as you float through powder on the return trip. Be careful, of course, to avoid obvious avalanche danger zones so you don't trigger an avalanche.

# --22--
# Ranger Lakes and Silver Creek

**Round trip:** 3 miles to saddle; 10 miles to upper creek
**Difficulty:** Moderate
**Skill level:** Novice to intermediate
**High point:** 9,600 feet to saddle; 10,200 feet to upper creek
**Elevation gain:** 300 feet to saddle; 900 feet to upper creek
**Avalanche danger:** None
**Map:** Trails Illustrated Rocky Mountain National Park
**Contact:** Colorado State Forest

This easy-to-find trail starts at the Ranger Lakes Campground (closed in winter) on State Highway 14 west of Cameron Pass. You can have an enjoyable and easy 3-mile round-trip jaunt to see the views or continue on for more of a workout, although the rest of the trail is primarily a tree tunnel on what is a road in summer, until you climb over the ridge into the next drainage, where it opens up onto a spectacular valley surrounded by peaks.

Take State Highway 14 west from Fort Collins 65 miles to Cameron Pass and continue approximately 5.8 to 6 miles west of Cameron Pass to the Ranger Lakes Campground on the left (south) side of the road. It is not heavily used, so you should be able to park in the entrance driveway. There is a recreational area parking lot another 0.8 mile west of the campground.

To find the trailhead go downhill and keep the restroom on your right.

Pass the campground loop road; you want the next trail on the right, which takes you west through the trees and then next to a somewhat open area in the trees. It is almost flat at the outset and swings around the Ranger Lakes, hidden in the trees, at about 0.5 mile. There are some trails on the left that go to the lakes if you want a short side trip. The main trail then goes slightly downhill and emerges from the trees to give you a gorgeous view of the ridge line of the Never Summer Mountains—Seven Utes Mountain and Mount Mahler in particular. Cross the Michigan River on a small bridge at a little past 0.5 mile. The trail then reenters the trees and climbs uphill steeply for more than a mile. There is an intersection a little before 1.5 miles with confusing signs. Don't go left as the sign suggests for Silver Creek; bear right toward Illinois Pass. A little past 1.5 miles the trail crests a saddle with a few glimpses. Turn around here if you don't want to descend toward the Silver Creek drainage; it's another 2 miles to meadows.

Though the trail is in a beautiful and peaceful forest, you might encounter an occasional snowmobile. At the intersection at 1.75 miles, turn left and follow the open, rolling trail into the Silver Creek drainage. Once you reach Silver Creek at 2.25 miles, follow it upstream and cross at about 2.75 miles. Wander through a beautiful meadow area to around 3.5 miles, where you can have a snack and reverse course or continue to climb another 1.5 miles higher along the creek into the foothills of the Never Summer Mountains.

## --23--

# Grass Creek Yurt Trails

**Loop:** 6 miles

**Round trip to end of trail:** 9.5 miles

**Difficulty:** Easy to moderate
**Skill level:** Novice to intermediate
**High point:** 9,200 feet on loop; 9,600 feet to end of trail
**Elevation gain:** 200 feet on loop; 600 feet to end of trail
**Avalanche danger:** Low
**Map:** Never Summer Nordic Yurt System/Colorado State Forest
**Contact:** Colorado State Forest; Never Summer Nordic, Inc.

This is one of the closest huts to visit and it is near two nice trails, one a very easy loop trail and the other an end-of-trail out and back. The setting is exceptional

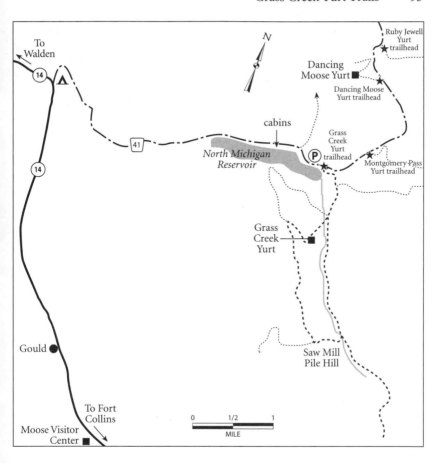

because of the backdrop of the Medicine Bow Mountains and its monarch, Clark Peak, towering above.

Take State Highway 14 west from Fort Collins 65 miles to Cameron Pass and continue west and then south over the pass 10 miles to Gould. Watch for signs on the right side of the highway for the State Forest campground and KOA. Turn right onto CR 41. Get a map from the unstaffed entrance station. Information is also available at the Moose Visitor Center south of Gould. Follow CR 41, a dirt and snowpacked road, approximately 4 miles east past the North Michigan Reservoir and cabins to the parking area for the Grass Creek Yurt trailhead on the left side of the road. Cross the road to the trailhead.

From the trailhead, travel east toward the yurt. At a trail junction in over 0.25 mile, continue straight (southeast). At about 0.75 mile you come to another trail junction.

**Loop:** Bear right and go directly past the yurt. (You can, of course, do the loop in either direction.) In about 1.25 miles go past the hut and climb more steeply up on top of a small ridge at 2.5 miles. Traverse the ridge and then turn left to meet the upper end of the loop at just past 3.5 miles. Go left to return to the trailhead, traveling the trail that parallels Grass Creek; this is a road in the summer that affords a nice view of the yurt without passing too closely. At about 5.25 miles complete the loop and go straight 0.75 mile to the trailhead.

**Out and back:** At the junction at 0.75 mile, take the left branch. It gradually climbs up the drainage for 1.5 miles. At the junction at a little past 2.25 miles, the other leg of the loop is to the right; continue straight ahead up Saw Mill Pile Hill and beyond to the end of the trail at about 4 miles.

(You can also combine the loop and the out and back, traveling up one leg of the loop and down the other on the way back, for 9 miles total.)

## OTHER TRAILS TO EXPLORE

All of the other yurt trails are enjoyable outings: Ruby Jewel Trail and Jewel Lake below Clark Peak, Montgomery Pass Yurt Trail, and Dancing Moose Trail.

*Chapter 4*
----------------

# STEAMBOAT SPRINGS AREA

Although the Steamboat Springs area is a fair distance from the Front Range, it's impossible not to mention it because it's one of the true winter wonderlands of the Rockies. The Steamboat Ski Area receives more than 300 inches of snow per year on average, and Rabbit Ears Pass usually gets much more. Much of it is the "champagne powder" that has made the Steamboat Ski Resort famous, which makes for a paradise on earth if you love snowshoeing and cross-country skiing. You'll find deep, fluffy, powdery snow; snow-draped fir trees; and ice crystals hanging in the air.

Rabbit Ears Pass (Routes 24 through 28) trails usually see enough use to be packed down, making for easier travel. However, you might encounter very deep, unpacked snow on parts of the trails. Note that the great snow at Rabbit Ears Pass comes from rapidly changing and intense weather that can go from blue skies to blizzard in short order. Always check the forecast and be prepared for anything. Don't be dismayed by the droves of snowmobiles. The east end of Rabbit Ears Pass is reserved for snow motorists; the west end is for snowshoers and skiers. North Walton Peak Trail (Route 25) is the only trail where some overlap occurs. A note on dogs at the pass: The West Summit Loop trails (Routes 27 and 28) are heavily used, with dogs usually outnumbering humans. The Forest Service requests that you leave your furry friends at home.

Approximately 40 miles south of the hustle of Steamboat Springs and Rabbit Ears Pass is Dunckley Pass and the Dunckley Flat Tops (Route 29). Nestled in the Dunckley Flattops are lightly used trails that offer a subtle beauty. This lesser-known area is a bit farther and less convenient than Rabbit Ears Pass but it doesn't draw the crowds and offers good snow and great scenery. Do not attempt the journey in midwinter unless you have a four-wheel-drive vehicle or a front-wheel-drive vehicle with good snow tires. Gravel Dunckley Pass Road is much lower than Rabbit Ears Pass, but it can be very slick and icy in the winter and doesn't get the attention from snowplows that Rabbit Ears does, though it is plowed.

To reach Rabbit Ears Pass from Fort Collins, drive State Highway 14 west 65 miles to Cameron Pass, cross the Continental Divide, and continue 30 miles to Walden; then drive south another 30 miles to US 40 at Muddy Pass; Rabbit Ears Pass is a couple of miles west. From Denver, take I-70 west 40 miles to Dillon, then take State Highway 9 north 38 miles to Kremmling, where you take US 40 north. It is 27 miles to Muddy Pass and the intersection with State Highway 14.

For Dunckley Pass, take US 40 from Rabbit Ears Pass west and north toward Steamboat Springs approximately 21 miles to State Highway 131. Turn south and go through Oak Creek to Phippsburg in 19 miles from US 40. From Denver take I-70 west about 100 miles to State Highway 131, just west of Vail/Beaver Creek. Take the Wolcott exit and turn north on State Highway 131 through Yampa to Phippsburg in 50 miles from I-70.

## --24--
# Hogan Park Trail

**One way:** 7 miles
**Difficulty:** Challenging
**Skill level:** Expert
**High point:** 10,385 feet
**Elevation gain:** 700 feet
**Avalanche danger:** Moderate
**Maps:** Trails Illustrated Rabbit Ears Pass, Steamboat Springs; USGS Mount Werner, Walton Peak
**Contact:** Hahns Peak Ranger District, Routt National Forest

This trail takes you from Rabbit Ears Pass to the Steamboat Ski Area; it is advisable to start the route at sunrise because it takes a long day. It is a major winter adventure that requires excellent routefinding skills and enough food and gear to survive an overnight stay just in case you end up making an unplanned camping stop. Even very experienced snowshoers and skiers who have taken this route have been caught short, so precautions are essential for a safe and enjoyable day (or night). Many, many snowshoers and skiers have also had successful and uneventful days on this route. If the snow isn't too deep and the wind hasn't intervened, the route is usually well marked. Good topographical maps and a compass or GPS unit are required for this route. The highly variable snow conditions on this trail are deceptive. Firm snow and easy traveling can

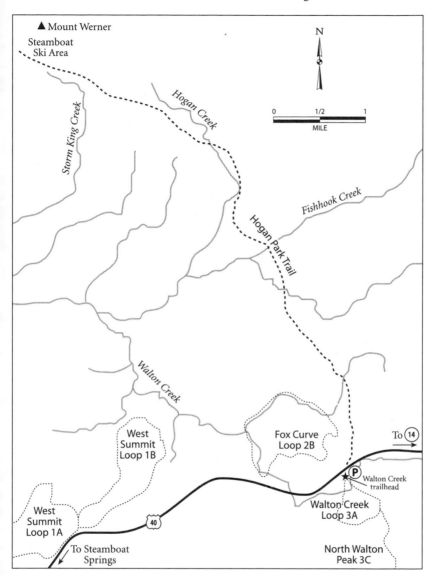

▲ Mount Werner
Steamboat
Ski Area

N

Storm King Creek

Hogan Creek

Fishhook Creek

Hogan Park Trail

0    1/2    1
MILE

Walton Creek

West
Summit
Loop 1B

Fox Curve
Loop 2B

To 14

P Walton Creek
trailhead

West
Summit
Loop 1A

40

Walton Creek
Loop 3A

To Steamboat
Springs

North Walton
Peak 3C

be replaced with deep powder that can sink down several inches with each step. The trail rolls through varying terrain with numerous ascents and descents. Unfortunately one of the more challenging ascents is at the end of the trek, when you have to climb up Mount Werner and descend through the ski area unless ski lifts are operating. From the backside ski lift you can consult with ski area employees for ski lifts that go to the base. The ski area does allow snowshoers or skiers to ride the lifts up the mountain and then down, assuming you can make it to the ski area before the lifts close at 3:30 to 4:00 P.M. Do a vehicle shuttle and park one car at the ski area, or have someone pick you up there.

From the intersection of State Highway 14 and US 40 at Muddy Pass, drive west 5 miles on US 40. The trailhead is 18 miles east from Steamboat Springs. Parking is at the Walton Creek trailhead on the south side of the highway; the trailhead for Hogan Park Trail is across the highway on the north side. To leave a car at the ski area, take US 40 to Mount Werner. Drive and follow signs for ski resort parking.

Starting from the north side of the highway, follow the old road east paralleling US 40; the trail then turns north. Climb up a small ridge at 0.5 mile (you can skirt this climb by tracking a bit farther east before heading north). Descend due north into a beaver pond/wetlands area of Walton Creek at 1 mile. Once you cross the wetlands, angle to the northwest; at 1.5 miles round a small ridge and descend into the Fishhook Creek drainage at about 2.75 miles.

Next climb out of the Fishhook drainage, heading northwest. Aim for a path that takes you between two hills to Hogan Creek at 3.5 miles. You then make a long stretch along Hogan Creek, crossing it at a little past 4 miles and reaching Hogan Park at about 4.5 miles. From Hogan Park climb northwest a mile or so into the Storm King Creek drainage. This is a tricky part of the trail, so take extra care picking your route. A little past 5.5 miles reach Storm King Creek. You then have a steady climb another mile up to the backside ski lifts and possibly the south slope of Mount Werner and into the ski area.

## --25--

# Walton Creek Loop 3A and North Walton Peak Trail 3C

**Loop 3A:** 1.6 miles
**Difficulty:** Easy to moderate
**Skill level:** Novice
**High point:** 9,600 feet
**Elevation gain:** 200 feet

**Round trip to peak:** 6 miles
**Difficulty:** Moderate
**Skill level:** Novice to intermediate
**High point:** 10,140 feet
**Elevation gain:** 640 feet

**Avalanche danger:** Low
**Maps:** Trails Illlustrated Rabbit Ears Pass, Steamboat Springs; USFS Rabbit
    Ears Pass Ski Route
**Contact:** Hahns Peak Ranger District, Routt National Forest

This is the first set of snowshoe and cross-country ski trails you come to if you
are traveling west on Rabbit Ears Pass. The Walton Creek trails are marked on
the Forest Service map as 3A (the campground loop), 3B (the connector to the
West Summit loops), and 3C (to North Walton Peak). There are no markings
on the trails to tell you where you are in the system, but there is a detailed map
at the trailhead, so it isn't too difficult to sort out. If you get confused, the best
strategy is simply to reverse course to your car; keep track of the distance and
time you have traveled in case you miss one of the trails. The scenery is comely
enough to support out-and-back travel too. Walton Creek Loop 3A is actually
side-by-side loops that circle through the campground, the pretty creek drainage, and the wetlands area, with the usual array of picturesque, snow-draped
blue spruce and fir trees. North Walton Peak Trail 3C is an easy route to follow
because after the first 0.25 mile it is actually a summer road that is shared with
snowmobiles. (The other trails in this area are for nonmotorized travel only.)
Once you reach the road, the firmly packed surface makes for a fast ascent to
the summit and sweeping views of Rabbit Ears Pass and part of the Yampa
Valley in the distance to the west.

    From the State Highway 14/US 40 junction at Muddy Pass, drive west on
US 40 approximately 5 miles to Rabbit Ears Pass. The trailheads are approximately 18 miles east of Steamboat Springs. The trail parking lot is on the south
side of US 40.

*Walton Creek*

**Walton Creek Loop 3A:** Look for the knoll at the south end of the parking lot and go to the right (west); follow the powerline for about 100 yards. Then turn left (southwest), cross Walton Creek (usually not visible), and go through the Walton Creek Campground. At 0.5 mile, reach a junction in the meadow just south of the campground (to the right is connector trail 3B to the West Summit loops); stay left. Walton Creek Loop 3A climbs steeply and at about 0.75 mile tops a ridge. You then go downhill through an open area back to Walton Creek, passing through wetlands and willows before reaching another trail intersection at just past 1 mile; North Walton Peak Trail 3C goes to the right. Go left and follow Walton Creek a mile back to the parking lot. (You can also combine the loop and the peak trail by going to the right here for a 6.5-mile trek.)

**North Walton Peak Trail 3C:** From the parking lot take the trail that is closest to the Walton Creek trail marker and map, on the left (east) side of the knoll. There is a trail on the right (the beginning of Loop 3A), which you should ignore. When you leave the parking lot, you go downhill to the southeast almost immediately, along Walton Creek. When you get to the bottom of the short hill, you are on the east side of a meadow that is a wetlands/creek in the summer. There is a blue trail marker to your left that marks the trail's entry into the trees; proceed straight/left when you pass trail junctions in the first 0.5 mile. At about 0.6 mile, stay left when another trail comes in from the right (the other leg of Loop 3A). You travel through a small but very pretty valley while climbing gently uphill, winding through the trees. At 1 mile, the trail dead-ends at North Walton Peak Road, which is shared with a few snowmobiles. Go to the right to reach the top of North Walton Peak. You will see two peaks with radio towers; North Walton Peak is the closest and least visible of the two. The firmly packed road surface makes for a fast ascent. The road is a bit of a tree tunnel at first, but the summit view is worth the trek. At about 1.5 miles the road veers sharply right (west) and follows just below a ridge line for 0.75 mile to a saddle at about 2.25 miles, then switchbacks south and west again before heading northwest the last 0.75 mile to the summit and sweeping views. Reverse course to return to the parking lot.

## OTHER TRAILS TO EXPLORE

Connector trail 3B travels west, paralleling the highway and taking you to the West Summit trails parking area in about 3.25 miles. This is a nice option with a car shuttle.

*The beginning of North Walton Peak Trail*

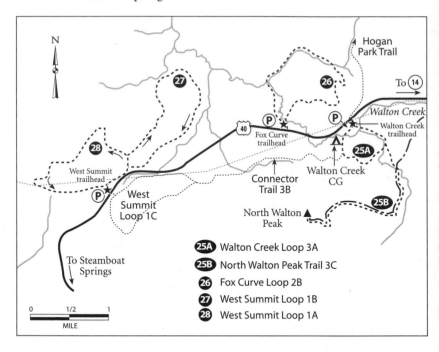

25A Walton Creek Loop 3A
25B North Walton Peak Trail 3C
26 Fox Curve Loop 2B
27 West Summit Loop 1B
28 West Summit Loop 1A

# --26--

# Fox Curve Loop 2B

**Loop:** 3.25 miles
**Difficulty:** Moderate
**Skill level:** Intermediate
**High point:** 9,600 feet
**Elevation gain:** 200 feet
**Avalanche danger:** None to low (steep slope at start)
**Maps:** Trails Illustrated Rabbit Ears Pass, Steamboat Springs; USFS Rabbit Ears Pass Ski Routes
**Contact:** Hahns Peak Ranger District, Routt National Forest

Featuring a variety of scenery and usually superb powder, this loop can also be done as a very satisfying out and back of any length. It starts on a steep downhill, travels through a beautiful meadow and the edge of the forest, and then rolls up and down a couple of hills. It isn't as heavily used as trails at the west end of Rabbit Ears Pass.

From the junction of State Highway 14 and US 40 at Muddy Pass, drive west on US 40 approximately 6 miles. The trailhead is 17 miles east of Steamboat Springs. The parking area is on the north side of the highway.

Start at the west end of the parking lot. Go around the low fence to the right and you will see the trail going into the trees. Follow the loop clockwise (turn to the left) because it is much easier to follow. It also makes for a better out-and-back journey if you don't want to complete the entire loop. The trail tracks north and down the steep hill, descending into a meadow area. There are often several routes down to the meadow. When you reach the meadow, stay left and track west to reach the foot of the hill on the north end of the meadow, and then angle north. The trail travels north along the bottom of the east-sloping hill and goes into the trees at the northwest corner of the meadow. (You can use this hill for a fun side excursion in the deep powder if avalanche danger is minimal.)

The trail finishes its 200-foot descent, crosses Walton Creek at a side stream at just past 0.6 mile, and then climbs fairly gradually as it tracks northeast, into and out of the trees following the stream drainage in a more heavily forested area. At about 1.25 miles the trail turns southeast, gently climbing toward an open beaver pond area at 9,400 feet. After crossing the wetlands at 1.75 miles, the trail begins to climb steadily and somewhat steeply for 200 feet to surmount the 9,600-foot ridge at just past 2 miles. This is a good place for a snack or lunch because of the view. Descend from the ridge top, heading south. The last mile of the trail can be difficult to follow if you are breaking trail, because it isn't well marked. At about 2.5 miles curve to the west, continuing your 300-foot descent; at about 2.8 miles, stay on the ridge line at about 9,300 feet and curve south to reach Walton Creek again at about 3.25 miles. Climb 100 feet to reach the parking lot.

*Fox Curve Loop*

## --27--

# West Summit Loop 1B

**Loop:** 4.2 miles
**Difficulty:** Moderate
**Skill level:** Novice to intermediate
**High point:** 9,520 feet
**Elevation gain:** 200 feet
**Avalanche danger:** Low (can be avoided; check conditions)
**Maps:** Trails Illustrated Rabbit Ears Pass, Steamboat Springs; USFS Rabbit
    Ears Pass Ski Routes
**Contact:** Hahns Peak Ranger District, Routt National Forest

The west end of Rabbit Ears Pass is a real treat for beginners or novices, although there are good intermediate-level trails here too. Trails here feature gradual climbs and beautiful vistas of the Yampa Valley, and are generally well marked. The very deep powder can at times make for challenging conditions, although the heavy usage usually means the trails are broken and well packed. Loop 1B is the easier of the two West Summit loops because Loop 1A (Route 28) has more ascents and descents.

From the State Highway 14/US 40 junction at Muddy Pass, drive west on US 40 approximately 10 miles and watch for a large sign alerting you to the last parking area on the right. The trailhead is 13 miles east of Steamboat Springs. There are places to park on both sides of the road; use the pulloff on the north side of the highway. (The pulloff on the south side of the highway is for intermediate/expert trails 1C and 3B.)

Go to the west end of the parking lot and look for a trail sign and a trail going to the right (north) up a short hill. This is the 0.15-mile connector trail. Though the hill is a short one, it will immediately let you know that you are at 9,400 feet and that pacing yourself is important. At the top of the hill you can go left (west) or right (east). Either choice takes you into Loop 1A; for Loop 1B, go right.

The trail goes slightly downhill on a former road, paralleling US 40 for a very short stretch, then goes left through the trees. There are some small hills on both sides of the trail that are fun for jumping or rolling in the snow, which is only recommended if you are dressed in waterproof gear. In just under 0.5 mile the trail descends to a wetlands area that is usually under several feet of snow at midwinter. Here you reach a junction. Loop 1B's return leg is to the right; stay left on the 0.15-mile section of trail that overlaps for both loops.

The trail takes a sharp left through a beautiful meadow area that is rimmed by stately aspen and pine trees and then goes up the hill. Your goal is the beautiful grove of aspen trees at the top of the hill. If the willows are still exposed early in the season, angle northeast and then back northwest to avoid them. At the trail intersection at 0.6 mile, Loop 1A goes left; bear right on Loop 1B. (You can include a side trip left to the top of the ridge in 0.4 mile on Loop 1A first if you like.) Near this junction there's a great view of the Hahns Peak area to the west and north of Steamboat.

Turning right, continue to climb northeast through the trees and then reach some ridgetop meadow areas with nice views as you approach the high point at 1 mile. You then descend north 400 feet in 0.75 mile, skirting a wetlands area with a colorful mixture of aspen, pine, and red willows. The trail climbs northwest and at 2.1 miles turns to the right (southeast) to 9,300 feet, following the ridge line south about 0.75 mile. You pass through a pretty forest with some nice views of the wetlands and creek covered in a thick blanket of powder. At about 3 miles the trail heads southwest, climbing about 100 feet in about 0.5 mile and then dropping again as you head west back toward the start. At 3.8 miles, reach the connector trail and turn left. The last 0.4 mile parallels US 40.

## --28--
# West Summit Loop 1A

**Loop:** 3.5 miles
**Difficulty:** Moderate
**Skill level:** Novice to intermediate
**High point:** 9,700 feet
**Elevation gain:** 400 feet
**Avalanche danger:** Low (can be avoided; check conditions)
**Maps:** Trails Illustrated Rabbit Ears Pass, Steamboat Springs; USFS Rabbit
    Ears Pass Ski Routes
**Contact:** Hahns Peak Ranger District, Routt National Forest

At the west end of Rabbit Ears Pass, the more difficult of the two West Summit loops, 1A, offers a variety of ascents and descents. You have a broad, easy start followed by a gradual climb up to the ridge line for great views. On a clear day, you will be treated to spectacular views of the Elk Valley to the north, the low hills of the Zirkel Range to the east, and the Flat Tops to the south.

Follow the driving directions for West Summit Loop 1B (Route 27).

Go to the west end of the parking lot and look for a trail sign and a trail going to the right (north) up a short hill. This is the 0.15-mile connector trail. Though the hill is a short one, it will immediately let you know that you are at 9,400 feet and that pacing yourself is important. At the top of the hill you can go left (west) or right (east). Either choice takes you into Loop 1A.

**Tip:** The easiest option for beginners is a short out and back to the left (clockwise) on part of Loop 1A. It has some very pleasing scenery and a good view of the Flat Tops, though it doesn't have the great views that doing the entire loop offers.

To do the entire Loop 1A, go right (counterclockwise) because the trail is easier to follow. The trail goes slightly downhill on a former road, paralleling US 40 for a very short stretch, then goes left through the trees. There are some small hills on both sides of the trail that are fun for jumping or rolling in the snow, which is only recommended if you are dressed in waterproof gear. In just under 0.5 mile the trail descends to a wetlands area that is usually under several feet of snow at midwinter. Here you reach a junction. Loop 1B's return leg is to the right; stay left on the 0.15-mile section of trail that overlaps for both loops. The trail takes a sharp left through a beautiful meadow area that is rimmed by stately aspen and pine trees and then goes up the hill. Your goal is the beautiful grove of aspen trees at the top of the hill. If the willows are still exposed early in the season, angle northeast, then back northwest to avoid them. At the trail intersection at 0.6 mile, Loop 1B goes right; bear left on Loop 1A.

Continue your climb northwest and then north up the hill and through the grove of aspen trees to reach the ridge line at 9,700 feet at just past 1 mile. On a clear day you will have spectacular 360-degree views. If there are beginners in your party, this is a good place to turn around.

Continue west and then south on Loop 1A to enjoy a ridge walk for more than 0.5 mile; the trail offers a nice variety of forested and open meadow trekking. At about 1.75 miles, begin a significant downhill that descends to 9,400 feet at 2.3 miles. When you reach the telephone line a short climb later, watch carefully for the trail marker because the trail turns sharply left. Descend 150 feet into a drainage and then regain it at a small saddle at about 3 miles. Descend 0.3 mile back to the connector trail and then climb gradually back to your car in 3.5 miles.

## OTHER TRAILS TO EXPLORE
West Summit Loop 1C, on the south side of Rabbit Ears Pass across from Loops 1A and 1B, is not as scenic but is a moderate, much less crowded trail.

# --29--
# Spronks Creek and Chapman/Bench Trails

**Loop:** 4.8 miles
**Difficulty:** Easy to moderate
**Skill level:** Novice to intermediate
**High point:** 9,400 feet
**Elevation gain:** 800 feet
**Avalanche danger:** Low
**Map:** USFS Dunckley Pass Ski Trails
**Contact:** Yampa Ranger District, Routt National Forest

Nestled in the Dunckley Flat Tops, these lightly used trails offer a subtle beauty away from the hustle of Steamboat Springs and Rabbit Ears Pass. The Chapman/Bench Trail–Spronks Creek Trail loop is a very rewarding adventure for the reasonably fit if you take your time and bring lots of water; you will work up a good head of steam chugging uphill. The mountainside gets lots of late-morning sun in the winter, the kind that warms both the body and the soul, and it can get quite toasty. Dress in layers that can be deposited in a pack on the way up; when you reach the summit and start down the north slope, and the wind whistles off the Flat Tops, you will want to fish those layers out and redeposit them on your rapidly cooling tendons, lest they talk back to you on the return trip.

The trail offers views of the Yampa Valley and, when you reach the heights of The Bench, superb views of the Dunckley Flat Tops and a beautiful high-mountain vale. The Chapman/Bench Trail, a steady, fairly steep climb that switchbacks uphill on an old road, is not recommended for small children or the marginally fit. Allow at least 3 hours; it might take you most of the day if the snow conditions are challenging. However, the Spronks Creek Trail is a relatively short but beautiful trail through a pretty aspen forest with nice views of the southern part of the Yampa Valley; you can do just this leg of the loop and retrace your route back to the trailhead for an easier route.

Take State Highway 131 to Phippsburg; when you are near the south boundary of Phippsburg, slow down and turn onto CR 16 to the west. Though this road is paved, you soon reach the unpaved Dunckley Pass Road at the first intersection; turn right. Dunckley Pass Road is closed in winter, but the closure is beyond the nonmotorized trails for snowshoers and cross-country skiers. Watch for the last cattle guard before the closure. The trails are on the left, just beyond the cattle guard. There is a Forest Service stand with a map; there are usually individual trail maps too.

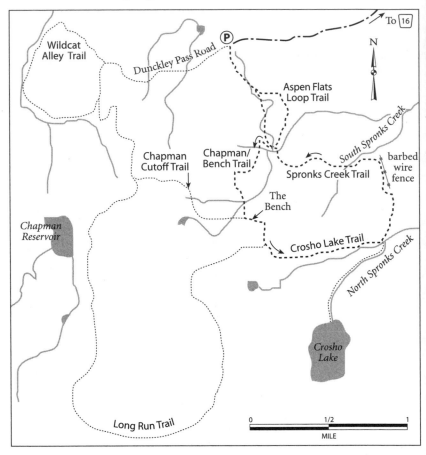

From the trailhead, the trail rolls fairly gently downhill for the first 0.75 mile or so. At about 0.4 mile there is an intersection (to the left is the Aspen Flats Loop Trail, your return leg, which continues to go downhill). The more challenging Chapman/Bench Trail goes to the right, continuing above Aspen Flats for 0.3 mile. At another trail junction at 0.7 mile (Spronks Creek Trail, your return leg, is to the left), stay right on the trail that goes charging uphill. After the trail stops switchbacking at about 1 mile, it climbs steadily through the very tall pine, fir, and aspens, cresting temporarily in a small meadow at a trail junction just past 1.25 miles. Before turning left here, go straight through the trees to the edge of the ridge and enjoy one of the better views in the Flattops. This is a good place to stop for photos and a rest break or snack. (You can retrace your steps back to the trailhead from here for a good 2-plus-hour out-and-back excursion of about 2.5 miles.)

Back at the trail junction, the trail to the right (west then northwest) is the Chapman Cutoff Trail; instead, bear left (east, then south); it is immediately scenic. The trail goes downhill through the trees close to the western edge of the ridge line. At about 1.75 miles it bottoms out and reaches another trail junction (to the right is the Long Run Trail); continue straight/left, gradually veering east. Now you're on the Crosho Lake Trail, which meanders 0.75 mile east to another trail junction at 2.5 miles. The Crosho Lake turnoff is to the right; keep going straight/left on the Crosho Lake Trail, which turns north downhill and at about 3 miles reaches a barbed wire fence.

Continue north to bottom out near the other end of the barbed wire fence at 3.25 miles, where the Spronks Creek Trail begins. Here, bear left (west) to make a climb back out to the trailhead. The draw is very narrow near the bottom, and deep snow can make it somewhat difficult to follow the actual summer trail. Just follow the drainage up the hill. You will be well rewarded for the effort by the colorful mixture of magnificent meadows, wetlands, and stately aspen, pine, and fir trees. The climb back out is certainly easier than the climb up to The Bench, but might seem longer or more difficult than it is because it is at the end of your trip. As you start ascending, stay on the left (south) side of the drainage; as the trail enters a small meadow at about 3.75 miles, stay on the left edge of the meadow. It is usually a little difficult to follow if you are the first to break trail.

Just before 4 miles, you encounter a trail intersection (straight ahead is the Chapman/Bench Trail you started on); go to the right on the east side of Aspen Flats Loop Trail. Bear right at all intersections now to head back to the trailhead. It is a short, easy climb to a flat spot at 4.25 miles that provides a nice overlook of the aspen forest rolling to the valley below, and of Rattlesnake Butte next to the Dunckley Pass Road. Once past the view, at about 4.5 miles, you encounter the other leg of the Aspen Flats Loop Trail—also the Chapman/Bench Trail you started on. You have nice views back toward Yampa; a good photo opportunity is just beyond the trail junction, on the right (east) side of the trail. The trail rolls fairly gently uphill for the last 0.3 mile or so.

(You can also do this return leg in reverse as a short out and back to Spronks Creek; when you bottom out at the fence line, simply retrace your route back to the trailhead for a 3.2-mile round trip.)

## OTHER TRAILS TO EXPLORE

The trail to Crosho Lake is an easy side trip that can extend either the large loop or a Spronks Creek out-and-back.

The Long Run Trail is an ambitious, challenging all-day adventure. The Dunckley Pass Road/Chapman Cutoff Trail loop winds considerably through

*Dunckley Flat Tops, Spronks Creek Trail*

thick tree cover and eventually tops out on The Bench. It is a steep, challenging route, and if it is early in the season and the snow cover is thin, it has a lot of fallen trees and stumps that are not snow covered. Because of the thick tree cover, you won't see much until you top out. The proximity to Dunckley Pass Road means the musical whine of snowmobiles will reach your ears, reminding you of buzzing bees. Wildcat Alley Trail is a nice short and easy loop side trip from Dunckley Pass Road.

*Chapter 5*
------------------------
# GLEN HAVEN AREA

Just east of Estes Park are Glen Haven and Drake, very small towns that consist of small stores, restaurants, and several houses visible from the road. The trails in this area are on the way to Rocky Mountain National Park. They offer access to beautiful areas near the national park or wilderness areas that are adjacent to the park and are less known and less crowded. Because their trailheads are at lower elevations, you have to wait for a good Front Range upslope snowstorm before they have enough snow. You might have to carry your snowshoes for a mile or two until you reach snow that is deep enough, but it is well worth it.

Nature makes it clear that it owns the Big Thompson Canyon and that we are visitors. In the summer of 2000, the Bobcat Fire flamed out of control for more than a week. In 1976 a flash flood scoured Glen Haven and the Big Thompson Canyon. A spectacular electrical storm brought a downpour in which 11 inches of rain fell over the canyon and its tributaries in a little more than 4 hours. A 20-foot wall of water swept down the canyon, reaching a speed of more than 150 miles per hour. One hundred forty-four people were killed as the flood carried away houses and cars and completely destroyed US 34. The force of the water carried debris nearly 30 miles out to I-25. It is these chaotic ways of nature that produce the dramatic scenery of cliffs and canyons.

Drake is 17 miles west of Loveland on US 34, Big Thompson Canyon Road. Turn right in Drake on CR 43, a windy, narrow road that is an alternative route to Estes Park, to reach Glen Haven in about 5 miles.

## --*30*--

# Crosier Mountain

**Round trip:** 9 miles
**Difficulty:** Moderate
**Skill level:** Novice to intermediate
**High point:** 9,250 feet
**Elevation gain:** 2,850 feet
**Avalanche danger:** Low
**Map:** Trails Illustrated Cache la Poudre, Big Thompson
**Contact:** Canyon Lakes Ranger District, Roosevelt National Forest

This hike is in a transition zone between lower foothills and higher mountains. It offers great views of the Glen Haven tributary of the Big Thompson Canyon, the Bobcat fire, and the snowcapped peaks of Rocky Mountain National Park. Take this trip after a heavy, midwinter storm to ensure good trail coverage.

From Drake, drive 2.4 miles west on CR 43 and watch carefully for the small turnout on the left side of the road. You will see a barbed wire fence, wooden gate, and the USFS trailhead sign, barely visible from the road, about 100 feet uphill from the Garden Gate entrance. This is the first and best access point for this trail because the trail from here is easy to follow and offers the best views, though there are two other accesses farther along CR 43 near Glen Haven.

The trail starts gradually uphill across an open field and then winds its way into the evergreens. The trail steepens as it enters the trees and begins to switchback. It gets very steep for the next 0.5 mile. Just when you are wondering if

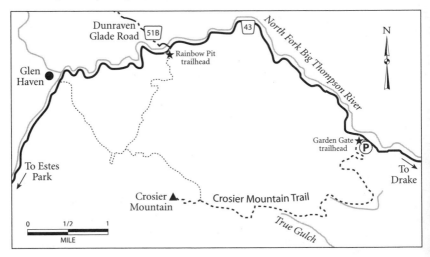

attempting this trail is a mistake, it levels out a bit. The forest is primarily tall fir trees. After catching your breath for 0.25 mile, the trail starts to climb steeply again and rewards you with nice views of the canyon before reentering the trees. This is a good place for a few photos of the valley because the trail levels out nicely as you mount a ridge line at about 1 mile and travel below a large rock outcropping. As the trail goes back into the thicker trees, it steepens again but not as much as previously. You can see signs of another forest fire that goes onto the highest cliff. That fire affected approximately 50 percent of the trees you can see, but stopped at a beautiful mountain meadow that at 1.5 miles stretches in front of you. This part of the hike can have wet or marginal snow if it is early or late in the season. The meadow is a good place for a break.

After crossing the meadow, the trail is not well marked. It is east of the peak. The trail enters the trees again, becomes more obvious, and climbs steadily toward Crosier Mountain, winding its way west next to a draw. At 2 miles the trail turns south and begins climbing steeply for 0.5 mile, then turns to the west at 2.5 miles. You switchback over a ridge and then go downhill into the head of True Gulch at 3 miles. The trail passes through a grove of aspen, around a ridge at 3.5 miles, and into another more level, open area. After winding your way around a ridge at 4 miles, you will finally see Crosier's summit. At about 4.25 miles there is a trail junction; the trail to the right goes to the Rainbow Pit trailhead or to Glen Haven (you could follow either of those trails another 3 miles if you have a shuttle vehicle). Stay left for Crosier Mountain. When you crest the top of Crosier at a little more than 4.5 miles, you will have panoramic views of the canyons, plains, and snow-crested peaks of the Continental Divide.

-- 31 --

# North Fork Trail

**Round trip:** 13 miles to Lost Falls; 16.2 miles to Lost Lake
**Difficulty:** Easy to challenging
**Skill level:** Novice to intermediate
**High point:** 9,900 feet
**Elevation gain:** 2,000 feet
**Avalanche danger:** None to low
**Map:** Trails Illustrated Rocky Mountain National Park
**Contact:** Rocky Mountain National Park; Canyon Lakes Ranger District

This lesser-known trail featuring varied topography in a riparian area winds its way through the short-forested canyon of the North Fork Big Thompson

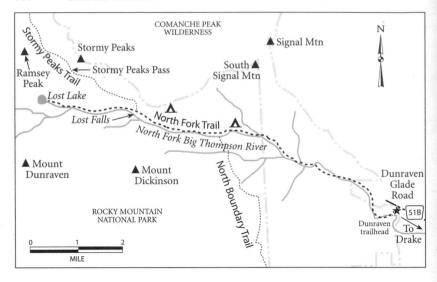

River, with its striking rock outcrops and meadows. Also known as the Lost Lake Trail, it goes through a narrow portion of the Comanche Peak Wilderness before entering Rocky Mountain National Park. The trail then climbs through a backcountry campground and more broad meadows, eventually venturing above tree line and to Lost Lake. Because of the low elevation at the start, this trail is only reliable if there has been a major Front Range snowstorm. However, if you are willing to unstrap your snowshoes and possibly hike for a mile or two, it can still be a great way to spend a day in a beautiful pine-forested valley. (You will need a way to fasten your snowshoes onto your pack to make it a hassle-free journey.) After the initial descent, the trail is very level for a considerable distance, making it a good choice for family excursions or mellow outings. The trail does have a few stream crossings on bridges suitable for snowshoes.

In Drake, turn right onto CR 43 toward Glen Haven and drive northwest 6 miles. Turn right on Dunraven Glade Road/CR 51B. Drive northwest for 2.4 miles on the well-maintained dirt or snowpacked road to its end, where you will find the Dunraven trailhead.

From the parking lot you can see the well-marked trailhead with a trail description and map. Proceed past the privy and up a slight hill. The trail then descends about 0.5 mile down to the North Fork Big Thompson River, losing perhaps 300 feet of elevation. At the bottom is a wonder world of pretty brookside winter settings, with tall pines and a meandering, babbling or frozen brook.

*North Fork Trail*

There are a few very narrow, potentially icy or wet spots in the first mile. The snow conditions can vary widely depending on sun exposure, and the first mile is likely to be snow free because it is open to southern exposure. The trail does gradually climb and enter a tree canopy, at which point you can safely don your snowshoes and feel confident you won't have to remove them again.

Though you are in a thick forest, the trees are tall so there are good views all the way. You go through open areas and a large meadow in the first 2 miles. There is a good bridge for a stream crossing. At this point the snow might be questionable for a while until you enter the trees again, but you are steadily gaining altitude so odds of better snow are good as you proceed. The trail climbs significantly before you enter Rocky Mountain National Park just before 4 miles, but then levels again. Reach park campsites about 4.25 miles from the trailhead.

At about 4.5 miles there is a trail junction (to the left is the North Boundary Trail); stay straight/right. As you travel the next 2 miles along the river, there are meadows and more backcountry campsites as the trees thin and the trail opens up. You reach Lost Falls at about 6.5 miles, where there is another trail junction (to the right is Stormy Peaks Trail, Route 8); stay straight/left.

**Warning:** Going all the way to Lost Lake means traveling below a high ridge just beyond Lost Falls. If you plan to go that far, check with the National Park Service or Arapaho-Roosevelt National Forest Office to see if there is avalanche danger, and proceed accordingly. Up to that point, about 7 miles from the trailhead, there are no avalanche hazards.

The last mile to the lake goes through Lost Meadow, finally reaching the stark beauty of the glacial cirque at 8.1 miles. You can decide to turn around at any point depending on the conditions and your ambitions.

# ROCKY MOUNTAIN NATIONAL PARK

*Beyond the wall of the unreal city . . . beyond the asphalt belting of superhighways . . . there is another world waiting for you. It is the old true world of the deserts, the mountains, the forests, the islands, the shores, the open plains. Go there. Be there. Walk gently and quietly deep within it.*

Edward Abbey, *Beyond the Wall* (1983)

*Chapter 6*

# BEAVER MEADOWS ENTRANCE

One of the gems of the national park system, some would even say the crown jewel, Rocky Mountain National Park features some of North America's most spectacular scenery. Its winter landscape casts an almost mystical spell.

Just west of the town of Estes Park is the park's Beaver Meadows entrance, Beaver Meadows Visitors Center, and park headquarters. Stop at the visitors center to see the 3-D map depicting the dramatic terrain you will be immersed in. There are also an overall map of the park and fairly specific trail maps for areas such as Bear Lake. Rangers can tell you about avalanche danger and where to find the best snow, and you can also fill water bottles.

From the Beaver Meadows entrance, you can reach Deer Ridge Junction (Route 32), Moraine Park (Routes 33 and 34), Glacier Basin (Route 36), and other trailheads on Bear Lake Road (Route 35 and Routes 37 through 43).

Moraine Park's ever-changing mountain weather and light make it a magical place where elk roam freely and birds of prey hover. This stunning setting features one of the most scenically impressive glacial moraines in the Rockies and also offers one of the nicest camping areas in the park. Moraine Park is relatively low (8,100 feet), so is best for snowshoeing in midwinter. If you are willing to strap your snowshoes on your back and hike through potentially sloppy trails up to the snow, you can try these trails earlier in the winter. You'll need a good 2 to 3 feet of snow to cover the rocky sections of the trails.

Along Bear Lake Road are the Hollowell Park trailhead to Mill Creek Basin (Route 35), Sprague Lake trailhead to Glacier Basin (Route 36), Glacier Gorge Junction trailhead (Routes 37 through 39), and Bear Lake trailhead (Routes 40 through 43).

Very appropriately named, Glacier Gorge is an entry point to one of the most magical parts of the park. Massive rock, frozen waterfalls of hanging ice, and the majestic cliffs of Mount Lady Washington and Longs Peak soar to the south, with views of the Mummy Range gracing the horizon to the north.

The first part of the Glacier Gorge Trail (Routes 37 through 39) is a very popular snowshoeing destination. The heavy use means that the first couple of miles, sometimes more, of the trails are hard packed unless you are first after a snowfall. This makes the first section of the trail good for beginners and families, though they are very steady uphill hikes.

The spectacular beauty of the Bear Lake area, its easy accessibility, wide variety of trails, and reliable snow conditions make it one of the most popular and populated areas in the park year-round. At 9,475 feet, the area is high enough to have good snow conditions when other areas in the park do not. Fortunately, most of the people don't get far from the parking lot or Bear Lake; enough do, however, to make an early start a good idea. At the trailheads there are chemical toilets but no drinking water in the winter.

From Denver, take I-25 north 40 miles and exit at Loveland/US 34. Take US 34 west through Big Thompson Canyon 40 miles to Estes Park. Allow at least 1 hour and 30 minutes. Other routes from Denver include US 36 northwest through Boulder and Lyons for 60 miles to Estes Park; and I-25 north for 30 miles to State Highway 66, west on State Highway 66 for 15 miles to Lyons, and northwest on US 36 for 20 miles to Estes Park. When you reach Estes Park, continue west to the third traffic light, where you will see a sign for the park. Turn left at the sign and go up a hill, bear right at the stop sign, and then bear right at the intersection 0.5 mile after the next traffic light. You will see signs for the Beaver Meadows Visitors Center.

## --32--
# Deer Mountain

**Round trip:** 6 miles
**Difficulty:** Easy to moderate
**Skill level:** Novice to intermediate
**High point:** 10,013 feet
**Elevation gain:** 1,075 feet
**Avalanche danger:** None
**Map:** Trails Illustrated Rocky Mountain National Park
**Contact:** Rocky Mountain National Park

This trail offers some of the best views of the Continental Divide and Longs Peak for the least amount of effort. The lower end of the trail is often snow free early or late in the season because of its elevation and exposure to the sun. You are likely to have enough snow after the first mile. There are nonstop views from the beginning and throughout. It offers good, short excursions for young families and beginners, or a nice moderate climb for more experienced snowshoers.

From the Beaver Meadows entrance, at the Bear Lake Road turnoff on the left, stay straight/right and drive 4 miles northwest to Deer Ridge Junction. There is parking on both sides of the road.

The trail begins in an impressive grove of tall, mature ponderosa pines, starting off on some stone steps. Look to your left as you begin the hike, and you will see a small hill with some rock outcrops on top. If you want a terrific view of the Mount Chapin, Mount Chiquita, and Ypsilon Mountain massif to the northwest, detour to the top of the rocks. This is a great photo opportunity at the start of the trek.

The trail rolls a bit at the start, goes slightly downhill, and then turns east and begins to climb more steeply. The panoramic views of Longs Peak (to the south and west) are superb until the trail enters the trees. There are numerous opportunities for photos on both sides of the trail for the first 0.75 mile. This trail is graced by a pleasing mixture of aspen, lodgepole pine, and limber pine trees. The snow depth on this trail can vary widely because of its sunny aspect, but it deepens with every switchback. At a little under 2 miles, you top out on the broad ridge; at 2.8 miles there is a trail junction with a short 0.2-mile spur trail to the right to the summit. The snow is usually several feet deep on the summit.

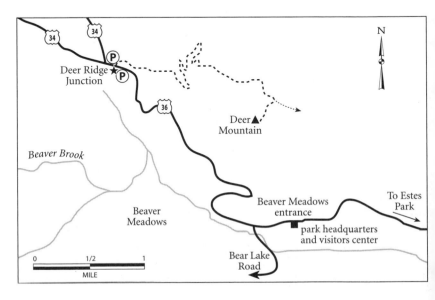

*Ypsilon Mountain from Deer Mountain Trail*

-- 🪶 --

# Cub Lake

**Round trip:** 4 miles
**Difficulty:** Easy to moderate
**Skill level:** Novice
**High point:** 8,600 feet
**Elevation gain:** 500 feet
**Avalanche danger:** None
**Map:** Trails Illustrated Rocky Mountain National Park
**Contact:** Rocky Mountain National Park

On this pleasant out and back, it isn't unusual to encounter elk along the way. It is a popular trail for elk viewing in late September and early October before there is enough snow for snowshoeing. Because the trail includes several sections of rock and starts and ends at relatively low elevations, wait until a good snow year or until there is good snow cover. Even then you might have to take off your snowshoes to get over the rocky sections and pick your way carefully around and over the rocks. You can snowshoe the route as a loop and return on the Fern Lake Trail, but you will have a mile of road walking back to Cub Lake trailhead.

From the Beaver Meadows entrance, take the first left at 0.25 mile, onto Bear Lake Road. After 0.5 mile there is a hairpin S turn and a sign for Moraine Park. Take the next right and then, at the next junction, turn left and continue 1 mile to the Cub Lake trailhead. (If you continue straight, you go into the Moraine Park Campground, which remains open in the winter.)

At the start the Cub Lake Trail goes south to cross two streams over wooden bridges, and it might be advisable to wait until you cross before putting on your snowshoes. You encounter the first rock crossing in about 0.5 mile; go to the left around the rocks. The trail turns west and climbs slowly, encountering another rocky section after another 0.25 mile or so; it then parallels a marshy area as the tree cover thickens and it starts its gentle climb. The first mile or so borders the open expanses of Moraine Park and offers nice views back to the east and south. You will have views of the ridge line that separates you from the Sprague Lake and Bear Lake area.

Eventually you enter a beautiful tree tunnel and then, as you get within 0.5 mile of the lake, at 1.5 miles the trail opens up and climbs steeply to the edge of the lake. This is the steepest section of the trail, but it isn't a very long climb.

(To intersect the Fern Lake Trail, Route 34, walk west past the west end of Cub Lake to a trail junction in 0.5 mile. The trail to the left goes to Bear Lake; stay straight/right. The trail climbs the ridge line to the north about 200 feet to meet the Fern Lake Trail in another 0.75 mile.)

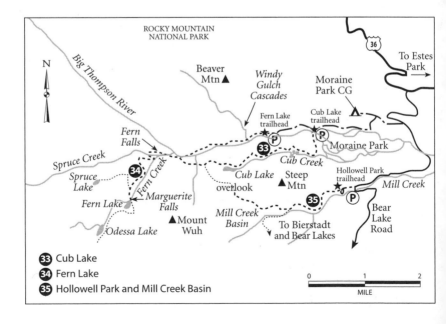

33 Cub Lake
34 Fern Lake
35 Hollowell Park and Mill Creek Basin

--*34*--

# Fern Lake

**Round trip:** 7 miles
**Difficulty:** Moderate to challenging
**Skill level:** Novice to intermediate
**High point:** 9,500 feet
**Elevation gain:** 1,345 feet
**Avalanche danger:** None
**Map:** Trails Illustrated Rocky Mountain National Park
**Contact:** Rocky Mountain National Park

This is a nice climb and a very striking trail as an out and back to Fern Lake. Although this trail has charms enough of its own—Windy Gulch Cascades, Fern Falls, and Marguerite Falls—it can also be used to climb another 500 feet and 0.6 mile higher up to Odessa Lake. That part of the trail is very steep and strenuous. For a major adventure you can also use the Fern Lake Trail by starting at Moraine Park and finishing at Bear Lake. That would require a car shuttle and an early start, especially in midwinter when the days are short. The Bear Lake trek is strenuous and should only be attempted by the very fit with good snowshoeing and winter routefinding experience.

From the Beaver Meadows entrance, take the first left at 0.25 mile onto Bear Lake Road. After 0.5 mile there is a hairpin S turn and a sign for Moraine Park. Take the next right, and then at the next junction turn left at the sign for the Cub Lake and Fern Lake trailheads. (If you continue straight you go into the Moraine Park Campground, which remains open in the winter.) After you pass the Cub Lake trailhead on the left in a mile, the Fern Lake trailhead is approximately a mile farther, with some parking at the end of the road.

The trail starts as a very gradual climb, covering terrain that is very similar to the Cub Lake Trail (Route 33). The major difference is that you climb out of the Moraine Park lowlands. In 0.5 mile you encounter Windy Gulch Cascades to the right, and then at around 1.5 miles the trail steepens considerably. At 1.6 miles reach a trail junction (the trail to the left goes to Cub Lake) where you continue straight/right.

After crossing Fern Creek, the trail begins to switchback at about 2.25 miles, rising for about a mile to surmount a higher plateau. At about 3.6 miles, there is a trail junction (the trail to the right goes up to Spruce Lake) and Marguerite Falls on the left; continue straight/left to the larger Fern Lake at 3.5 miles.

(From there you can continue around the lake and up Fern Creek a steep mile to Odessa Lake, switchback high onto the ridge and gain spectacular views of the entire Moraine Park valley, and even climb up and over into the Glacier Gorge–Bear Lake drainage—another 4.5 miles or so to Bear Lake—if you have the time, ambition, and a car shuttle. It is one of the more spectacular jaunts in the park without going up to the very highest reaches.)

## --𝟑𝟓--
# Hollowell Park and Mill Creek Basin

**Round trip:** 5 miles to overlook
**Difficulty:** Easy to moderate
**Skill level:** Novice
**High point:** 9,200 feet
**Elevation gain:** 800 feet
**Avalanche danger:** None
**Map:** Trails Illustrated Rocky Mountain National Park
**Contact:** Rocky Mountain National Park

Hollowell Park is an expansive, classic high-mountain meadow of yellow grass rimmed by stately pine trees interspersed with aspen. As you head south on Bear Lake Road, this is the first trailhead after Moraine Park. It is a fairly gradual climb. The snow might not be very good in the meadow, but it improves dramatically as you gain altitude. The trail can be turned into an out and back of

any length, and also offers a very nice view of Cub Lake from above. This trail can be used for a steeper 1-mile trek up to Bierstadt Lake from Mill Creek Basin or as the beginning of a 6.4-mile loop back to the Cub Lake trailhead.

From the Beaver Meadows entrance, take the first left onto Bear Lake Road. After a hairpin S turn, the road travels downhill past the Moraine Park Campground and Museum and then goes uphill through a pine forest that is adjacent to the YMCA camp. When you emerge

*Mill Creek, Hollowell Park*

from the trees, you are looking at Hollowell Park straight ahead. Just as the road reaches the turnoff approximately 3.5 miles from the Beaver Meadows entrance, it makes a hairpin turn to the left; bear right, into the parking area.

Take the trail west across the meadow and bear left at the first intersection in 0.25 mile. Go up a gradual hill into the trees. You'll soon be next to pretty frozen or babbling Mill Creek, lined with pine and aspen trees. At the next intersection, at 1.25 miles, the trail to the left climbs steeply up to Bierstadt Lake; go straight (west) for the overview of Cub Lake. If this sign is completely covered by snow, just bear right or go straight—don't take the first stream crossing to the left (southwest), and you will know you are on the Cub Lake branch of the trail.

The trail climbs gradually through the trees; at 1.7 miles reach another junction, where you stay right (the trail to the left goes to Bear Lake). Soon the trail opens up to a couple of nice small meadows in Mill Creek Basin. It then winds back into the trees, alternating with steeper and flatter sections, until it opens up into a great view back up the moraine onto Cub Lake at about 2.5 miles. This is a good place to turn around because the trail descends steeply to Cub Lake.

## --*36*--

# Sprague Lake Trails

**Loop:** 3.3 miles
**Difficulty:** Easy to moderate
**Skill level:** Novice
**High point:** 8,900 feet
**Elevation loss:** 200 feet
**Avalanche danger:** None
**Map:** Trails Illustrated Rocky Mountain National Park
**Contact:** Rocky Mountain National Park

The Sprague Lake area offers a couple of nice easy loops for beginners or intermediate snowshoers as well as trailheads for more ambitious adventures such as the Boulder Brook and Storm Pass Trails. The easiest trip is simply around the lake itself, which is only 0.5 mile with no elevation gain. The easy longer loop can actually be started at either Glacier Basin Campground (closed during winter) or Sprague Lake. The best views are at Sprague Lake or at the campground, with some nice views through the heavy tree cover along the way. Part of this loop can be done as a one way with a shuttle if you want a very easy trip for small children or beginners who aren't acclimated to the altitude.

From the Beaver Meadows entrance, take the first left at 0.25 mile onto Bear Lake Road. In 5.25 miles, approximately 1 mile after Hollowell Park, the Glacier Basin Campground is on the left. Parking is on the right (north) side of road, and the trailhead is on the south side of the campground. Approximately 0.5 mile from the Glacier Basin Campground parking lot is the turnoff for the Sprague Lake picnic area and parking lot on the left (south) side of the road. When you enter the Sprague Lake parking area, you follow a one-way road to the right; at around 10 o'clock on the road loop, you will see the small picnic area and the trailhead.

The longer 3-mile loop can be planned to end on either a long downhill or a gradual uphill; to start and end your trek on uphill sections, start at the Sprague Lake picnic area and follow the route counterclockwise. After ascending a 200-yard, somewhat steep hill, you level out to an easy climb and enter the lodgepole pine forest. The trail is marked with orange markers on tree limbs. After about 0.5 mile you reach a trail junction (the trail to the right goes out to Bear Lake Road); the trail entering from the left has a sign that says "Glacier Gorge/Bear Lake." Turn left onto this trail and continue to climb a short distance to another trail intersection. This is where the trail intersects the Boulder Brook Trail (straight ahead) and Glacier Gorge Trail (to the right). Follow the sign to the left to the Glacier Basin Campground.

The trail now goes downhill and over Boulder Brook twice, rolling somewhat before beginning another short climb. At the crest of the hill you intersect the Storm Pass Trail on the right at about 1 mile. Stay to the left and continue downhill toward the campground. You enjoy some views across to the Beirstadt

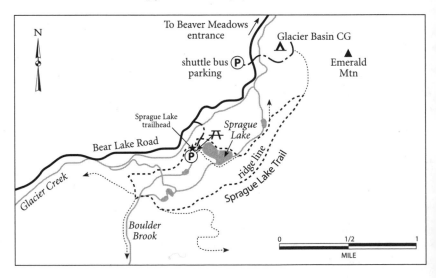

*View from Glacier Basin Campground near Sprague Lake*

Lake ridge and Mount Wuh and into some glades of aspens and pines. At about 2.25 miles the trail breaks out of the trees for the best view of the route, with the Mummy Range in the distance to the north and Flattop Mountain and Hallett Peak to the west. If the wind isn't blowing, this is a nice sunny spot for a snack or photo break. From here you can add another pleasant mile by continuing straight ahead 0.5 mile to the campground and back; to complete the loop, go left to take the short switchback down to the return trail to Sprague Lake.

At the end of the switchback in about 0.25 mile, there is a junction. The trail to the right returns to the picnic area along the creek; go to the left to reach the lake. Once you reach Sprague Lake at about 3 miles, there is another spectacular view to the west, and another trail junction. Either option is a short hop around the lake back to the picnic area. To the left is a trail to a picnic area for the handicapped, which is a nice short detour if you need a sunny spot out of the wind; the picnic tables are in the shade, but the nice glade below is a windbreak. To complete the loop, take the trail to the right.

**Options:** Though the trail between Glacier Basin Campground and the Sprague Lake picnic area is fairly flat, the easiest one-way trek for a young family is to use a car shuttle and start at the high point at Sprague Lake, following the loop described above and walking downhill 2.75 miles to the campground.

For a simple 2.5-mile out and back for young families—though it's not quite as interesting, it's a way to avoid the need for a shuttle—start from Glacier Basin Campground, the flattest part of the route, and you can entirely avoid the ridge walk. At the trail intersection at 0.5 mile, stay right and walk another 0.75 mile before turning around.

Another short out and back of about 3 miles starts with the gradual downhill to Glacier Basin Campground and ends on a short, steep downhill. Start from the Sprague Lake picnic area and walk around the northeastern shore of the lake to the trail to the Glacier Basin Campground, on the left. The trail marker might not be visible if the snow is deep. At the next junction stay right; at the one after that, stay left. When you reach the campground, return the way you came.

-- 37 --

# Alberta Falls and The Loch

**Round trip:** 1.2 miles to Alberta Falls; 5.4 miles to The Loch
**Difficulty:** Easy to moderate
**Skill level:** Novice to intermediate
**High point:** 9,400 feet at falls; 10,180 feet at lake
**Elevation gain:** 160 feet to falls; 940 feet to lake
**Avalanche danger:** None
**Map:** Trails Illustrated Rocky Mountain National Park
**Contact:** Rocky Mountain National Park

The trip to Alberta Falls is strictly a beginner family excursion if you have small children or people very reluctant to participate. The trail is usually quite safe because of the hard snowpack. You'll have to take off your snowshoes if you want to walk on the rock, which is not a good idea with small children because it can be slick and ice coated. Alberta Falls is a short, easy round trip that can easily be extended. The trail continues on up to The Loch on one of the prettiest hikes in the park. As you climb away from Alberta Falls and Prospect Canyon, you enjoy ever better views of the canyon and the Mummy Range behind you.

From the Beaver Meadows entrance, take the first left at 0.25 mile onto Bear Lake Road. Drive 8.2 miles (0.8 mile short of the Bear Lake parking lot) to the Glacier Gorge parking lot. Bear Lake Road makes a major curve around the parking lot, which fills up early, summer or winter. If it is full, park in the Bear Lake lot and walk back on the road or, preferably, on the trail connecting the two, which is a pleasant, short jaunt of about 0.4 mile. There is also a small overflow parking area approximately 200 yards short of the Glacier Gorge lot.

The trail crosses a bridge and then begins a steady but not very steep climb. It eventually climbs next to a small gorge carved out by a small stream that can boil for a short time during the spring runoff. In the winter its rock shoulders are snow covered, and the color contrasts among the rock, trees, snow, and ice can be striking. In 0.6 mile you reach the frozen Alberta Falls, which can take on a wide variety of shapes and make for some interesting photography.

After you reach the falls, if all is well, try venturing farther up the trail, because with every step the views get better. If you go high enough, you have a spectacular view of the Mummy Range in the distance and the cliffs of the Bierstadt Moraine across Prospect Canyon.

The trail climbs steadily through loose switchbacks to the intersection with the North Longs Peak Trail (Route 38) to the left at 1.1 miles; go right.

The trail then climbs around one of the Glacier Knobs on the north side of the Icy Brook drainage, which is icy and rocky. At 1.5 miles reach an intersection with the Black Lake Trail to the left (up this way about 0.25 mile is Glacier Falls) and the Dream Lake trail to the right; continue straight ahead.

The scenery gets even more interesting as you near the entrance of the Loch Vale (valley). After about 0.5 mile the switchbacks level out and you

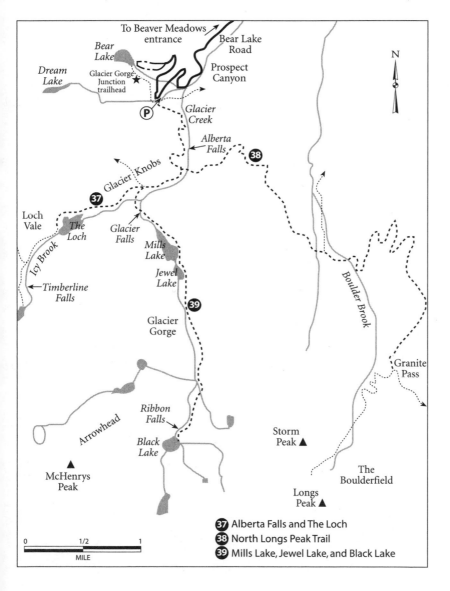

37 Alberta Falls and The Loch
38 North Longs Peak Trail
39 Mills Lake, Jewel Lake, and Black Lake

enter between steep, canyonlike walls. Then, after winding your way 0.5 mile through the canyon, reach The Loch. The Loch, Scottish for "lake," is in a magnificent setting surrounded by Otis, Taylor, and Powell Peaks, offering great photographic opportunities.

Beyond The Loch, the trail climbs again with switchbacks to Timberline Falls, Glass Lake, and Sky Pond in another mile.

## --*38*--
# North Longs Peak Trail

**Round trip to Granite Pass:** 12.4 miles
**Difficulty:** Easy to challenging
**Skill level:** Novice to expert
**High point:** 12,080 feet
**Elevation gain:** 2,840 feet
**Avalanche danger:** None to high
**Map:** Trails Illustrated Rocky Mountain National Park
**Contact:** Rocky Mountain National Park

This trail is a rarity because of its beautiful views and relatively low use. Few people take it in the winter. The first 3 miles or so to the Boulder Brook Trail intersection has low to no avalanche danger most of the year. It also offers superb views on the return, of Glacier Gorge, Flattop Mountain and Hallet Peak, the Mummies, and the entire valley.

From the Beaver Meadows entrance, take the first left at 0.25 mile onto Bear Lake Road. Drive 8.2 miles (0.8 mile short of the Bear Lake parking lot) to the Glacier Gorge parking lot. Bear Lake Road makes a major curve around the parking lot, which fills up early, summer or winter. If it is full, park in the Bear Lake lot and walk back on the road or, preferably, on the trail connecting the two, which is a pleasant, short jaunt of about 0.4 mile. There is also a small overflow parking area approximately 200 yards short of the Glacier Gorge lot.

From the trailhead it is about a 400-foot gradual gain to the intersection with the North Longs Peak Trail in 1.1 miles. Here, The Loch Trail (Route 37) continues straight ahead; turn left. From this intersection it is 5.1 miles one way, or a total of 6.2 miles one way, to Granite Pass—an ambitious winter or summer round trip.

The trail goes downhill from the intersection for approximately 100 to 200 feet and you are immediately greeted by great views of the Mummies (not

British for Mommies) and valley as well as Glacier Gorge. This part of the trail is very open to sun and wind, and can have sections that are in need of snow. Don't be dismayed, because you will soon be on a north-facing portion. Climb back out of the draw after crossing Glacier Creek. The trail levels out for a bit and enters a short new-growth forest of lodgepole and spruce. After another 0.25 mile or so, you round the bend into the Boulder Brook drainage, where you can get an impressive view of the summit of Longs Peak. You can also see the north shoulder of the mountain's massif soaring above and daring you to make the climb above tree line to Granite Pass.

At about 1.5 miles from the trailhead, you enter a more mature forest of taller trees; this is a reasonable turnaround point because the view is obscured until you near tree line. At about 2.25 miles the trail reaches approximately 10,000 feet. Going higher above tree line is only advisable if avalanche danger is minimal. When the snow has consolidated in the late spring it is safer. From here it is another 1 mile or so to a small stream crossing and the intersection with the Boulder Brook Trail on the left. This also makes a good turnaround point for a great round-trip trek of approximately 6.6 miles.

To continue on to Granite Pass, go straight/right. At about 3.5 miles you cross Boulder Brook and begin climbing. This requires steep switchbacking about 1.5 miles through an avalanche zone that should only be crossed if avalanche danger is low. The switchbacks can be tricky in winter and require a map, compass, GPS, and good routefinding skills. After emerging above tree line the route can be windswept, with scarce snow.

The trail levels out at about 5 miles and climbs much more slowly for the next 0.25 mile before steepening again on the shoulder of Battle Mountain. At about 5.5 miles the ascent eases for the last 0.7 mile or so. The view from Granite Pass is a 360-degree wonder, but don't risk life or limb getting there. Turn around if avalanche conditions are dicey.

*View from North Longs Peak Trail*

*-- 39 --*

# Mills Lake, Jewel Lake, and Black Lake

**Round trip:** 4 miles to Mills; 5 miles to Jewel; 8 miles to Black
**Difficulty:** Moderate to challenging
**Skill level:** Novice to expert
**High point:** 9,940 feet at Mills; 9,950 feet at Jewel; 10,620 feet at Black
**Elevation gain:** 700 feet to Mills; 710 feet to Jewel; 1,380 feet to Black
**Avalanche danger:** None to low; last hill moderate to high
**Map:** Trails Illustrated Rocky Mountain National Park
**Contact:** Rocky Mountain National Park

If you want a superb winter adventure, Black Lake Trail is one of the park's better offerings short of climbing a peak. As with many of these destinations, it takes on an almost mystical quality in the winter that is not quite as profound on a nice summer's day. The trail visits three spectacular frozen lakes. The journey to the first two can be nice day trips in themselves. Venturing all the way to Black Lake in the winter can make for a very satisfying day for the experienced and very fit; it can be challenging for anyone, depending on conditions that often vary between bare rock and deep powder. You can usually expect to take your snowshoes off and on at different points during the trip, even if snow conditions are generally good, so be adept at doing so. Do not attempt this route unless snow conditions in the park are very good, because after about 3 miles it is usually necessary to cross rocky, windswept stretches of trail that are only snow covered after mid-January (if at all). Check with the park's backcountry office to find out if there is adequate snow.

From the Beaver Meadows entrance, take the first left at 0.25 mile onto Bear Lake Road. Drive 8.2 miles (0.8 mile short of the Bear Lake parking lot) to the Glacier Gorge parking lot. Bear Lake Road makes a major curve around the parking lot, which fills up early, summer or winter. If it is full, park in the Bear Lake lot and walk back on the road or, preferably, on the trail connecting the two, which is a pleasant, short jaunt of about 0.4 mile. There is also a small overflow parking area approximately 200 yards short of the Glacier Gorge lot.

The first 1.5 miles of this route follow the Alberta Falls Trail (Route 37). Once you get beyond Alberta Falls, you continue winding back and forth over Glacier Creek next to the small gorge that gives you more than one overlook photo opportunity. Eventually the gorge opens up, with cliffs soaring above on both sides of the trail.

At 1.1 miles you come to the North Longs Peak Trail on the left, which goes

*Flattop Mountain and Hallett Peak from Glacier Gorge*

toward Granite Pass (high on the flank of Longs Peak), Boulder Brook, and the infamous Boulderfield on Longs Peak. Take the right branch toward Mills Lake and Loch Vale. The trail steepens here but there are views of the Arrowhead and Chiefs Head Peak in the distance straight ahead, with Glacier Gorge on your left.

The trail then goes downhill for a short distance and eventually goes back into the trees. At 1.5 miles you reach the next trail intersection. To the right is the trail to Dream Lake; straight ahead is the trail to The Loch. Take the left branch, the Black Lake Trail, and you soon encounter a stream crossing that uses a log as a bridge. That can be quite tricky in snowshoes and you will have to decide whether you want to cross without them on. Snow depth and ice conditions will determine what you feel is safest. There is a second stream crossing in a relatively short distance that features wooden steps and rocks, which should be snow covered unless it is early in the season. You might also find some exposed rocks and cairns as well as bare wooden steps that might require taking off your snowshoes temporarily. At 1.75 miles you reach Glacier Falls.

From here, there are at least two good routes to Mills Lake, so pick your way through the best snow or take off your snowshoes and scramble over the large rock formations if they aren't icy. You are 0.25 mile from the lake at this point, so it is well worth the trouble of surmounting the rocks and taking a circuitous route through the trees to stay in the snow. Once you reach the north shore of Mills Lake at 2 miles there are stunning views of Mount Lady Washington, and you can see the Keyboard of the Winds on the southwest side of Longs Peak. This is a great place for photos or a snack or lunch break. You might have to find a wind-sheltered spot to enjoy it. Mills Lake is a good place to turn around if you find the mixture of snow and rocks annoying and don't want to encounter more of the same. If it has been a snowy season, you won't have to remove snowshoes more than a couple of times. That is one of the interesting aspects of more challenging and remote trails: They require more flexibility, creativity, and thought than just marching down the easy path.

From the north end of Mills Lake, you are 1 mile from the Glacier Gorge backcountry campsite if you're spending the night and 2 miles from Black Lake. The varied trail continues with lots of interesting options over, under, and around large outcroppings and towering trees. Don't fret too much about staying on the trail. As long as you don't wander too far upslope to the left (east), and stay relatively close to the shores of Mills Lake and its neighbor, Jewel Lake, you'll be safe. Jewel Lake, whose south end is 0.5 mile beyond the north end of Mills Lake, is barely distinguishable as a separate body of water. It can be a very long 0.5 mile under windy, whiteout conditions. If the lakes are firmly and solidly frozen, you can use the surface to avoid some obstacles, though you'll have to walk lightly or you'll damage your snowshoes.

At 3 miles you reach the backcountry campsite. In another 0.5 mile the main trail wanders rather far to the east away from the shore of Glacier Creek, reaching an open meadow area with great views of Stone Man Pass, Arrowhead, and Chiefs Head Peak as well as McHenrys Peak. You are then only about 200 yards from the very steep stretch that takes you the last 0.5 mile up to the edge of Black Lake. The standard trail is to the left but sometimes, snow permitting, it is easier to get off the trail because the snow cover is better on the steeper slope. You'll have to use your best judgment to make the route decision, but avoid running water and ice if it is visible or you discover it under the top layer of snow. Shortly before you reach Black Lake, Ribbon Falls should be a frozen spectacle, depending on the severity of the winter. At last, at 4 miles, you reach Black Lake in its spectacular setting.

## --40--

# Bear Lake Loop

**Loop:** 1 mile
**Difficulty:** Easy
**Skill level:** Novice
**High point:** 9,495 feet
**Elevation gain:** 20 feet
**Avalanche danger:** None
**Map:** Trails Illustrated Rocky Mountain National Park
**Contact:** Rocky Mountain National Park

The easiest trail at Bear Lake is the loop around the lake. The wide, paved trail is nice for small children or people not accustomed to the altitude. This trail is usually so hard-packed that snowshoes aren't necessary.

*Bear Lake Loop*

From the Beaver Meadows entrance, turn left (south) in 0.25 mile onto Bear Lake Road and follow it 9 miles to its terminus to reach the Bear Lake parking lot.

From the parking lot, walk to the lake; you can circumnavigate it in either direction. Go to the right for a counterclockwise loop. In about 0.2 mile reach the intersection with the trail to Mill Creek Basin on the right; go left. At the northwest side of the lake at about 0.5 mile there is a small and very popular sliding hill for sleds and tubes. This far side of Bear Lake is also a good spot for practicing running up and downhill in snowshoes, rolling, and tumbling—while avoiding trees and rocks, of course. Many a snowshoer and skier has discovered that those pretty aspen trees don't bend or break easily upon impact with any part of their body.

As you continue around the lake, now heading south, the view of Hallett Peak is one of the most spectacular you can enjoy with so little effort. Near the parking lot, you reach the intersection with the trail to Nymph Lake on the right; go left to return to your car.

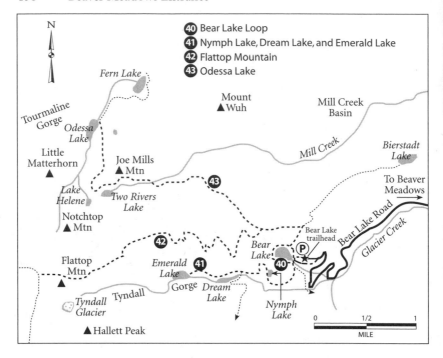

40 Bear Lake Loop
41 Nymph Lake, Dream Lake, and Emerald Lake
42 Flattop Mountain
43 Odessa Lake

--*41*--

# Nymph Lake, Dream Lake, and Emerald Lake

**Round trip:** 1 mile to Nymph; 2.2 miles to Dream; 3.6 miles to Emerald
**Difficulty:** Easy to moderate
**Skill level:** Novice to intermediate
**High point:** 9,700 feet at Nymph; 9,900 feet at Dream; 10,100 feet at Emerald
**Elevation gain:** 225 feet to Nymph; 425 feet to Dream; 625 feet to Emerald
**Avalanche danger:** Low to moderate
**Map:** Trails Illustrated Rocky Mountain National Park
**Contact:** Rocky Mountain National Park

The trail to Nymph, Dream, and Emerald Lakes features some of the most beautiful scenery in the park, and, because the trail is relatively short and easy to navigate, it is not difficult to understand why the lakes are also among the most popular in the park. The hard-packed snow on the lower trail can make snowshoes superfluous, unless there has been fresh snow. From the parking lot, it is only 0.5 mile to Nymph Lake, so it is not a difficult hike. However (there is always a caveat, isn't there?), the trail starts at 9,500 feet, it is uphill, the snow can be unpredictable (though it is usually firmly packed), and small children might find it to be quite enough. For an average, fit adult, it is a stroll in the park and well worth the view.

From the Beaver Meadows entrance, turn left (south) in 0.25 mile onto Bear Lake Road and follow it 9 miles to its terminus to reach the Bear Lake parking lot.

The trail heads south and then curves west and north 0.5 mile to Nymph Lake. It is usually frozen solid and safe to cross at the height of winter, but err on the side of caution. You can loop around the lake to the right in or very near the trees to enjoy views of Hallett Peak, Thatchtop, and Flattop Mountain. Turning around Nymph Lake is a nice, short family outing that can be combined with some off-trail walking on the way back to Bear Lake.

From the north side of Nymph Lake, the trail continues uphill to the left. It requires a traverse over steep terrain that can be trying after a heavy, fresh snowfall. Once you emerge from the trees, if the snow is deep, the trail can be hard to find. What is an easily identifiable trail in summer becomes a bit tricky under several feet of fluffy powder. Magically, things just don't look the same. Don't be drawn straight uphill to the right even though you are likely to see tracks going that way. That is a route taken by the adventuresome and foolhardy and will probably lead you into avalanche danger. Bear left and stay fairly low angle. Stay above the picturesque valley spreading out on the left, and below the impressive rock cliffs looming on the right. A steady climb uphill is what you want, though there is more than one route to Dream Lake. The various paths eventually merge at the top, but bearing to the right after the initial slope is the most common route. On the return trip, the hillside that will be on the right is a nice place to run and jump through powder, if you have a good landing spot picked out and are very energetic and waterproof.

*On the way to Emerald Lake*

The hike from Nymph to Dream Lake is eye candy. Stately, magnificently healthy evergreens climb the mountainsides; their branches and needles seem etched in the crystal high-altitude atmosphere, and you soon have a striking view of Longs Peak. Just before you reach Dream Lake there's an intersection with the trail to Lake Haiyaha on the left; continue straight/right. In 0.6 mile from Nymph, moderate switchbacking gets you to the sleepy shoreline of Dream Lake. Weave your way through a few rocks, climb the last hillock, and then see the stunning setting of Dream Lake, true to its name. This is definitely a terrific photo opportunity because of its exquisite surroundings: towering mountains and cliffs, scruffy wind-sculpted trees with gnarled roots, and the mists, clouds, and blowing and drifting snow of the high country in winter.

The 0.7-mile trail to Emerald Lake is straightforward. Track around the north side of Dream Lake and climb steadily over the rolling terrain with views on all sides. This can be a challenging section of trail in deep, untracked powder as you continue up Tyndall Gorge. OK, who can resist calling this lake a real gem? Emerald Lake has a frozen, slippery surface of mottled, rough ice, with patches of dry, windblown snow covering its pate. Frozen bubbles lurk just below the surface, and viewing the ice is like looking into jumbled, chaotic, transparent, volcanic rock. Its setting is also impressive. The shoulder and cliffs of Flattop Mountain soar on the north, while Hallett Peak and Tyndall Glacier complete the panorama. Snowsqualls on the peaks can be an interesting spectacle, and make you grateful you aren't in the windchill on the ridge top.

## --42--
# Flattop Mountain

**Round trip:** 8 miles
**Difficulty:** Easy to challenging
**Skill level:** Intermediate to expert
**High point:** 12,324 feet
**Elevation gain:** 2,849 feet
**Avalanche danger:** Low to considerable on upper slopes (check with RMNP)
**Map:** Trails Illustrated Rocky Mountain National Park
**Contact:** Rocky Mountain National Park

The addition of snow and snowshoes in winter make this challenging summer hike unlikely for all but the very physically fit and more experienced winter adventurers. However, most people can handle snowshoeing at least part of the trail to enjoy some of the great views. The trail offers views of Bear Lake and the tops of Glacier Gorge and Longs Peak. If you get an early start and get lucky with the weather, summiting is a distinct possibility. You just have to restrain the compulsive, goal-oriented side of your personality if conditions are dicey, and you can have a fun shorter climb and descent.

From the Beaver Meadows entrance, turn left (south) in 0.25 mile onto Bear Lake Road and follow it 9 miles to its terminus to reach the Bear Lake parking lot.

Starting from the parking lot, walk to the right, toward the lake. When you reach the shoreline, you can see the impressive massif of Hallett Peak and the unimpressive summit of Flattop behind. Go to the right and watch for the sign that takes you first gradually uphill through the pretty aspens that frame the lake and Hallett Peak. At the first intersection, about 0.2 mile, the trail to

*Glacier Gorge from Flattop Mountain Trail*

the left continues around Bear Lake; stay to the right. At the first major switchback, at 0.4 mile, you come to the Bierstadt Lake Trail straight ahead; take a left to stay on the Flattop Mountain Trail.

The next steep stretch parallels Bear Lake, affording you some of the best views of Longs Peak, Bear Lake, Glacier Gorge, and the glacier-carved U-shaped valleys. It's a perfect place for photographs because it will be a while until you break into the clear again. In about 0.25 mile the trail veers north into Engelmann spruce trees and you can see east into Mill Creek Basin. Overall you climb steadily for approximately 0.8 mile to reach the intersection with the Odessa Lake Trail. The rangers try to keep the sign uncovered, but deep snow can obscure most of it.

Going this far is a nice, quick trip for a family with kids. You could turn around and go back to circle Bear Lake, having enjoyed some spectacular views and gotten the heart rate up. Though the time will vary, making it this far and circling Bear Lake could easily be an hour-plus family jaunt with small children.

At the trail intersection, the Odessa Lake Trail goes straight ahead; stay to the left on the Flattop Mountain Trail, which switchbacks up. The trail climbs steadily, mostly in fir and spruce trees, until you reach the Dream Lake overlook, which is not obvious or well marked. Here once again are great views of both Longs and Hallett Peaks. Depending on the depth of the snow, just getting to tree line can easily take a couple of hours or more if you stop frequently for breaks and have to break trail through very deep powder. If you are determined, very fit, and on the move, and the snow isn't too powdery, you can make tree line in an hour or so. Tree line is approximately 2.5 miles from the Bear Lake trailhead. When you reach tree line you likely will encounter wind, and possibly severe windchill. This is a good time to have a snack and decide if discretion is the better part of valor. Depending on the time of the year, particularly during early season, the wind can blow some of the trail clear of snow. You can usually pick your way through to find more snow. If there have been recent heavy snowfalls, this part of the trail can also be avalanche prone. From tree line you still have another 1.5 miles of very steep hiking to make the summit.

How long it takes from tree line to the summit is very dependent on the condition of the trail and the individuals. Turning around is highly recommended if it is snowing or whiteouts are possible. If you have a beautiful day and plenty of time to make the return trip, you can have a lot of fun. The views are nonstop above tree line. As you near the summit there are breathtaking views of Bear Lake valley and the pointy false summit and actual summit of Hallett Peak. You can also see the Tyndall Glacier. On the flat, windswept summit that is your destination, you can see over the Continental Divide into the west side of the park and the trails that lead into the Grand Lake and Colorado River drainage.

# --43--
# Odessa Lake

**Round trip:** 9 miles
**Difficulty:** Moderate to challenging
**Skill level:** Intermediate
**High point:** 10,020 feet
**Elevation gain:** 1,215 feet
**Avalanche danger:** Low to moderate (check with RMNP)
**Map:** Trails Illustrated Rocky Mountain National Park
**Contact:** Rocky Mountain National Park

This trail isn't for the fainthearted in the winter after heavy snow. It branches off from the Flattop Mountain Trail (Route 42) about 0.8 mile from Bear Lake. As with all of the routes in this book, you can bite off a smaller morsel to savor, rather than attempting the whole enchilada, and have a great time.

*Hallett Peak from Flattop Mountain Trail*

From the Beaver Meadows entrance, turn left (south) in 0.25 mile onto Bear Lake Road and follow it 9 miles to its terminus to reach the Bear Lake parking lot.

Start at Bear Lake and follow the signs for Flattop Mountain or Odessa Lake. From Bear Lake it is a fairly steady and somewhat steep climb before the trail eventually levels. At about 0.2 mile the Bear Lake Trail goes left; stay right. At 0.4 mile there's a trail junction (the Bierstadt Lake Trail continues straight—northeast); take a sharp left (west) to stay on the Flattop Mountain/Odessa Lake Trail as it heads uphill.

There are great views as you climb above Bear Lake and look out across the valley at Glacier Gorge and Longs Peak. This is a good place for photos. You then enter the trees but after 100 yards the trail breaks out and affords a nice view of the Mill Creek Basin and the rounded, thickly forested shoulder of Mount Wuh. The trail travels more northwesterly, leveling out and climbing at a slower rate. You then climb to the second trail junction at 0.8

*Author on Odessa Lake Trail*

mile (the Flattop Mountain Trail switchbacks sharply left—west—uphill); continue straight ahead/right (northwest) on the Odessa Lake Trail. Though the trail isn't steep, the slope it is carved into is. In fact it becomes a moderate avalanche area after a heavy snowfall because its gradient exceeds 30 degrees. The trail is usually well traveled and obvious, but might become obscured by deep snow and be somewhat difficult to negotiate if you are the first one on it. It is not well marked beyond this point, but remember that it climbs steadily to the northwest and does not descend northeast as some errant tracks might indicate. You generally can follow tracks another mile until you reach tree line at about 1.8 miles. At that point the summer trail is hard to find and you need good routefinding skills to angle your way west and then north first up to Two Rivers Lake and then Odessa Lake. You definitely want to have a compass and topo when you break out of the trees. You do not want to climb the steep, open slopes of Joe Mills Mountain. The route in winter can seem much steeper than in summer because of the several feet of deep, fresh powder. Ask the rangers at Bear Lake for the status and proceed cautiously. Much of the winter it is quite safe because the snow is older and more stable and the trail is heavily used.

The trail steadily climbs in and out of the more sporadic and wind-twisted trees for the next approximately 2 miles and 600-plus feet of elevation gain, crossing Mill Creek at about 2.3 miles and winding past the small Two Rivers Lake and Lake Helene at about 3.5 miles. The unconsolidated snow can make it seem like much more than 2 miles and 600 feet of gain! The mind has a way of shortening or lengthening distances depending on the level of exertion needed.

The trail reaches the impressive Tourmaline Gorge after you round a bend to the left at just over 4 miles, and there are majestic, windswept winter visages of Notchtop (12,129 feet), Knobtop (12,331 feet), and the Little Matterhorn. Their snow-covered slopes make what seems like a rather casual jaunt in the summer much more of an achievement and wilderness experience in winter. In a long 0.5 mile you reach the northern shore of Odessa Lake. Fern Lake is another 1.25 miles but is an unlikely destination from here in the winter because it is downhill and you would have a tough climb back out (for an easier trek to Fern Lake, see Route 34).

If it is late in the day, it is wise to reverse course and make sure you are back to the parking lot by sundown. The way back is much easier because you can often enjoy sliding and floating down the steep parts rather than gasping your way up. If you do get off track, it is fairly easy to keep Mill Creek Basin on your left and go south until you reach the Bear Lake Basin and cliff band.

*Chapter 7*

# LONGS PEAK TRAILHEAD

South of Estes Park is the Longs Peak trailhead (not a park entrance). The peak was considered unclimbable from the time of its discovery by Stephen Long in 1820 until fearless, one-armed Grand Canyon navigator John Wesley Powell did it in 1868, from the south side. His approach was especially remarkable because his party had to climb all the way up and over the Continental Divide through uncharted terrain from Grand Lake before attempting the summit. However, it is likely that Native Americans climbed the peak before him.

Longs Peak is one of those places you never tire of no matter how many times you have visited, summited, or attempted to summit it. Many an expert climber has spent an unplanned bivouac among its frigid granite cliffs, praying for dawn. The towering northeast face of Longs Peak, known as the Diamond, is one of the most challenging technical climbs in North America. It requires superb technical high-altitude rock-climbing skills in radically variable weather between 11,000 and 14,000 feet.

The true beauty of Longs Peak is the wide variety of trails that crisscross its massive expanse and makes it possible for trekkers of all skill levels to partake of its high-altitude glory. Winter months are less crowded because making the summit is impossible for all but a very select set of winter mountaineers. Another bonus is that even when there is little snow in Estes Park, this trailhead generally offers good snow because of its elevation of 9,500 feet. The trails also have excellent tree coverage that protects the snow below tree line. If it is late or early in the season, you might have to do some intermittent hiking between snowshoeing.

From Estes Park, take State Highway 7, the Peak to Peak Highway, south 7.5 miles to the turnoff on the right (west) side of the road for the Longs Peak Campground and trailhead. Go up the hill about a mile to the intersection with the campground road and bear left into the trailhead parking lot. From Lyons, drive west 14 miles then north 10 miles on State Highway 7 to the trailhead on the left. From Denver the route through Lyons is the best.

--44--

# Estes Cone

**Round trip:** 6 miles
**Difficulty:** Moderate
**Skill level:** Novice
**High point:** 11,000 feet
**Elevation gain:** 1,600 feet
**Avalanche danger:** Low
**Map:** Trails Illustrated Rocky Mountain National Park
**Contact:** Rocky Mountain National Park

The pleasant trek to Estes Cone offers striking views of Longs Peak and Mount Meeker as well as Twin Sisters Peaks to the east. The final climb to the summit is not recommended for young children.

Drive to the Longs Peak trailhead, off State Highway 7, at the Longs Peak Ranger Station.

The route starts on the Longs Peak Trail for about 0.5 mile of gradual uphill through the lodgepole pine forest. At the junction, trail signs say it's 2.7 miles to Estes Cone (the Longs Peak Trail goes left—south—to Chasm Lake in 3.7 miles, according to the trail sign); turn right (north). Shortly you arrive at another junction (the trail to the right goes down into Tahosa Valley); continue straight/left. At around 1 mile the trail veers to the northwest and levels off somewhat before climbing gradually to Inn Brook at 1.25 miles. Just after crossing the brook, you reach the site of Eugenia Mine, where some aspen trees are mixed in with the pine. This is a good place for a snack and water break.

Then the trail travels northeast downhill into Moore Park, reaching a trail junction at 1.7 miles (the trail to the right goes down into Tahosa Valley); turn left to join the Storm Pass Trail. It goes northwest, gradually climbing to Storm Pass at 2.4 miles, where the trees begin to thin out and there is another trail junction. To the left, the Storm Pass Trail continues down to Sprague Lake; turn right (northeast) to reach the rock summit of Estes Cone.

The trail switchbacks more steeply uphill. The most challenging section is the last, long switchback section because it climbs the last 1,000 feet in approximately 0.6 mile. This rocky part of the trail will reward you with the best views of Longs Peak and Mount Meeker.

**Warning:** If you make it to the summit area at 2.8 miles, you will have to shed your snowshoes and climb very carefully on the sometimes slick, wet, and icy rock to reach the top of the summit rocks. You can still have a very enjoyable outing by going as far as Storm Pass and walking up enough of the switchbacks to catch a few photo ops, or to the bottom of the summit rocks, and then turning around—especially if you are fortunate and catch a sunny day or fresh snow.

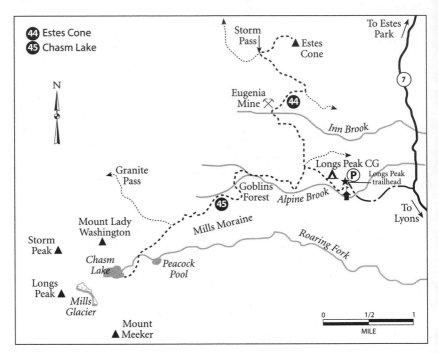

## --45--

# Chasm Lake

**Round trip:** 8.4 miles
**Difficulty:** Challenging
**Skill level:** Novice to expert
**High point:** 11,800 feet
**Elevation gain:** 2,400 feet
**Avalanche danger:** Low to moderate (can be avoided; check with RMNP)
**Map:** Trails Illustrated Rocky Mountain National Park
**Contact:** Rocky Mountain National Park

This spectacular trek offers striking views of Longs Peak and Mount Meeker as well as Twin Sisters Peak to the east. The entire trail should be attempted only

*Longs Peak from the trail to Chasm Lake*

by those experienced in high-mountain, midwinter travel above tree line. You have to cross one avalanche chute and a couple of slopes that could avalanche in moderate to high conditions. Check for avalanche conditions in the area before attempting the route and consider digging a snow pit if danger is moderate. It is usually safe, but the trail is easy to lose if it isn't already broken, and even then people tend to blaze their own paths in the snow cover of winter when the standard route gets obliterated by drifts. The route to Chasm Lake follows the Longs Peak Trail most of the way, until the Longs Peak Trail goes northwest to Granite Pass and the Chasm Lake Trail follows Mills Moraine south and then west to Chasm Lake.

**Tip:** As with most of the trails in this book, you can have a very satisfying, moderate-level family adventure by using only the first 1.5 miles of the trail. You emerge from the tree tunnel at around 10,000 feet and have nice views of the summit of Longs Peak. At that point you can simply enjoy lunch or a snack and then head back to the trailhead. The 500-foot climb is a good workout, and there are ample opportunities to get off the generally hard-packed trail to enjoy softer powder.

Drive to the Longs Peak trailhead, off State Highway 7, at the Longs Peak Ranger Station.

Walk 0.5 mile of gradual uphill through the lodgepole pine forest to an intersection where trail signs say it's 3.7 miles to Chasm Lake. The Storm Pass Trail splits off to the right (north—the trail sign says it's 2.7 miles to Estes Cone); continue straight/left (southwest). After the trail splits it steepens, climbing with occasional short switchbacks. Unfortunately one of the steepest sections of the trail is at the beginning, when you aren't sufficiently warmed up to enjoy it. It climbs up past 10,000 feet fairly quickly in thick tree cover over the next 0.5 mile. It then levels a bit and climbs more gradually for the next 0.25 mile before climbing more steeply for another 0.25 mile and gaining another 500 feet. The trees thin out at about 1.5 miles and allow you coy views of the summit of Longs looking down from on high, daring you to climb it. On a clear day you will enjoy an impressive view of the Diamond.

As the trail starts to climb again and switchbacks, it turns more due south, edging its way up toward the stunted wind- and weather-gnarled trees of Goblins Forest. You have to cross one avalanche chute to reach the small footbridge that crosses Alpine Brook. Don't dawdle in the chute, and listen for that hollow sound to see if the snow is stable. If you hear a hollow sound and the avalanche danger is moderate to high, consider the risk of the crossing before attempting it. Under those conditions, loosen all of your straps and remove large backpacks. Cross one at a time in single file.

In a good to average snow year, the trail can be difficult to follow from this point on, though there is bound to be more than one trail that is broken because of the heavy usage. You might need intermediate snowshoeing skills and ski poles to make it up some of the next sections if there is fresh, deep snow. Sometimes the snow is so old and hard-packed you won't need snowshoes. Don't hesitate to turn around if conditions become challenging. Soon the stunted trees reveal a spectacular view of the slope all the way to the summit. In about a mile you reach tree line, at about 2.5 miles from the trailhead.

Once you are above tree line at 11,000 feet you have a panoramic view in all directions. In a thin snow year, you might have to take off your snowshoes and hike because the intense sun can melt the snow off the very rocky ridge. Always keep an eye on the weather, the time of day, and the amount of daylight left. The trail down might not be as straightforward as you remember; allow extra time for slower members of your party to make it back to the trailhead without the duress of a too-rapid descent. Once above tree line, you gradually make your way to a ridge and somewhat steep snowfield that you have to traverse to the south to reach the final stretch up Mills Moraine. Here, at about 2.8 miles, the trail splits again (to the right the Longs Peak Trail goes almost due north to Granite Pass); stay straight/left to veer to the south toward Chasm Lake.

Follow the ridge about a mile to 11,600 feet, on the way crossing Roaring Fork, then walk around a corner and be startled by the views of Longs Peak, Mount Meeker, Chasm Lake itself, and Peacock Pool almost 600 feet below. At this Chasm Lake overlook at 3.8 miles, there is a privy. It can be a bit of a difficult and precarious ridge walk a short 0.4 mile across another snowfield to a second privy and a Rocky Mountain National Park hut that is locked up and not usable. It is then another 200 feet up to the lake surrounded by soaring Mount Meeker and Longs Peak.

*Chapter 8*

# WILD BASIN ENTRANCE

Rocky Mountain National Park's Wild Basin entrance is south of Estes Park and the Longs Peak trailhead. The subtle beauty of this area never ceases to amaze. You can see the rounded shape of Copeland Mountain from I-25, and the high mountain valley looks magical even from that distance. If you want a relaxing snowshoe outing along a delightful mountain stream and through a beautiful forest, then this is the place for you. On the other hand, if you are very fit and ambitious, you can hike above tree line to the Continental Divide and enjoy some magnificent vistas. Because it is farther from Estes Park, it also doesn't get the number of people that visit the Bear Lake area. And the usual rule applies: The farther from the parking you go, the fewer people you see.

Wild Basin is just west of State Highway 7, the Peak to Peak Highway, between the small towns of Meeker Park on the north and Allenspark on the south. From Estes Park, take State Highway 7 south approximately 12 miles through Meeker Park; the Wild Basin road is on the right and Allenspark is another 2.5 miles south. From Denver, take I-25 to State Highway 66 and go west 16 miles to Lyons. From Fort Collins drive US 287 south to State Highway 66 and go west to Lyons. At Lyons take State Highway 7 west, bearing left at the first intersection west of Lyons. In 14 miles, at the intersection with State Highway 72 at Raymond, bear right to stay on State Highway 7 as it turns north to Allenspark in about 4 miles. From Allenspark look for the Wild Basin road about 2.5 miles north of town on the west side of the highway.

## --46--

# Copeland Falls, Calypso Cascades, and Ouzel Falls

**Round trip:** 3.8 miles to Copeland Falls; 6 miles to Calypso Cascades; 7.4 miles to Ouzel Falls
**Difficulty:** Easy to moderate
**Skill level:** Novice
**High point:** 8,515 feet at Copeland Falls; 9,200 feet at Calypso Cascades; 9,450 feet at Ouzel Falls
**Elevation gain:** 195 feet to Copeland Falls; 880 feet to Calypso Cascades; 1,130 feet to Ouzel Falls
**Avalanche danger:** None
**Map:** Trails Illustrated Rocky Mountain National Park
**Contact:** Rocky Mountain National Park

If you have young children who aren't very ambitious, the short hike from the road closure near Copeland Lake to Copeland Falls might just be enough adventure for one day. For those ready for a little more distance and climbing, continue on to Calypso Cascades and Ouzel Falls, one of the most popular winter treks in Wild Basin. It features the subtle beauty of a frozen stream with snow-covered ice sculptures that can be enjoyed by adventurers of all ages and abilities. Call park headquarters to make sure the snow cover is adequate for snowshoes.

From State Highway 7, drive west on the Wild Basin road; proceed past the lodge to Copeland Lake and around the lake to the left. The road narrows to almost single-car width. The road is closed near Copeland Lake (8,320 feet).

From the parking area, walk about 1.5 miles, either on the flat road or the adjacent horse trail on the left side of the road, to the summer trailhead at Wild Basin Ranger Station (8,500 feet; closed in winter). The trail, which is a bit more pleasant and interesting than the road, rolls gently and gains approximately 200 feet to the ranger station. On the trail, you can enjoy the trees and solitude a bit; you will see lots of nice streamside scenes and pretty open meadows along the way. Or stay on the road and occasionally leave it to wander into the trees.

From the ranger station, proceed to the left through the parking lot to a route map and sign. Bear left and take the trail across the bridge; take the well-marked side trail 0.4 mile from the ranger station to see Copeland Falls. The multilevel, subtle beauty of the frozen falling water is worth exploring with young children and camera in hand. At that point you can take a rest break and decide if you want to venture farther up the trail, or retreat to Allenspark for hot chocolate.

The trail continues up North Saint Vrain Creek, offering a lot of variety as it winds, rolls, and steadily climbs through a pretty mixed forest of aspen and a variety of evergreens. Parts of the trail are next to the beautiful frozen water-falls and ice of the creek, while at times you move some distance from it. At about 2.5 miles there is a trail junction (to the right is the trail to Rocky Mountain National Park campsites and Thunder Lake); continue straight/left.

Shortly you come to the bridge that crosses the creek about 0.4 mile below Calypso Cascades. This is a good spot for a snack break; it usually offers nice photo opportunities of the hillocks of snow and ice crystals that dress the creek in the winter and make it look like a diorama. In approximately another 0.25-mile climb, reach the intersection of North Saint Vrain Creek and Cony Creek; just a bit farther at the 3-mile mark is the magic of the Calypso Cascades, which never look the same.

*Continental Divide summit above Wild Basin*

At the cascades, the Allenspark Trail is on the left; bear to the right, and cross Cony Creek over two more bridges. Above the bridges are countless frozen-water cascades. At this point the trail levels for a bit and then steepens as it switchbacks straight uphill. From Calypso Cascades it is another steep 0.7 mile to Ouzel Falls. If you don't plan to go all the way to Ouzel Falls, it is worth going another 200 yards—even if it takes some gentle persuasion—to enjoy the views that open up of the west slopes of Longs Peak and Mount Meeker. When you break out of the trees, you can also see the dramatic scenery from the 1978 lightning-ignited fire that swept through this area and burned more than 1,000 acres.

Once you get beyond the steep switchbacks you soon cross Ouzel Creek and see Ouzel Falls in the near distance. In another 100 yards you reach an overlook at 3.7 miles with spectacular views of Longs Peak, Mount Meeker to the northwest, Meadow Mountain to the southeast, and Wild Basin and the North Saint Vrain Creek below to the north. The view of the majestic peaks is the primary attraction here; Ouzel Falls are unremarkable in comparison. (Ouzel Lake, another 1.5 miles farther, is a great winter campsite; you need a backcountry permit for camping.)

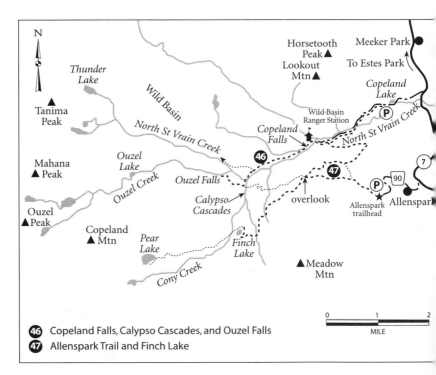

**46** Copeland Falls, Calypso Cascades, and Ouzel Falls
**47** Allenspark Trail and Finch Lake

--*47*--

# Allenspark Trail and Finch Lake

**Round trip from Allenspark:** 3.2 miles to overlook; 7 miles to lake
**Difficulty:** Moderate to challenging
**Skill level:** Novice to expert
**High point:** 9,760 feet at overlook; 9,912 feet at lake
**Elevation gain:** 800 feet to overlook; 952 feet to lake

**Round trip from Wild Basin road closure:** 7.6 miles to overlook; 11.4 miles
to lake
**Difficulty:** Moderate to challenging
**Skill level:** Intermediate to expert
**High point:** 9,760 feet to overlook; 9,912 feet to lake
**Elevation gain:** 1,440 feet to overlook; 1,592 feet to lake

**Avalanche danger:** None to low (can be avoided; check with RMNP
backcountry office)
**Map:** Trails Illustrated Rocky Mountain National Park
**Contact:** Rocky Mountain National Park

This trek offers two starting points that both take you high above Wild Basin.
You can begin at either the Wild Basin road closure at Copeland Lake, climbing up from the Wild Basin Valley, or the Allenspark trailhead higher up. The
Allenspark trailhead is about 640 feet higher than the trailhead on the Wild
Basin road and is about 2 miles shorter. From either, you snowshoe to an overlook where the two trails intersect, continuing up to Finch Lake if desired. You
don't have to snowshoe all the way to the lake to enjoy a great view of Wild
Basin. It is an interesting short side trip (out and back) to climb to the ridge
above Wild Basin. At the overlook, you are rewarded with spectacular views
from above of this glacier-carved valley and the peaks that surround it. Mount
Meeker and Chiefs Head Peak are just a couple of visible gems.

    **Wild Basin road closure to overlook:** From State Highway 7, drive west
on Wild Basin Road; proceed past the lodge to Copeland Lake and around the
lake to the left. The road narrows to almost single-car width. The road is closed
about 0.5 mile past Copeland Lake (8,320 feet).

    From the parking area, walk about 1.4 miles, either on the flat road or the
adjacent horse trail on the left side of the road, to the Finch Lake–Pear Lake
trailhead on the left before you reach the ranger station. It is about a 1.5-mile

trek from this trailhead and about 3.8 miles (one way) from the road closure to the overlook near the top of the ridge, with an approximately 1,440-foot climb on switchbacks to reach the ridge. Upon arriving you have great views of Meeker, Longs, Chiefs Head, Pagoda and the entire Wild Basin stretched before your feet. At this point you could turn around and have a satisfying round trip; to continue to Finch Lake, see below.

**Allenspark trailhead to overlook:** From State Highway 7 follow signs for the Allenspark/Ferncliff business route. When you reach the center of this small town, near the post office and church turn west on CR 90. Stay on this road as it meanders for several miles. When you see Meadow Mountain Drive, turn right and reach the trailhead and parking lot in approximately 200 feet. The road from this point might not be passable unless you have four-wheel drive. Park along the road and walk up to the trailhead; it will not add much mileage or effort to the trip.

The Allenspark Trail is more scenic than the trail from the Wild Basin valley floor; it is a steady climb with some variation all the way to the overlook. At about 0.8 mile there is a trail on the right (it is a short connector to the Wild Basin Trail); continue straight/left. After approximately the first mile, there are breaks in the trees and you start getting nice views of Chiefs Head, Pagoda Mountain, Meeker, and a bit of Longs Peak. The last 0.5 mile to the overlook provides even more nice views, with the grand finale the overlook itself at 1.6 miles, where you get a 180-degree view of the peaks and the valley.

**Overlook to Finch Lake:** This is a challenging addition to either of the overlook routes. From the trail junction at the overlook, the Allenspark Trail

continues straight ahead, and the trail down to the right goes to Wild Basin Road; take the Finch Lake–Pear Lake Trail to the left (southwest). You reenter the trees and climb steadily toward the lake, passing through a small section of trail that was burned in the 1978 fire. In about 1 mile you cross a stream. After the first stream crossing, you dip into and out of the drainage and reach another stream crossing in about 0.5 mile. The trail then follows a small ridge 0.4 mile down to the lake in 1.9 miles from the overlook. There you have an impressive view of Copeland Mountain for photographs.

*Copeland Mountain and Lake*

# INDIAN PEAKS AREA

*I am glad I shall never be young without wild country to be young in. Of what avail are forty freedoms without a blank spot on the map?*
Aldo Leopold, *A Sand County Almanac* (1949)

*Chapter 9*

# PEACEFUL VALLEY AREA

True to its name, Peaceful Valley is a tranquil riparian area northwest of Boulder, just outside of the Indian Peaks Wilderness. Enjoy spectacular views of jagged Sawtooth Mountain and its soaring 12,000 foot unnamed neighbor that guard Buchanan Pass on the south and north, respectively. Meander the Middle Saint Vrain Creek drainage and experience a mixture of high mountain meadows, rock outcrops, and a variety of evergreen and aspen trees. At 8,500 feet, this heavily forested, below treeline area, offers some of the lowest and easiest trails with consistent snow.

The area absorbs a lot of weekenders because it offers many snowshoeing routes to choose from. Begin just before the Peaceful Valley Campground at a trailhead known by several monikers: Middle Saint Vrain, Buchanan Pass, and Peaceful Valley. This gives you the option of using either Middle Saint Vrain Road or the Buchanan Pass Trail for an out and back or loop (Route 48). Other options would be to start at trailheads near Beaver Reservoir off of CR 96 to explore Coney Flats Trail (Route 49) or the Sourdough Trails (Routes 50 and 51).

From Lyons on State Highway 7, drive south 14 miles to State Highway 72, the Peak to Peak Highway, then turn south on State Highway 72 toward Nederland. The Peaceful Valley area is west of State Highway 72 a couple of miles south of Raymond. From Nederland, drive north on State Highway 72 about 5 miles past Ward.

*--48--*

# Buchanan Pass Trail and Middle Saint Vrain Creek

**Round trip:** 10.8 miles to tree line
**Difficulty:** Easy to moderate
**Skill level:** Novice
**High point:** 9,880 feet at tree line
**Elevation gain:** 1,360 feet at tree line
**Avalanche danger:** None to low
**Map:** Trails Illustrated Indian Peaks, Gold Hill
**Contact:** Boulder Ranger District, Roosevelt National Forest

This is an easy trek on a heavily used trail that starts on a road and then parallels it while passing through rolling, heavily forested terrain. It is wise to arrive early to avoid the large, midday weekend crowds. This trail is good for snowshoers of all ages and skill levels, and it is a good place to go on windy days because of the heavy tree cover that shields you from the wintry blasts once you get beyond Camp Dick Campground.

On State Highway 72 heading south, when you see the turnoff for Peaceful Valley about 3.5 miles south of Raymond, you are close, but don't take the Peaceful Valley turnoff. Take the second turnoff on the right (west) after Peaceful Valley. Look for signs for Peaceful Valley Campground, Forest Access, or Camp Dick. The highway marker is a small brown sign with a tent symbol on it. Turn onto FR 114. The turnoff is approximately 6 miles north of Ward. (This is an alternative trailhead for the Sourdough Trail, Routes 50 and 51, which goes south toward Beaver Reservoir, Red Rock Lake, and Rainbow Lakes Road.)

At the beginning of this route, the snow can be a bit thin because it is very open and sun exposed. Some of the best views for photography are at the beginning of the trail and in the Peaceful Valley Campground. If it is pictures of peaks you want, snap away at Mount Audubon and Sawtooth Peak here, because in about a mile you reach heavy forest. For the first mile, the route follows the road between Peaceful Valley Campground and Camp Dick Campground, crossing Middle Saint Vrain Creek twice. Past the gate at the far end of the road, the unpaved road continues along the south side of the creek; take the trail, which crosses to the creek's north side on a small footbridge; the snow improves dramatically once you enter the trees. The streamside and short hill are a pretty setting here, and after a mile of walking it's a good place for a water break and/or photos.

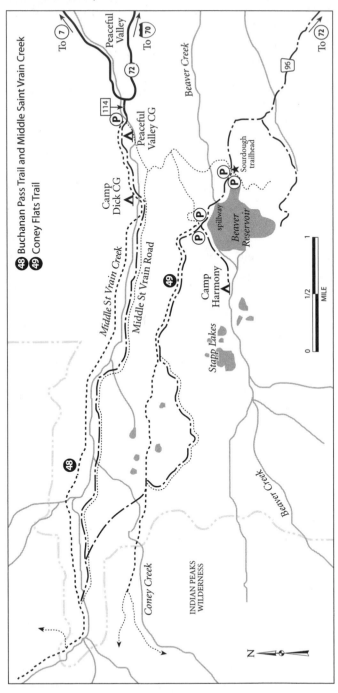

48 Buchanan Pass Trail and Middle Saint Vrain Creek
49 Coney Flats Trail

At around 2 miles you pass through some open meadows; enjoy the warm sunshine before entering the cool forest. Some nice rock outcrops are good for lounging in the sun while you have a snack. It is a very wide valley; the road and trail climb very gently, offering a variety of mountain scenery. There is a side trail for horses that, because it is less traveled, offers powder rather than the hard-packed snow on the main trail. Though the horse trail isn't shown on maps, it is within view of the main trail. It offers more rolling terrain and rock outcrops to climb for variety.

On the main trail, at 2.5 miles cross a side stream; at 3 miles is another open meadow. The challenging spots on the horse trail are at about the 3-mile mark, where the trail narrows around a rock, and above a drop into the creek where there is a bypass with extra climbing. The main trail crosses another side stream at 3.5 miles. At 4.5 miles, the end of the road crosses the creek and joins the trail; it's about 0.4 mile farther to the Indian Peaks Wilderness boundary and a trail junction. A tree line of sorts, another 0.5 mile beyond the wilderness boundary, offers nice views but a very long return trek. Go as far as you like before turning around. You have to start very early and move very fast if you want to make it to tree line and back.

## --49--

# Coney Flats Trail

**Round trip:** 7 miles
**Difficulty:** Easy to moderate
**Skill level:** Novice
**High point:** 9,800 feet
**Elevation gain:** 600 feet
**Avalanche danger:** None to low
**Map:** Trails Illustrated Indian Peaks, Gold Hill
**Contact:** Boulder Ranger District, Roosevelt National Forest

This lightly used, relatively easy, out-of-the-way trail is primarily in the trees but does offer some nice views along the way. There are some great views of the Indian Peaks from Beaver Reservoir. If the weather is iffy and you want peak pictures, take them before using the trail in case the weather socks in. Go as far as you like before turning around.

In 3 miles past the Peaceful Valley turnoff, past the Middle Saint Vrain/ Camp Dick Campground turnoff (see Route 48), look on the west side of the highway for the one sign for CR 96 and a Boy Scout camp. The CR 96 turnoff is approximately 2.5 miles north of Ward and the Brainard Lake Recreation Area. Drive west on CR 96, passing the entrance to the Boy Scout camp, the Sourdough trailhead on the south side of the road in 2 miles, and the spillway of Beaver Reservoir at 2.75 miles; then look for the trail on the right (north) side of the road. You can turn around at a wide spot about 0.25 mile west and then park as close as you can get to the trailhead gate.

The road/trail starts a bit steeply in a lodgepole pine forest tree tunnel, and then mixed aspen and pine, for the first mile or so before the trees open up to some nice views of Sawtooth Mountain and Paiute Peak. At a trail junction at about 1.5 miles the road branches off to the left (south). You can use the road for a short side trip to a small lake, but the road isn't marked and eventually becomes difficult to follow; if you're careful about retracing your steps, you can enjoy the rolling terrain over to the lake and back. Unless you are experienced with a compass and topo map and/or GPS, stay to the right on the trail, which then levels and rolls gently. You will have some nice views of Peaceful Valley through the trees. At 2.25 miles you pass by several small lakes. At 2.5 miles the other end of the road comes in from the left; the trail follows it for about 0.25 mile and then the road heads to the right toward Middle Saint Vrain Creek. At 3 miles you cross Coney Creek and enter Indian Peaks Wilderness; at 3.5 miles reach the Coney Lake Trail junction. Here the trees open up and you can see the flanks of Sawtooth Peak.

## --*50*--

# North Sourdough Trail

**One way to Middle Saint Vrain Creek:** 1.25 miles
**Difficulty:** Easy to moderate
**Skill level:** Novice
**High point:** 9,140 feet at trailhead
**Elevation loss:** 540 feet

**One way via Beaver Reservoir Cutoff Trail:** 1.5 miles
**Difficulty:** Easy
**Skill level:** Novice
**High point:** 9,200 feet
**Elevation gain:** 60 feet

**One way to Red Rock trailhead:** 5 miles
**Difficulty:** Moderate to challenging
**Skill level:** Novice to intermediate
**High point:** 10,000 feet
**Elevation gain:** 860 feet

**Avalanche danger:** Low
**Map:** Trails Illustrated Indian Peaks, Gold Hill
**Contact:** Boulder Ranger District, Roosevelt National Forest

From Beaver Reservoir you can take the North Sourdough Trail either north or south. The snow is generally better to the north. The route to the south, between Beaver Reservoir and Red Rock trailhead, is often plagued by spotty snow and is quite rocky. If there has just been a major spring snowfall in the area it will be OK; the route south from Beaver Reservoir to Red Rock Lake is best done one way with a vehicle shuttle. More accessible, popular access points for the South Sourdough Trail are in the Brainard Lake Recreation Area at Red Rock trailhead, or farther south at Rainbow Lakes trailhead; the South Sourdough Trail from Red Rock trailhead to Rainbow Lakes has more reliable snow (see Route 51).

In 3 miles past the turnoff for Peaceful Valley, past the Middle Saint Vrain/ Camp Dick Campground turnoff, look on the west side of the highway for the one sign for CR 96 and the Tahosa Boy Scout Camp. The CR 96 turnoff is approximately 2.5 miles north of Ward and the Brainard Lake Recreation Area. Drive west on CR 96, passing the entrance to the Boy Scout camp. The Sourdough trailhead is 2 miles west of State Highway 72, about 0.25 mile before Beaver Reservoir, on the south side of the road. Another access point is at the Coney Flats trailhead, on the right (east) side of the road a little more than 0.75 mile farther. It is called the Beaver Reservoir Cutoff Trail on some maps.

From the Sourdough trailhead, the trail to the north is a short route to Middle Saint Vrain Creek (Route 48). In 0.25 mile it crosses Beaver Creek, and at about 0.75 mile the Beaver Reservoir Cutoff Trail comes in on the left. Continue straight to reach Middle Saint Vrain Creek.

You can also turn left onto the hilly, heavily forested Beaver Reservoir Cutoff Trail at 0.75 mile, which takes you uphill to the Coney Flats Trail in another 0.75 mile. It can be a fun, short trip with a car shuttle, or you can take your snowshoes off and walk 0.75 mile on the road back to your car to close the loop at 2.25 miles.

From the Sourdough trailhead, the trail to the south climbs between two

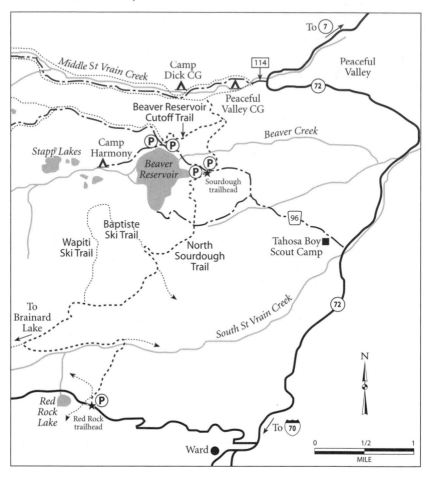

hills, crosses a gated road at about 0.75 mile, and intersects with the Baptiste Ski Trail at about 1.4 miles and with the Wapiti Ski Trail at about 2.4 miles. It travels down- and then uphill until a trail junction at about 3.1 miles. From there the South Saint Vrain Trail goes straight/right up to Brainard Lake; go left on the South Saint Vrain Trail toward the Red Rock trailhead.

In about a mile is another trail junction at 4.2 miles; the South Saint Vrain Trail continues straight/left; go right on the Sourdough Trail and cross South Saint Vrain Creek. In about another mile reach the Red Rock Lake trailhead at a little over 5 miles. It is a long, very hilly trek.

*Chapter 10*

# BRAINARD LAKE RECREATION AREA

This recreation area bordering the Indian Peak Wilderness Area is one of the most popular places in the state for snowshoeing and cross-country skiing. When you see the stunning setting, you will know why. The Indian Peaks are a formidable and thoroughly enticing backdrop that makes it worthwhile to endure the crush of humanity. This glacier-carved Continental Divide mountain "wall" was once proposed to become part of Rocky Mountain National Park to protect it, but it was feared the designation would cause it to be overrun with people. It is hard to imagine that it could be used more heavily than it is; however, it absorbs a large number of people very well because of the large number of trail options. The moral of this story is that weekday visits are highly recommended if you want to avoid your fellow *Homo sapiens*. If that isn't possible, then early arrival for a parking space on the Brainard Lake Road is strongly suggested.

The Forest Service strives to spread out the users and maintain the wilderness appeal of the area. First, the USFS asks that, if at all possible, you leave your pets at home. The heavy usage in the relatively small area would be much more palatable if there were fewer dogs. There are three trails that are designated dog-free trails: Little Raven, Waldrop, and the Colorado Mountain Club (CMC) Trails. The USFS also has some separate trails for skiers and snowshoers, so that snowshoers don't have to walk in skiers' tracks and skiers don't have to zoom around 'shoers.

From Boulder, take State Highway 119, the Boulder Canyon Road, west 14 miles to Nederland. At Nederland, turn right (north) on State Highway 72, the Peak to Peak Highway, for approximately 9 miles. The funky town of Ward is on the right (east) side of the road. Watch for the Brainard Lake Recreation Area turnoff immediately on the left (west) side of the road after the Ward turnoff.

## --*51*--

# South Sourdough Trail

**One way to Rainbow Lakes Road:** 5.5 miles
**Difficulty:** Moderate
**Skill level:** Novice to intermediate
**High point:** 10,000 feet (Red Rock trailhead)
**Elevation loss:** 900 feet
**Avalanche danger:** Low
**Maps:** Trails Illustrated Indian Peaks, Gold Hill; USGS Ward
**Contact:** Boulder Ranger District, Roosevelt National Forest

The South Sourdough Trail, though popular, has much less traffic than other trails in and around Brainard Lake Recreation Area. You won't get quite the stunning views of the Indian Peaks Wilderness, but you will get beautiful views of the foothills and plains, and even James Peak in the distance to the south. From the Red Rock trailhead, you can go either north (see Route 50) or south; both routes offer a rolling trail that is sheltered from the wind. This route to the south, which is a bit easier overall than going north toward Beaver Reservoir, is the most popular segment. A car shuttle is a good way to enjoy the trail unless you're a fleet snowshoe runner.

From State Highway 72, drive west on the Brainard Lake Road to the gate closure in about 3 miles. The Sourdough Trail is just east of the gate closure, crossing the road at the Red Rock trailhead parking area.

From the Red Rock trailhead parking area, take the Sourdough Trail south and cross Left Hand Creek. In about 0.4 mile the Little Raven Trail (see Route 52) goes off to the right; continue straight/left in thick trees. The trail rolls up and down for a mile, and opens up to spectacular views of the plains and foothills. It then climbs to another stream crossing at about 1.75 miles. The trail levels and continues due south for 0.75 mile, affording a nice view of snowcapped James Peak to the southwest. Then it turns sharply west (right) at about 2.6 miles, and in another 0.5 mile drops to Fourmile Creek at 3 miles. This is a good turnaround point for an out and back—or turn around before descending into the drainage and save the climb back out.

Switchbacking into the drainage to cross the creek and then climbing back up, the trail continues due south another 0.75 mile or so. At about 4 miles, the trail winds to the east and then south for a mile, descending the ridge line to the Rainbow Lakes Road at 5.5 miles.

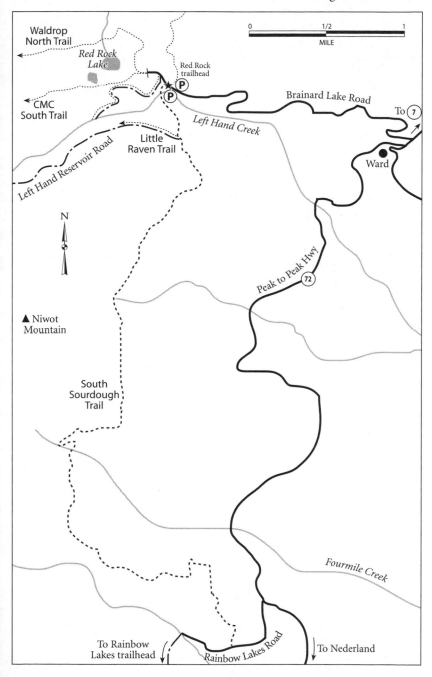

--*52*--

# Niwot Mountain and Ridge

**Round trip:** 6 miles
**Difficulty:** Challenging
**Skill level:** Intermediate to expert
**High point:** 11,557 feet
**Elevation gain:** 1,557 feet
**Avalanche danger:** Low to high
**Map:** Trails Illustrated Indian Peaks, Gold Hill
**Contact:** Boulder Ranger District, Roosevelt National Forest

This high ridge towering to the south of the Brainard Lake area can offer an interesting winter adventure. It has a grand view of the majestic Indian Peaks and Longs Peak without requiring you to travel the length of Brainard Lake Road. There are two approaches to Niwot Ridge, but one of them—the western approach from Long Lake—is not recommended in winter because of high avalanche hazard. You can reach the eastern approach from either the Left Hand Reservoir Road or the Sourdough and Little Raven Trails. There is no marked trail on this approach to the ridge top, so good routefinding and bushwhacking skills are required, plus a topo map and compass or GPS. This climb is best attempted on a calm, warm, late winter or early spring day. Niwot Mountain and Ridge are often windswept, so be prepared for hiking as well as snowshoeing if some of the route is snow free. Because the ridge is often wind-blown, the snow is usually consolidated, which makes for safer travel. Most of the slopes are low angle, and avalanche-hazard areas can be avoided—but avoid the route if the avalanche danger or winds are high.

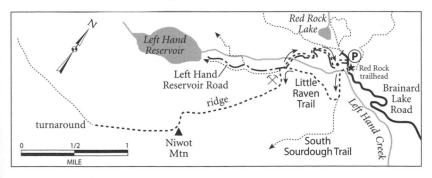

*South Sourdough Trail*

From State Highway 72, drive west on the Brainard Lake Road to the gate closure in about 3 miles. The Red Rock trailhead parking lot is just east of the gate closure. Left Hand Reservoir Road is at the entrance station about 200 yards west of the Red Rock trailhead parking lot; the Sourdough Trail heading south is across the road from the parking area and about 100 feet east. The route described here takes the trails on the way up and then the road, which is about 0.3 mile shorter, on the way down.

Take the Sourdough Trail south and cross Left Hand Creek. The trail rolls gently approximately 0.5 mile to reach the intersection with the Little Raven Trail; there should be a sign marking the Little Raven Trail. Turn right (west) onto the Little Raven Trail (the South Sourdough Trail continues straight/left to Rainbow Lakes to the south; see Route 51). The Little Raven Trail alternates between steep and moderate climbing. As it nears Left Hand Reservoir Road, it levels out a bit and climbs more slowly. In approximately 0.6 mile reach the intersection with Left Hand Reservoir Road at 1.1 miles. Turn left (southwest) onto the road (to the right is your return path). There is a sign on the right for the Little Raven Trail, which goes on to Brainard Lake; stay on the road. Climb approximately 150 yards up the Left Hand Reservoir Road to an old gravel pit or mine on the south side of the road, where you leave the road for the ridge at about 1.2 miles.

Climb up the hill to the left (east) side of the mine, then bear southeast (left) when you enter the trees. You climb steeply and gain about 200 feet in the first 0.25 mile through thick trees. After 0.15 mile you are on a more gradual ascent path at around 10,600 feet, about 1.5 miles from the trailhead; pick the best route and angle to the southwest. After climbing another 0.25 mile and another 200 feet to 10,800 feet, you encounter stunted pine trees at 1.7 miles. At this point, you already have a great view of Longs Peak to the north and Mount Toll, Pawnee Peak, and Mount Audubon to the west. If the wind is howling, you can turn around and still have had a nice adventure.

If it is one of those rare beautiful, calm spring days, note carefully where you have emerged from the trees and pick your way southwest up the ridge for 0.5 mile. Look back frequently so you'll know where to reenter the trees on your return. Decide how high and how far you want to go based on weather and snow conditions. At about 2.3 miles, angle south toward the rock shelter visible on the top of the ridge. It offers a nice windbreak for a snack or photos. The Niwot Mountain/Bald Mountain summit is the high point at the east end of the ridge at 11,471 feet. Continue about a mile southwest along the ridge to the second high point at 11,557 at about 3.25 miles. (If you are in a high point–bagging mood, you can continue slightly northwest another mile to 11,679 feet.) Snowshoe or hike the ridge for as long and as far as you like, and then turn around. You must turn around before the Boulder watershed boundary.

On the return when you reach Left Hand Reservoir Road, stay on it. About 0.1 mile after the intersection to the right with the Little Raven Trail, cross Left Hand Creek. The road continues with some nice views to the north, and then descends for a mile through thick trees back to Brainard Lake Road.

## --53--

# Red Rock Lake and Brainard Lake

**One way to Red Rock Lake:** 0.75 mile
**Difficulty:** Easy
**Skill level:** Novice
**High point:** 10,100 feet
**Elevation gain:** 100 feet

**One way to Brainard Lake via road:** 2 miles
**Difficulty:** Easy
**Skill level:** Novice
**High point:** 10,300 feet
**Elevation gain:** 300 feet

**One way to Brainard Lake via snowshoers-only trail:** 2.3 miles
**Difficulty:** Moderate
**Skill level:** Novice
**High point:** 10,300 feet
**Elevation gain:** 300 feet

**Brainard Lake loop:** 1.2 miles
**Difficulty:** Easy
**Skill level:** Novice
**High point:** 10,370 feet
**Elevation gain:** 70 feet

**Avalanche danger:** None to low
**Maps:** Trails Illustrated Indian Peaks, Gold Hill; USGS Ward
**Contact:** Boulder Ranger District, Roosevelt National Forest

One of the reasons the Brainard Lake Recreation Area is popular is its proximity to Denver and Boulder; another is its ease of use for family or novice

outings. It is almost impossible to get lost, and views of the surrounding Indian Peaks are spectacular. The Red Rock Lake Trail is a very short, easy, and
scenic out and back for families with very young children that can also be a
warmup for a trip to Brainard Lake. Brainard Lake Road can be snowshoed
as an out and back to Brainard Lake—or any distance short of the lake. The
road rolls gently and is usually packed down firmly by midmorning. You pay
for the convenience, however, by encountering the greatest number of dogs
and people on the road. If you don't like furry friends or friendly people, or if
you want to avoid having skiers zoom up and around you, then the snowshoers-
only trail is for you. It is a pleasant and fairly easy tromp through the trees that
shelter you from the wind, with some viewpoints. You can also do a loop between Red Rock and Brainard Lakes by combining the road and the snowshoers-
only trail.

From State Highway 72, drive west on the Brainard Lake Road to the gate
closure in about 3 miles. Do not confuse this with the Red Rock trailhead just
east of the gate that is the entry point for the superb but challenging Waldrop,
Saint Vrain Creek, and Sourdough Trails.

Walk from the Red Rock trailhead parking area west to the Brainard Lake
Road closure and walk around the gate. Take Brainard Lake Road west. In 100
yards, just past the CMC Trail, the snowshoers-only trail is on the left (it is
described below); stay right, on the road. As you walk up Brainard Lake Road,
in about another 50 yards the Red Rock Lake Trail/side road is on the left
(Waldrop North Trail is on the right, directly across the road); Brainard Lake
Road continues straight ahead.

**Red Rock Lake Trail:** Go left for a nice, short, easy side excursion to the
south side of Red Rock Lake. It gives you a spectacular view of the peaks without having to walk all the way to Brainard Lake; the Red Rock Lake area is the
best place for photos until you reach Brainard Lake. If you have very young
children and want a short excursion, this detour to Red Rock Lake may be
enough of an outing. If you want a little bit of adventure and a short challenge
on the way to Brainard Lake, you can take the short trail to Red Rock Lake and
then walk along its shores to return to Brainard Lake Road.

The Red Rock Lake Trail climbs a bit steeply from Brainard Lake Road
through trees; bear right at any intersections. The trail levels and rolls gently
before descending to the lake at 0.3 mile. Red Rock Lake offers spectacular
views of some of the Indian Peaks along the Niwot Ridge. Once you reach the
lake, you can go to the right to follow the east edge of the lake back to Brainard
Lake Road. At the road, if you feel a bit more adventuresome and don't mind a
small hill, continue along the north edge of the shoreline around the lake toward the west. You are rewarded with additional views of the peaks and a nice

view of Red Rock Lake. Be careful that you are not walking on the lake itself, because the ice might be thin in early winter or late spring, and the shoreline is exceedingly narrow. When you reach the west end of the lake bear right, climb the short hill, and you will see the short Red Rock Lake Road coming in from the left. Turn left (west) on the road to return to Brainard Lake Road.

**Brainard Lake Road:** Back at the trail intersections near the gate closure, the road climbs gradually northwest; in 0.5 mile you cross Red Rock Lake's outlet stream. The Brainard Lake Road climbs slightly, curving southwest and then leveling off, reaching the midpoint intersections with the snowshoers-only trail at 1.25 miles. The south branch is on the left first and then the north branch is on the right. The road resumes climbing southwest, and in 0.5 mile reaches the side loops for Pawnee Campground. In another 0.25 mile, at approximately 2 miles you reach the stunning high-mountain panorama at Brainard Lake.

**Snowshoers-only trail:** On the south side of Brainard Lake Road 100 yards from the closure gate, the south leg of the trail starts off gradually climbing. At about 0.25 mile the trail goes around the north side of a small lake, enters thicker tree cover, then steepens as it goes along another mile. This definitely is *not* an early or late-season trail because it needs several feet of snow and very

*Red Rock Lake*

cold weather to make passable the small streambed that comprises much of it. The next segment of the trail opens up and offers nice views of the majestic peaks that surround Brainard Lake. At approximately 1.25 miles the trail reaches Brainard Lake Road.

Cross the road, walk about 100 yards west, and continue on the north leg of the trail, on the north (right) side of the road. On this trail segment you get to avoid the crowd on the road and enjoy the solitude of the trees, but there aren't as many viewpoints because the trees are rather dense. It starts off gradually for the first 100 yards and then turns left up a steep hill. Don't be dismayed; it levels out after the first 0.25 mile and you have a nice view of Niwot Ridge as a reward for making the very short climb. The trail is quite moderate after that; the hill tops out at around 10,200 feet and then you actually lose some elevation. It parallels the road from atop the hill and then eventually drops down almost next to it before swinging west into the Pawnee Campground at 1.8 miles. If you're hungry, early in the season the campground might have some usable picnic tables with southern exposure for a snack break. Later in a very heavy snow year they could be covered in snow. After the campground you cross through the Pawnee Picnic Area and might be tempted to go directly to Brainard Lake. Stay on the trail, which takes you directly back onto the road and to Brainard Lake in 0.5 mile, where you can enjoy the full panorama of the Indian Peaks (weather permitting).

**Brainard Lake loop:** From the end of either the road or the snowshoers-only trail, you can continue on the road around the lake to enjoy views of the Indian Peaks or reach the roads to the trailheads for Mitchell and Blue Lakes and for Long Lake and Lake Isabelle. From where Brainard Lake Road first reaches the lake, go right (counterclockwise). In 50 yards the north leg of the snowshoers-only trail comes in from the right; in another 25 yards you cross the lake's outlet stream and see the Arickeree Picnic Area, and in another 25 yards a trail goes off to the right. At a little over 0.3 mile you cross Mitchell Creek, and less than 100 yards later is the Mitchell Creek Picnic Area, which is at the intersection with the road to Mitchell, Blue, and Long Lakes and Lake Isabelle, on the right at 0.4 mile.

At the west end of the lake, where the other trailheads split off, you are in the trees. From there, you can turn right to proceed to another trailhead (see Routes 54 and 55); stay straight/left on the road to continue around the lake. On the loop road, in another 50 yards cross South Saint Vrain Creek. At 0.7 mile the Niwot Cutoff Trail comes in from the right. Past here the tree cover thins and you have nice views to the north and west across Brainard Lake. Now the road climbs a small hill in 0.1 mile, then descends through an open meadow area in 0.4 mile to the start of the loop.

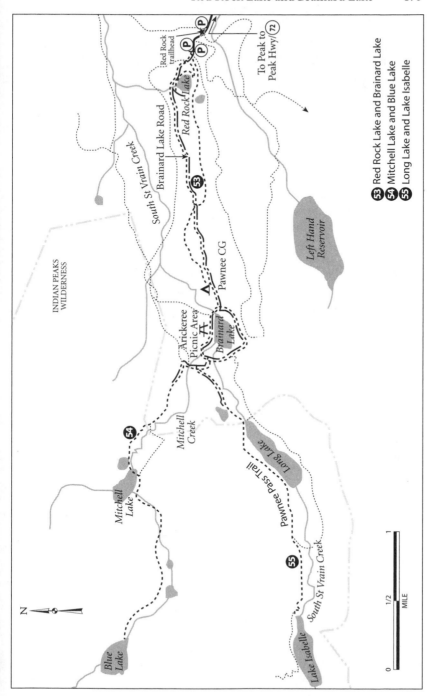

INDIAN PEAKS WILDERNESS

South St Vrain Creek

Brainard Lake Road

Red Rock trailhead

Red Rock Lake

To Peak to Peak Hwy (72)

Pawnee CG

Arickeree Picnic Area

Brainard Lake

Mitchell Creek

Mitchell Lake

Blue Lake

Long Lake

Pawnee Pass Trail

South St Vrain Creek

Lake Isabelle

N

53 Red Rock Lake and Brainard Lake
54 Mitchell Lake and Blue Lake
55 Long Lake and Lake Isabelle

53
54
55

0    1/2    1
MILE

Left Hand Reservoir

## --*54*--

# Mitchell Lake and Blue Lake

**Round trip:** 7.2 miles to Mitchell; 10 miles to Blue
**Difficulty:** Moderate to challenging
**Skill level:** Intermediate to expert
**High point:** 10,700 feet at Mitchell; 11,300 feet at Blue
**Elevation gain:** 700 feet to Mitchell; 1,300 feet to Blue
**Avalanche danger:** Low
**Map:** Trails Illustrated Indian Peaks, Gold Hill
**Contact:** Boulder Ranger District, Roosevelt National Forest

You have to have good weather and snow conditions and/or get an early start to make the round trip to Mitchell Lake from the Brainard Lake Road gate closure. It is worth the trip to see the setting of this large, high-mountain lake and the backdrop of the Indian Peaks. If conditions permit, you can continue on the Mitchell Lake Trail 1.4 miles to Blue Lake. This is a tougher hike than the hike from Long Lake to Lake Isabelle (Route 55). Fortunately, the return is mostly downhill except for one small hill.

See Route 53 for driving directions. From the Brainard Lake gate closure, follow Brainard Lake Road 2 miles one way (or the snowshoers-only trail 2.3 miles one way) to reach the lake, then follow the loop 0.4 mile around the lake to the turnoff for summer trailheads at 2.4 miles (see Route 53). At the well-marked turnoff for Mitchell and Long Lakes on the right (north) side of Brainard Lake Road, the trailhead road turns to the north and in 0.1 mile forks; take the righthand branch (the left goes to Long Lake and Lake Isabelle, Route 55). In about 100 yards the road crosses Mitchell Creek, and Waldrop North Trail comes in from the right here. At 0.25 mile from the turnoff the South Saint Vrain Trail comes in from the right, and the road curves left (west). Meander through a thick tree cover gradually uphill to the summer trailhead parking lot (10,500 feet) at 0.4 mile (200-foot elevation gain) from the turnoff from Brainard Lake Road, 2.9 miles from the gate closure.

From the summer trailhead, the trail levels before climbing steadily next to Mitchell Creek. You continue in trees most of the way. In about 0.3 mile, at the boundary for Indian Peaks Wilderness, a path comes in from the left at 3.2 miles. Shortly after, the trail opens up for several nice views of the pointed summit of Mount Toll. In a little more than 0.3 mile you cross the southern shore of a little lake at 3.5 miles, and about 0.1 mile after, at 3.6 miles, you reach the shore of Mitchell Lake. If it is a windy day, the wind will likely be whipping across the lake into you, so your viewing time will be limited unless you have a ski mask, goggles, or a weatherproof face.

After the first shoreline access to Mitchell Lake you cross its outlet and continue to climb around its southern shore; there are several more opportunities to descend to the lakeshore and enjoy the views of Mount Toll, Pawnee Peak, and Shoshoni Peak. Reach the inlet stream from Blue Lake at 3.9 miles. If you don't want to go all the way to Blue Lake but would like a nice view above the trees, continue on the trail and climb the steep hill just west beyond Mitchell Lake. It is worth the price of admission to see the view back to the east and won't add much to the return-trip mileage.

Continuing up to Blue Lake, the trail is steeper throughout, although there are a few flat stretches. It is not a good early-season trail unless you don't mind shedding your snowshoes and negotiating multitudinous rocks. It is much more enjoyable when it is under several feet of fluffy powder. At 4.1 miles cross the stream, and then again at 4.2 miles. After the first steep hill beyond Mitchell Lake, you are well out of the trees. On a clear day you have a steady diet of nice views all the way of Niwot Ridge while the numerous waves of ridges roll away under your feet as you climb one false summit ridge after another. Several little lakes to your left are not the real thing.

Finally, at 5 miles from the gate closure, you reach the southeastern shore of Blue Lake at its outlet; the lake is above tree line in a glacial cirque beneath Mounts Toll and Audubon. As with many of the trails in this book, even if you turn around short of Blue Lake, you will have had a very enjoyable, physically demanding, and satisfying snowshoeing adventure. Just remember that the return trip will seem much longer and might actually take more time because you will be tired. Be conservative in your turnaround time deadline unless you are prepared to make it back to your car in fading twilight or darkness—or will have a full moon.

## OTHER TRAILS TO EXPLORE

Some hardy souls actually haul skis to the summit of Mount Toll and ski down. Needless to say, it is a precarious adventure under the best of circumstances. You also have to negotiate a very steep snowfield that requires experience with an ice ax if you want to navigate it safely. The Mitchell Lake Trail also offers access to Mount Audubon, which is climbable in the winter and worth a major adventure. The best strategy is to ski to the trailhead with your snowshoes on your pack and then snowshoe when skiing is no longer tenable. Its higher reaches are often blown free of snow, so expect to alternate between snowshoeing and hiking. The summit is 7.4 miles one way from the gate closure, so intermediate to expert skills are required.

## --55--

# Long Lake and Lake Isabelle

**Round trip:** 6.3 miles to Long; 9.3 miles to Isabelle
**Difficulty:** Moderate to challenging
**Skill level:** Intermediate
**High point:** 10,600 feet at Long; 10,800 feet at Isabelle
**Elevation gain:** 600 feet at Long; 800 feet at Isabelle
**Avalanche danger:** None
**Map:** Trails Illustrated Indian Peaks, Gold Hill
**Contact:** Boulder Ranger District, Roosevelt National Forest

Long Lake enjoys a stunning setting, and the trek has its own rewards. Lake Isabelle, another 1.5 miles beyond, is reached on one of the more beautiful trails in the Front Range. It is a steady climb from Long Lake but not particularly steep until you are very near Lake Isabelle. From this lake you can also safely venture another 0.5 mile up the Pawnee Pass Trail before entering an avalanche hazard area.

See Route 53 for driving directions. From the Brainard Lake gate closure, follow Brainard Lake Road 2 miles one way (or the snowshoers-only trail 2.3 miles one way) to reach the lake, then follow the loop 0.4 mile around the lake to the turnoff for summer trailheads at 2.4 miles (see Route 53). At the well-marked turnoff for Long and Mitchell Lakes on the right (north) side of Brainard Lake Road, the trailhead road turns to the north and in 0.1 mile forks; take the lefthand branch (the right goes to Mitchell and Blue Lakes, Route 54). The road gradually climbs southwest 0.4 mile to the summer trailhead parking lot (10,500 feet) at 2.9 miles from the gate closure.

*Indian Peaks from Lake Isabelle in early season*

*Along the Pawnee Pass Trail to Lake Isabelle*

From the trailhead you have nice views of Niwot Ridge along the way to Long Lake, and it is well worth the 0.25 mile to the lake—also the boundary of Indian Peaks Wilderness, and on the left is a short connector to Jean Lunning Trail (it's mostly in the trees and doesn't offer the great views of the Pawnee Pass Trail); stay straight/right. When you reach the lake at about 3.2 miles, there is a spectacular and unique view of the Indian Peaks. If it's a windy day, hang on to your hat and nose to enjoy the view for any length of time. If it isn't windy, the lakeshore is a delightful place for a lunch or snack break.

As you continue west and then southwest along the shore of Long Lake for 0.5 mile, you are rewarded with superb views almost all the way, since most of the trail has openings through the trees to Niwot Ridge. There is a trail junction at 4 miles with the other end of the Jean Lunning Trail to the left; for Lake Isabelle, stay straight/right. In about 0.4 mile beyond the intersection you come to a very nice, open meadow area at 4.4 miles that affords a terrific view of the ridge and some of the peaks beyond. It is a good place for a rest break because it has southern exposure and is still relatively sheltered from the wind. After this, the trail steepens considerably and switchbacks up through trees 0.25 mile to Lake Isabelle at 4.6 miles. The view from here of this section of the Indian Peaks is nothing less than stunning.

## OTHER TRAILS TO EXPLORE

From Lake Isabelle you can continue higher up the Pawnee Pass Trail, but stop when the trail starts to near the ridge line with cliffs above. This area is very avalanche prone. The route is safe up to that point. You need a very early start, a good day, good snow conditions, and fit people to safely make the round trip. Or be prepared to spend the night in a snow cave or tent, or to walk out in the dark.

*Chapter 11*

# ARAPAHO PEAKS AREA

The majestic high alpine terrain of the Arapaho Peaks is heavily trod in the summer but rarely used in the winter, making it a treat for snowshoers. Access Rainbow Lakes (Route 56) or approach the Arapaho Glacier (Route 57) and encounter the massive spectacles of Niwot and Caribou Ridges, brooding Pomeroy and Klondike Mountains, and the high and distant summit ridge of the Arapaho Peaks. The area is south of the busy Brainard Lake area and west of a bustling parking lot that is at the south end of the Sourdough Trail. Even if the road beyond the Sourdough parking lot it is impassable, a trek on the road to the Rainbow Lakes Trailhead will reward you views of the area's rugged peaks.

From Boulder take Boulder Canyon Road, State Highway 119, west for 14 miles to Nederland. Here turn right (north) onto State Highway 72, the Peak to Peak Highway, and drive north about 6.75 miles to CR 116 on the left (west) side of the road.

# --56--
# Rainbow Lakes

**Round trip:** 2 miles
**Difficulty:** Easy
**Skill level:** Novice
**High point:** 10,300 feet
**Elevation gain:** 300 feet
**Avalanche danger:** Low
**Map:** Trails Illustrated Indian Peaks, Gold Hill
**Contact:** Boulder Ranger District, Roosevelt National Forest

The Rainbow Lakes are in a spectacular high-mountain setting nestled next to the soaring tundra of the glacier-carved Caribou ridge line. This trail is heavily used in the summer and rarely used in the winter. Much of the rough road to the trailhead enjoys southern exposure and is relatively snow free much of the winter. If the road is not passable to the trailhead, it can be used for a nice snowshoe to the trailhead. You have good views of both the Caribou and Niwot Ridges and some of the Indian Peaks on the way.

From the turnoff on State Highway 72, take CR 116 west. The road is plowed to about 0.5 mile at the large parking lot for the Sourdough Trail, but you will likely need a four-wheel-drive vehicle from that point to the trailhead, 4.2 miles farther. The road to the University of Colorado Research Station is on the right at 0.75 mile, then the road turns sharply south (bear left) for a mile or so. At about 2 miles the road turns west; at about 3.25 miles it crosses

*At 11,000 feet, Caribou Ridge is blown free of snow.*

North Boulder Creek. The trailhead is at the end of the road at the western edge of the Rainbow Lakes Campground. The Rainbow Lakes Trail is at the very end of the campground road loop, next to the trailhead map.

The trail rolls gently to the northwest alongside a creek; you'll have some nice views along the way. In a mile reach the lakes, which are surrounded by Caribou and Arapaho Ridges. The real treat is the view from the lakes; ice fishing is also an option if the wind isn't howling.

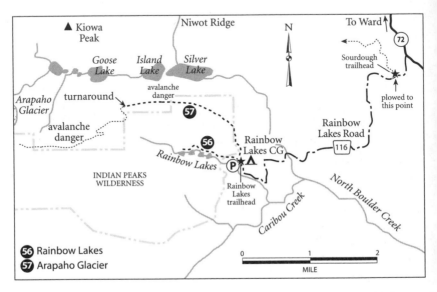

## --57--

# Arapaho Glacier Trail

**Round trip:** 5 miles
**Difficulty:** Moderate to challenging
**Skill level:** Intermediate to expert
**High point:** 11,240 feet
**Elevation gain:** 1,240 feet
**Avalanche danger:** Low to high
**Map:** Trails Illustrated Indian Peaks, Gold Hill
**Contact:** Boulder Ranger District, Roosevelt National Forest

The Arapaho Glacier Trail is more challenging than the trail to the Rainbow Lakes (Route 56), but it's an even more stunning spectacle. You will have a great view of the rest of the Caribou Ridge route to North and South Arapaho Peaks as well as the Arapaho Glacier (all to the west), Kiowa Peak to the northwest, and Niwot Ridge to the north. There is usually a prevailing cold west wind that makes your visit above tree line a brief one. The Arapaho Glacier overlook is a distant 5 miles from the trailhead, but this complete trek is not recommended because of potential high avalanche danger; you can make it to tree line and a stunning view in about half that distance. This trail is heavily used in summer and rarely used in winter. If the road is not passable to the trailhead, you can snowshoe to the trailhead, with good views of both the Caribou and Niwot Ridges and some of the Indian Peaks on the way. Much of the road is relatively snow free much of the winter because of its southern exposure.

From the turnoff on State Highway 72, take CR 116 west. The road is plowed to about 0.5 mile at the large parking lot for the Sourdough Trail, but you will likely need a four-wheel-drive vehicle from that point to the trailhead, 4.2 miles farther. The road to the University of Colorado Research Station is on the right at 0.75 mile, stay left. Then the road turns sharply south for a mile or so. At about 2 miles the road turns west; at about 3.25 miles it crosses North Boulder Creek. The trailhead is at the end of the road at the western edge of the Rainbow Lakes Campground. The well-marked Arapaho Glacier trailhead is on the northwest end of the campground.

The initial mile or so of the trail is easy to track because it's next to the City of Boulder's watershed fence, and has a few blue ribbons after you leave the watershed boundary. Once it starts to climb and steepen, the switchbacks are difficult to see and are not well marked because this is primarily a summer trail. You'll need a topo and good routefinding skills to be safe, but if you keep the lakes to your left (south) and the ridge line to the right (north), you will generally be traveling first north and then west on the south side of Caribou Ridge. There is much fallen timber everywhere *but* on the trail, and that is always a good clue.

After winding your way to tree line at 11,000 feet at 2 miles, you can walk up and over to the north side of the ridge and enjoy a superb view of the Boulder watershed, which includes the panorama of the Indian Peaks' glacier-carved Arapaho Moraine. In another 0.5 mile, where the trail turns sharply southeast, end your trek at 2.5 miles. The trail continues for another 2.5 miles one way to the actual overlook, but the avalanche danger increases significantly beyond tree line, so turning around is advisable for all but the very experienced who know how to analyze a snowpack for stability.

# CENTRAL COLORADO

*The horizon is bounded and adorned by a spiry wall of pines, every tree harmoniously related to every other; definite symbols, divine hieroglyphics written with sunbeams. Would I could understand them!*
John Muir, *My First Summer in the Sierra* (1911)

*Chapter 12*

# I-70 CORRIDOR

Winter weekend traffic on I-70 west of Denver is extremely crowded due to downhill skiers. But if you go midweek or are determined to brave the roadwarriors, you'll find easy, quick access to superb scenery.

## --58--

## Saint Marys Glacier and James Peak

**Round trip to glacier top:** 4 miles
**Difficulty:** Moderate
**Skill level:** Intermediate to expert
**High point:** 11,716 feet
**Elevation gain:** 1,316 feet

**Round trip to peak:** 7.5 miles
**Difficulty:** Challenging
**Skill level:** Intermediate to expert
**High point:** 13,250 feet
**Elevation gain:** 2,850 feet

**Avalanche danger:** Moderate to considerable
**Map:** Trails Illustrated Winter Park, Central City, Rollins Pass
**Contact:** Clear Creek Ranger District, Arapaho National Forest

This is a very climbable glacier in a spectacular setting that is an easy drive from Denver. It is a permanent glacier and, though it shrinks in the summer, there is usually enough snow for year-round use. You have a lot of recreational options

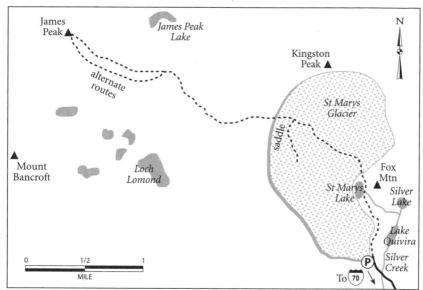

when visiting Saint Marys Glacier. Many people enjoy the climb from the lake to the top of the glacier, take in the nonstop round-trip views of the Front Range, and call it a day. If you have an ice ax, know how to self-arrest, and want to do some glissading, that is an option. When you reach the area near the summit of the glacier, you can see an impressive panorama of James Peak and its Front Range neighbor, Mount Bancroft. Some find this sight to be an irresistible invitation and extend their adventure to the summit of James Peak. Avalanche danger on the slopes of the peak could be high, and there have also been avalanches on the glacier, so check on conditions with the avalanche information center or Forest Service before attempting the route. Heavy usage by other snowshoers and skiers doesn't necessarily mean it is safe. This area is not recommended for families with children; it requires sound mountaineering skills.

From Denver take I-70 west about 30 miles to the Fall River Road/Saint Marys/Alice exit. Follow the signs approximately 8 miles north to the old Saint Marys Glacier Ski Area parking lot. In the winter it is essentially a dead-end road, so you can't miss it. On a clear day, you can see the glacier from the road.

From the parking lot, follow the drainage north toward Saint Marys Lake. On this approximately 0.5-mile trek, you might have to carry your snowshoes. When you reach the edge of the lake, go to the right along its east shore less than 2 miles; this is as far as families or the inexperienced should go. Climb steeply up the slope another 0.3 mile, gradually turning northwest; the ascent is not so steep for the next 0.5 mile. At 1.5 miles reach a saddle. From here, turn south/southeast to hike 0.5 mile to the top of the glacier and a stunning 360-degree view.

To continue to James Peak, from the saddle continue west and then northwest on a very obvious, well-traveled route that is relatively flat and easy for about 1.5 miles. If it is socked in and/or snowing and you cannot see James Peak, or there are no tracks to follow, reconsider unless you are an experienced mountaineer and have a topo and compass or GPS unit and are a good routefinder. Don't track too far to the northeast or you will climb a false summit and be on steep slopes. Reach the foot of the peak at about 3 miles from the trailhead. From here the route steepens considerably and you'll have to employ some routefinding skills. Once you reach the base of the peak, continue to follow the righthand (northeast) slope. Stay just below the ridge and you can angle your way to the summit in another 0.75 mile.

## --*59*--

# Jones Pass Trail

**Round trip:** 3.5 miles
**Difficulty:** Easy to challenging
**Skill level:** Novice to intermediate
**High point:** 11,000 feet
**Elevation gain:** 720 feet
**Avalanche danger:** Low (can be avoided; check with USFS)
**Map:** Trails Illustrated Winter Park, Central City, Rollins Pass
**Contact:** Clear Creek Ranger District, Arapaho National Forest

This beautiful mountain valley close to Denver doesn't require a drive over Berthoud Pass. There are several trails you can explore at this popular location

*Avalanche class going to dig snowpit along the Jones Pass Trail in order to determine snow stability*

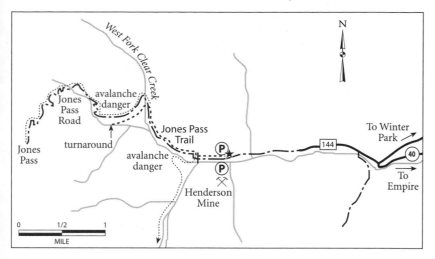

near the Henderson Mine on Red Mountain. You will have to share this trail with some snowmobiles. Off-trail slopes can be hazardous, moderate to high avalanche zones.

From Denver take I-70 west about 40 miles and exit at Empire/US 40 for Berthoud Pass/Winter Park. Drive west on US 40 through Empire toward Berthoud Pass for about 12 miles until you come to the first sharp hairpin turn to the right. Before the hairpin turn, exit to the left onto CR 144 for Henderson Mine. Continue west on the mine road until you come to the designated parking area. The road is closed at the trailhead that serves both the Jones Pass Trail and the Butler Gulch Trail.

Travel west through the trees on the joint trail until the junction at approximately 0.3 mile (left is the more difficult and advanced Butler Gulch Trail); bear right for the Jones Pass Trail. You have some glimpses of the ridge line as you travel northwest through the trees. At a little less than 0.5 mile you break out of the trees and enjoy the panorama of the valley and soaring ridge line. Avalanche run-out zones are observable across the valley on the steep slopes to the west. Gradually bear northwest and then north, following West Fork Clear Creek; at 1.25 miles cross the creek.

On the other side, where the trail veers sharply southwest, stay about 120 feet lower than the trail, in the flat meadow area, rather than traversing the ridge. The trail travels west through a varied landscape of high mountain meadows and trees, gradually curving southwest. At about 1.75 miles, when you reach another creek, turn around because the avalanche danger can be high beyond this point. (You can go all the way to the summit of the pass, but this is only advisable in late spring after the snow has consolidated; check snow conditions with the avalanche information center or Forest Service before doing so.)

*Chapter 13*

# GUANELLA PASS AREA

This popular area south of Georgetown offers many recreational options that are close to Denver and don't require a trip through the Eisenhower Tunnel. A bonus is Georgetown, a turn-of-the-nineteenth-century mining village that features restored Victorian architecture and a wide variety of great dining options. Allowing for a snack or meal in Georgetown will add to your appreciation of this once bustling mining region.

From Denver take I-70 west about 40 miles and take the Georgetown exit (exit 228). Drive toward town and turn right toward Georgetown at the first four-way stop; look for signs to Guanella Pass. Climb west and then south out of town on Guanella Pass Road/State Highway 381 to the pass in about 10 miles. The pass can be a challenging road in the winter, but it is plowed and generally negotiable in a car with snow tires.

# --60--

# Silver Dollar Lake

**Round trip:** 4 miles
**Difficulty:** Easy to moderate
**Skill level:** Novice to intermediate
**High point:** 12,000 feet
**Elevation gain:** 1,150 feet
**Avalanche danger:** None to low
**Maps:** USGS Mt. Evans, Montezuma; Trails Illustrated Idaho Springs, Georgetown, Loveland Pass
**Contact:** Clear Creek Ranger District, Arapaho National Forest

This short, fairly easy trail to a pristine mountain lake surrounded by soaring cliffs is one of the best trails on Guanella Pass, within easy driving distance of Denver. The only disadvantage is the possibility of snowmobiles or SUVs on the road to the trailhead.

On Highway 381, drive to Guanella Pass Campground (about 8.5 miles south of Georgetown) and at the first road past it, turn right. Park here, on the west side of the road.

Take the Silver Dollar Lake road southwest; it is steep. At about 0.5 mile the route levels somewhat and you follow a small creek for a short distance. At approximately 0.6 mile reach the Silver Dollar Lake trailhead on the left; it is well marked. From the trailhead cross the creek. The trail then leaves the drainage, climbing to the right (west) and winding through the trees.

It then climbs out of a hollow at about 1.25 miles and traverses along a

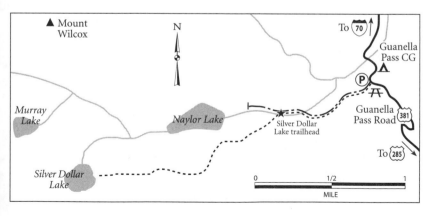

*Silver Dollar Lake*

narrow section with a small drop-off for about 0.5 mile until you emerge from the trees to a spectacular view of the lake and the surrounding rock wall cirque that towers above. You will have a unique view of Mount Wilcox, 13,738-foot Argentine Peak, and Decatur and Squaretop Mountains. From the lake you can climb the peaks in the summer, but in winter the avalanche danger could be significant above the lake, so check conditions with the avalanche information center or Forest Service or by digging a snowpit before climbing higher.

## --*61*--
# Mount Bierstadt

**Round trip:** 1.6 miles to Scott Gomer Creek; 5.8 miles to Mount Bierstadt
**Difficulty:** Easy to challenging
**Skill level:** Novice to expert
**High point:** 11,669 feet at trailhead; 14,060 feet at Mount Bierstadt
**Elevation loss/gain:** 269-foot loss to creek; 2,600-foot gain from creek to peak
**Avalanche danger:** None to high
**Map:** Trails Illustrated Idaho Springs, Georgetown, Loveland Pass
**Contact:** Clear Creek Ranger District, Arapaho National Forest

Mount Bierstadt, one of Colorado's highest peaks (topping out at 14,060 feet), is also one of Colorado's most accessible 14,000-foot peaks, as it is close to

Denver. It is climbable in winter because much of the western side of the mountain gets blown free of heavy snow, and there is a ridge on the northern edge of the western side that is relatively safe. If you plan to summit, start at dawn. Its upper slopes are not without avalanche danger, but you can also enjoy safe, shorter excursions in the grand high-mountain terrain at the base of the Evans-Bierstadt massif. The first 0.75 mile can be hiked before encountering any danger, and the setting is magnificent. Simply start at the Guanella Pass trailhead and go as far as you like before turning around. Use your own judgment based on snow reports and the area you are crossing.

On State Highway 381, when you break out into the open and see the striking view of the Bierstadt-Evans massif to the east, look for the Guanella Pass trailhead for Bierstadt on the left (east) side of the road 10 miles from Georgetown.

The first part of the trail is virtually without avalanche danger and it actually goes downhill to the east for 0.8 mile. Using this first section as an out-and-back trek is worth the trip in combination with another nearby jaunt just for the view. At 0.8 mile you are near Scott Gomer Creek at around 11,400 feet. In crossing the creek you encounter the infamous willows that befuddle many climbers. The newly designed trail makes avoiding them easy.

After you make it through to the other side, the trail climbs very gradually to the southeast for another 0.5 mile before you encounter steeper slopes and avalanche danger. But remember, the danger is relative to the conditions on the day you are climbing and vary greatly. Make your way south around a

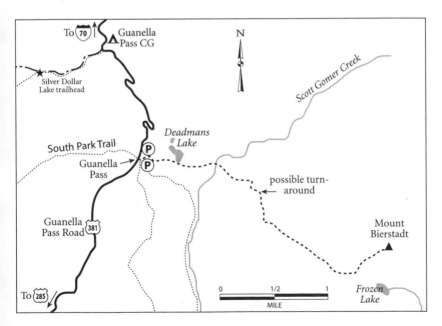

*Route up Mount Bierstadt*

pyramid-shaped rock and then climb southeast. After 0.5 mile of steep climbing almost due south, at about 1.5 miles the trail settles down to a steady incline heading southeast for a mile up the wide west ridge. The last 2 miles are often windswept, and snowshoes might be optional. At about 2.5 miles the trail curves northeast for the steep rise to the summit.

## OTHER TRAILS TO EXPLORE

A trail on the west side of the highway from the Bierstadt trail, the South Park Trail, is another short out and back with great views. It starts out on a short hill, travels around 100 yards or so on a flat area, and then descends to a creek before climbing again. After another 100 yards it starts to meander and climb under avalanche zones and becomes unsafe to travel unless the snow is very thin or very stable.

# SOUTHERN COLORADO

*I wish to preach not the doctrine of ignoble ease, but the doctrine of the strenuous life.*
President Theodore Roosevelt, speech before the Hamilton Club (1899)

*Chapter 14*

# COMO AREA

Kenosha Pass at 10,000 feet offers easy access to the popular Colorado Trail. It offers a magnificent view of South Park and the 14,000-foot peaks of the Mosquito and Tenmile Ranges. This group of mountains is much more impressive when snowcapped and viewed from a distance than they are dotted by droves of people climbing them in the summer.

One of the hidden treasures of the state, Como has a magnificent backdrop; it is the gateway to Boreas Pass (Route 64) and the Gold Dust Trail (Routes 65 and 66), both of which are delightful ways to enjoy the scenic Tarryall Mountains, Tenmile Range, and Mosquito Range. Como features only a grocery store, so don't expect any support services. The road to Como is plowed and generally passable to passenger cars with good snow tires, but a four-wheel-drive vehicle is advisable. Be aware that the road may be passable in the morning and *not* passable by afternoon.

From Denver go southwest on US 285. At about 55 miles, State Highway 381 to the north is another approach to the Guanella Pass area (see chapter 13). In another 10 miles on US 285, you reach Kenosha Pass, and in 10 miles more you reach Como. At the Como turnoff, turn right (northwest) and drive west through Como on CR 33, also known as the Boreas Pass Road, a good snow-packed gravel road.

# --62--

# Kenosha Pass and Colorado Trail West

**Round trip:** 10 miles; 0.8-mile side trip
**Difficulty:** Easy to challenging
**Skill level:** Novice
**High point:** 10,300 feet
**Elevation gain:** 300 feet; elevation loss, 400 feet
**Avalanche danger:** None to low
**Map:** Trails Illustrated Tarryall Mountains, Kenosha Pass
**Contact:** South Park Ranger District, Pike National Forest

This very popular summer trail is also used frequently in the winter, but still relatively lightly compared to many trails closer to Denver. This segment of the Colorado Trail on the west side of Kenosha Pass makes for short, easy out-and-back family excursions or more ambitious adventures. The first 2 or 3 miles of the trail are a very gradual climb, emerging out of the trees to a panoramic view of South Park and the massive backdrop of the 14,000-foot wall of the Mosquito Range. On the way up the trail, you get some scenic glimpses of the Tarryall Mountains to the east too. Unless it has been a very heavy snow year and the south slope has been undermined by spring melt, avalanches are unlikely. Always check with the Colorado Avalanche Information Center to be absolutely sure.

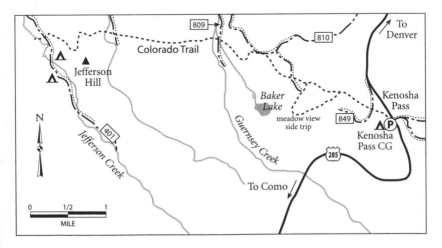

Park on the west side of US 285 outside of the Kenosha Pass Campground, which closes for the winter. Go through the main, gated entrance to the campground and immediately you see a sign for the Colorado Trail.

Follow the trail/road up to some rest rooms. Bear left and keep going; do not walk into the campground area on the right; eventually you come to another sign for the Colorado Trail. Go to the right (northwest) on the trail. At first you are in a very thick tree tunnel as you climb steadily but gradually to about 0.6 mile.

**Tip:** If you are adventurous and want to see the view of South Park sooner, you can go off trail to the left (southwest) at this point and perhaps enjoy some deep, unpacked powder. This might also mean breaking trail and sinking down into the powder, depending on snow conditions. Go across this small, low-angle, open meadow. You top out in the view area at about 0.6 mile from the trail; gradually angle your way back northeast to the trail at its 1-mile mark and turn left to continue the main route. This 1.2-mile side trip only adds about 0.8 mile to your excursion because you skip about 0.4 mile of the trail. You could do the side trip on the way out and the trail on the way back.

From about 0.6 mile on the trail, you gain another 100 feet before it levels off and then starts to go downhill to emerge from the trees. There is a stunning view of South Park; this is the best spot for a photo or snack break. This part of the trail slants to the south so the snow can be very thin to nonexistent early or late in the season. After about 200 yards of downhill travel, it reenters the trees so the snow should improve.

The trail continues fairly level; at about 1 mile the side-trip route through the meadow rejoins the trail from the left. At just short of 1.5 miles the trail overlooks Baker Lake (which is on private land); if you turn around near here, you will have about a 3-mile round trip and about 350 feet in total elevation gain. In another 0.25 the trail starts dropping down to Baker Lake's outlet stream, the low point of this route.

From the Baker Lake overlook, you lose around 250 feet as you drop down 0.75 mile to the creek, crossing it and Guernsey Creek at 2.5 miles. Then you climb steadily but gradually (regaining those 250 feet and gaining another 250 feet in the next mile) as you meander into and out of the trees. At about 3.75 miles you drop to cross another stream, rising again on the other side, then at about 4.25 miles you descend 200 feet on the side of Jefferson Hill to Jefferson Creek Campground at around 5 miles (9,900 feet). As always, be cautious and turn around early if the weather is changing and a storm is blowing in.

## --63--
# North Twin Cone Peak

**Round trip:** 8.8 miles
**Difficulty:** Moderate to challenging
**Skill level:** Novice
**High point:** 11,300 feet
**Elevation gain:** 1,300 feet
**Avalanche danger:** None to low
**Map:** Trails Illustrated Tarryall Mountains, Kenosha Pass
**Contact:** South Park Ranger District, Pike National Forest

This route follows FR 126 (closed to traffic in winter), meandering gradually up toward the summit of North Twin Cone Peak (12,323 feet). This little-used road is a good way to escape the crowds and enjoy a trail that is primarily tree covered but does offer some tree breaks and views of the Tarryall Mountains. Climbing steadily and switchbacking, it is not well marked for winter use but is a fairly obvious route.

The trailhead is across US 285 from the Kenosha Pass Campground (see Route 62), but parking is available on both sides of the road.

From the highway the route heads east across a meadow and then enters the mixed forest of aspen and evergreens. At about 0.6 mile the road/trail rounds a small hill with a radio tower, offering some views of the Tarryall Mountains and gradually curving southeast to reach Kenosha Creek at 1 mile. There are

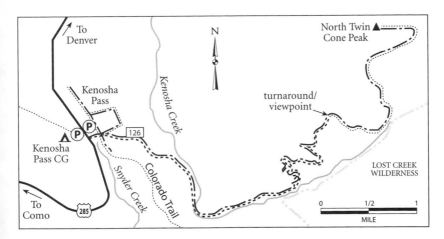

*North Twin Cone Peak from the Colorado Trail east of Kenosha Pass*

breaks in the trees with nice views of the Lost Creek Wilderness Area. The road follows the creek closely for the next mile and a half, crossing it at about 1.25 miles. At about 2.5 miles the switchbacks begin in earnest from about 10,400 feet; you could turn around here for a pleasant 5-mile out and back with only about 400 feet of elevation gain. The higher you go on the switchbacks, the better the view of South Park and the distant fourteeners of the Mosquito Range.

The intense switchbacks take you up 900 feet in 0.75 mile, then at about 3.25 miles settle down to more moderate but steady climbing that takes you up 400 feet in about a mile. You reach a good viewpoint at 11,300 feet at about 4.4 miles; turn around after enjoying the view of the Tarryalls, Lost Creek Wilderness, and South Park.

## OTHER TRAILS TO EXPLORE

The Colorado Trail east of Kenosha Pass wanders up and down 6 miles into Johnson Gulch, offering some nice views of South Park.

## --64--

# Boreas Pass Road and Halfway Gulch

**Round trip:** 5 miles
**Difficulty:** Easy to moderate
**Skill level:** Novice
**High point:** 10,550 feet
**Elevation gain:** 450 feet
**Avalanche danger:** Low to high
**Map:** Trails Illustrated Breckenridge, Tennesse Pass
**Contact:** South Park Ranger District, Pike National Forest

The road to Boreas Pass is a steady and then eventually steep climb that offers superb views of part of South Park and the Tarryall Mountains. You might have to share the road/trail with snowmobiles, but it is worth the price of admission. The road is usually well packed because of snowmobile use, and with a little luck there won't be a major fleet of them starting off or returning when you are. You can do an out and back of any distance if the snow is stable and there is no avalanche danger—you could go up to the pass and continue all the way to Breckenridge for a winter mountaineering overnight, but only if the snow has consolidated and there is no avalanche danger. If the snow is unstable, then an out and back of 4 or 5 miles is recommended because the road passes next to slopes that are steep enough to produce avalanches. Keep your eyes on the north side of the road and turn around when the slope equals or exceeds 35 degrees.

From from US 285 at Como, take CR 33, Boreas Pass Road, northwest. In approximately 5 miles there is a fork; Boreas Pass Road is on the north (right); the road you are on continues straight ahead and becomes CR 50. Park near Boreas Pass Road, which is closed in winter and isn't plowed; sometimes it is usable by high-clearance four-wheel-drive vehicles for a short distant from the turnoff.

The road heads east then south to round a hill in a mile, then heading north around another one in 0.5 mile. It quickly gains enough elevation to give you nonstop views of the surrounding mountain ranges and part of the South Park valley. At 1.5 miles you reach Davis Overlook; this is a good turn-around point if you aren't ambitious or it is a family expedition. The road then heads northwest, gradually descending over the next mile. As the road swings to the northwest, the views diminish for about 0.5 mile; you will see more views of Iron and Little Baldy Mountains if you trek another 0.5 mile to Halfway Gulch. At 2.5 miles you reach the gulch.

Beyond Halfway Gulch the road curves north, and at around 3 miles, there is considerable avalanche hazard for a mile. It's possible to cross the drainage and continue another 0.5 mile to enjoy the views, but at the 3-mile mark where avalanche danger begins, it is definitely time to turn around. A 3- to 6-mile round trip on this road/trail can be very rewarding for anyone, including families.

*Boreas Pass from near Como*

Attempt the pass only when the snow is consolidated and only if you are an experienced winter mountaineer with survival gear and skills. At 4.5 miles the road reaches Selkirk Gulch, then heads northwest to reach the pass in another 2.5 miles.

## --*65*--

# Gold Dust Trail South

**One way:** 4 miles
**Difficulty:** Easy
**Skill level:** Novice
**High point:** 10,600 feet
**Elevation gain:** 600 feet
**Avalanche danger:** None
**Map:** Trails Illustrated Breckenridge, Tennessee Pass
**Contact:** South Park Ranger District, Pike National Forest

This very enjoyable trail isn't heavily used and does not allow motorized traffic. It offers a scenic tour of the creek valleys off the beaten path. This southern segment is good only in a snowy midwinter; the snow is very spotty to nonexistent early and late in the season because of sun and wind exposure. With good snow cover, this is a pleasant, meandering trail that rolls in and out of trees and over gentle terrain, offering views of the Tarryall Creek valley and surrounding mountains. It is described here as an easy one-way trip with a vehicle shuttle to the north trailhead (see Route 66), but it can also be done as an out and back.

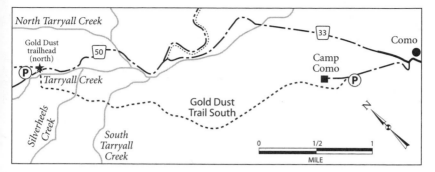

In Como when you turn off US 285 onto CR 33, Church Camp Road is the first road on the left (south). It is not well marked; follow signs to Camp Como. Church Camp Road travels northwest a little less than a mile. Park on the side of the road near the entrance gate to the camp.

The trailhead is on the left; look for a blue diamond on the left gate post. Follow blue diamonds through tight aspens approximately 0.3 mile to a wider trail marked with orange diamonds in a clearing. Follow uphill approximately 200 yards and keep your eyes open for a trail to the right, once again marked with blue diamonds. The trail travels northwest around the shoulder of Little Baldy Mountain, gradually rising to 10,600 at about 1.75 miles. Drop about 300 feet to cross scenic South Tarryall Creek at 3 miles, and in another 0.5 mile cross equally pretty Silverheels Creek. Just before intersecting with the road in 0.5 mile, the trail crosses Tarryall Creek before reaching CR 50 and the north trailhead.

## --66--
## Gold Dust Trail North

**Round trip:** 8.5 miles
**Difficulty:** Moderate to challenging
**Skill level:** Novice to intermediate
**High point:** 11,482 feet
**Elevation gain:** 782 feet
**Avalanche danger:** Low to moderate near the pass
**Map:** Trails Illustrated Breckenridge, Tennessee Pass
**Contact:** South Park Ranger District, Pike National Forest

On the Gold Dust Trail, an enjoyable, lightly used trail that does not allow motorized traffic, this is the better option of the two segments. It is more interesting

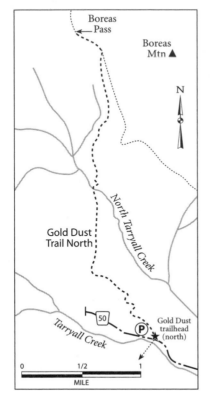

and challenging because it makes the exhilarating climb all the way up to Boreas Pass Road without as much exposure to avalanche hazard as the road itself presents. A narrow, somewhat steep pine-tree tunnel at the beginning, the trail opens up into a mixed forest of aspen and evergreens with very nice views of the peaks and Tarryall Creek valley. As is almost always the case, the climb up takes considerably longer than the descent, but allow a long day and get an early start for the entire round trip. Though the view from the Boreas Pass Road is well worth the effort, the round trip is suitable for only the very fit and experienced; a shorter out and back can be accomplished by novices.

From US 285 at Como, take CR 33, Boreas Pass Road, northwest. In approximately 5.5 miles there is a fork; Boreas Pass Road is on the north (right); continue straight ahead, now on CR 50. In 0.75 mile the road forks again; stay left and in a mile reach the trailhead. It is easy to miss the brown Forest Service sign on the south side of the road because it is set back from the road and parking is 0.3 mile west past the trailhead. The trailhead is signed, though not easy to spot from the road.

The trail climbs northwest for the first 0.5 mile through a pretty mixed forest to offer some views, and then climbs again before leveling out on a ridge top. This is a good place for a snack and photo of Iron Mountain and the beautiful Tarryall Creek riparian area below. The trail then travels north 1.5 miles in an old water flume, and so is relatively flat, crossing North Tarryall Creek at about 2.25 miles. This is another good place for a wind-sheltered break in a pretty open meadow/wetland. If your ambitions have faded, this is also a good turnaround point. Otherwise, climb steeply for a mile to the Boreas Pass Road at 3.75 miles, and another short 0.5 mile of gradual uphill to the pass itself.

-------------------------

# Chapter 15

# LEADVILLE AREA

Leadville, the highest-altitude incorporated city in the United States, is a historic mining town surrounded by some of the most stunning scenery—and devastation—in the state. Colorado's highest mountain, 14,433-foot Mount Elbert, is to the southwest, and the views of it and its neighbor, Mount Massive, would be the envy of any city. Unfortunately Leadville is just a dozen miles south of the infamous open-pit mine at Climax, with its massive tailings pond. It is also surrounded by the scars of the gold and silver mines that scoured the area during the mining boom that started in 1878 and peaked by 1890, swelling the town to its highest population of 24,000 people. In spite of tailings that decorate the south end of town, the historic downtown is well worth a visit; it has been admirably rebuilt and refurbished, and now offers a variety of dining and lodging options.

Don't be fooled by the somewhat funky state of Leadville and the surrounding area where mine waste and tailings dominate some of the scenery. Though little of the surrounding terrain has not been mined or turned over, it still offers some spectacular and unique recreational opportunities. Tennessee Pass north of Leadville is replete with railroading history dating back to the narrow-gauge lines of the nineteenth century. Because of the mixed reputation created by mining, the trails around Leadville aren't overrun by people. The very forgiving white carpet of snowfall does a thorough job of hiding the warts that are obvious during the warmer months.

Leadville is on US 24, 38 miles south of I-70 at the Minturn/Vail area. From Denver, drive west on I-70 about 80 miles to Copper Mountain and take exit 195, before Vail Pass, to State Highway 91. Drive southwest about 38 miles to reach Leadville.

--*67*--

# Vances Hut

**Round trip:** 5.5 miles
**Difficulty:** Moderate
**Skill level:** Novice to intermediate
**High point:** 11,200 feet
**Elevation gain:** 800 feet
**Avalanche danger:** None to low (can be avoided)
**Map:** Trails Illustrated Breckenridge, Tennessee Pass
**Contact:** Holy Cross Ranger District, White River National Forest

One of the most accessible of the Tenth Mountain Division huts is less than 3 miles from the trailhead at Tennessee Pass. It is an easy trail to follow, featuring superb views of the Holy Cross Wilderness Area, Mount Elbert and the Mount Massive massif, and Ski Cooper.

*From Vances Hut Trail*

From Leadville drive north on US 24 approximately 8 miles to Tennessee Pass. The Ski Cooper Ski Area is on the right (east) side of the road. Pull into the parking lot and as you near the main lodge, look for a small one-story building on the right (south) side of the road, on the west side of the parking lot. It is the Nordic ski and snowshoe rental hut, where you can get information about trail conditions and permission to park overnight. The trailhead is a cat-tracked road actually across the road from the Nordic building, 100 yards from the main lodge, on the left (north) edge of the ski area.

Follow the road—Piney Gulch/Cooper Loop Nordic trail—downhill into the drainage toward Chicago Ridge, crossing Burton Ditch at about 0.3 mile, and reach the intersection with the turnoff for Vances Hut at about 0.6 mile. The Tenth Mountain Trail was not marked at this writing. To the right, the trail climbs higher, going south around Cooper Hill; take the trail to the left (north) alongside the irrigation canal.

The trail then climbs gradually northeast along the edge of the trees and Burton Ditch into an open wetlands and meadow area where there is a trail junction at about 1.25 miles. The other leg of the Cooper Loop goes to the right (east); go left (due north)—don't take the trail hard to the left (due west), which goes back down Piney Gulch to the highway. Shortly you reenter thick tree cover and cross the confluence of the ditch and Piney Gulch; follow the gulch upstream in a narrow drainage for 0.5 mile to another intersection, at 1.5 miles. Here, the trail to Taylor Hill continues straight/right to the northeast up the drainage; take the hut trail to the left (northwest).

Begin the steep slog 600 feet up toward the shoulder of the ridge. The Tenth Mountain Trail climbs sharply uphill to the northwest/north and switchbacks. There are times when you have to look sharply to see the trail markers. There are widely spaced blue diamonds but, because of the switchbacks, they are easy to miss, especially if it is snowing. Once you reach the shoulder of the ridge in a little over 2 miles, the trail levels considerably and you have views of the mountains that surround the area. If it is early or late in the season, you will have to detour around fallen trees.

In another 0.5 mile the trail rounds the ridge and you come to a beautiful open meadow with spectacular views of the Holy Cross Wilderness Area to the west, Turquoise Lake to the south, and Mount Elbert and the Mount Massive massif also downvalley. If you aren't staying at the hut, this is a good place to turn around because the trail goes steeply downhill to the left (west), edging the left side of the meadow and dropping in 0.3 mile to the hut. It is hidden below the lower left quarter of the meadow in the trees. The cabin has a nice deck with a superb view of Ski Cooper and the Holy Cross Wilderness.

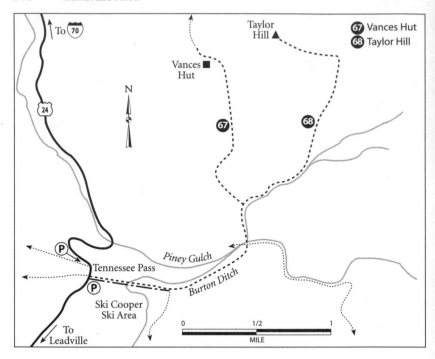

--*68*--

# Taylor Hill

**Round trip:** 6 miles
**Difficulty:** Challenging
**Skill level:** Intermediate to expert
**High point:** 11,725 feet
**Elevation gain:** 1,325 feet
**Avalanche danger:** Moderate to considerable (can be avoided)
**Map:** Trails Illustrated Breckenridge, Tennessee Pass
**Contact:** Holy Cross Ranger District, White River National Forest

Climbing Taylor Hill gives a panorama of the Tennessee Pass area, with 360 degrees of great views. You get a closeup look at Chicago Ridge to the east, the spectacle of the Holy Cross Wilderness to the west, and the Sawatch Range to the south. It is not a good route to attempt at times of high avalanche danger.

See Route 67 for driving directions.

Follow the route for Vances Hut (Route 67) for the first 1.5 miles. At the junction where the trails separate (the trail to Vances Hut tracks to the left, northwest), stay to the right for Taylor Hill, and continue straight up the Piney Gulch drainage heading northeast.

Watch for tree blazes. Stay on the left side of the Piney Gulch stream as the trail follows the creek and weaves through some open meadows and trees. When you reach a secondary drainage coming in from the left at about 2 miles, turn north (left) and shoot for the saddle on the east side of Taylor Hill. Avoid open slopes that are more than 30 degrees as you make your own switchbacks to the saddle. This is the steepest section of the trek and requires patience, given the altitude. From the top of the saddle at about 2.75 miles, follow the ridge line west/northwest to the summit of Taylor Hill for a real treat. Enjoy the panorama and have a nice break before retracing your steps through the powder to the trailhead. There are lots of opportunities for romping through the powder on the return, but stay off the steepest slopes and weave your way through the trees where possible in order to avoid avalanche danger.

*Early season along Piney Gulch with Chicago Ridge in the distance*

## --*69*--

# Mitchell Creek Loop

**Loop:** 6.5 miles
**Difficulty:** Moderate
**Skill level:** Novice to intermediate
**High point:** 10,600 feet
**Elevation gain:** 200 feet
**Avalanche danger:** Low
**Map:** Trails Illustrated Breckenridge, Tennessee Pass
**Contact:** Leadville Ranger District, San Isabel National Forest

The Mitchell Creek Loop follows the Tennessee Pass portion of the Colorado Trail, part of which is a former railroad bed. The loop offers great views of the Holy Cross Wilderness and Homestake Peak to the west. It is a good trail for beginners but interesting enough in location and terrain to be fun for snowshoers of all skill levels. Even though it is on Tennessee Pass, there is no avalanche terrain.

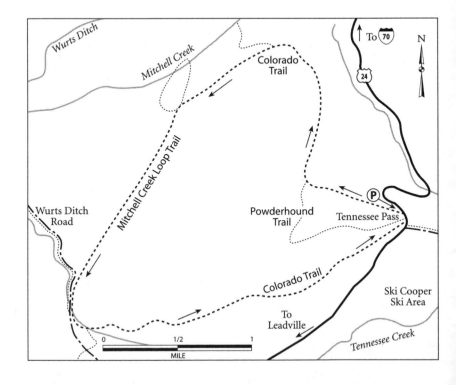

From Leadville drive north on US 24 approximately 8 miles to Tennessee Pass (the Ski Cooper Ski Area is on the right—east—side of the road). The loop trailhead is on the west side of Tennessee Pass, across the road from Ski Cooper, at the end of a large parking lot.

**Tip:** At this writing, the Trails Illustrated map of this trail is in revision and is not accurate or in agreement with the USFS description provided by the Leadville USFS office. The map provided here is accurate.

The loop starts on the Colorado Trail, an old railroad grade that descends gradually traveling to the northwest. After you climb back up a bit, at approximately 0.25 mile you pass old charcoal kilns and then the trail descends about 200 feet over the next mile. For the first 0.6 mile you enjoy great views of Homestake Peak. When you come to the Powderhound Trail junction at about

*Homestake Peak from Tennessee Pass*

0.7 mile (it goes uphill to the left), stay to the right. The trail then turns right, to the north. At about 1.5 miles it levels out at 10,200 feet, then turns left to round the toe of the ridge, heading west.

At a junction just before 2 miles, the Colorado Trail turns off to the right and goes west then north; stay left on the Mitchell Creek Loop Trail as it travels southwest into the Mitchell drainage, where it bottoms out at around 10,110 feet at 2.5 miles. A trail on the right goes down Mitchell Creek to the highway; stay to the left. The railroad grade ends and the terrain becomes more difficult as the trail begins to climb again for about 1.5 miles. The trail climbs steadily up to 10,600 feet and intersects the Wurts Ditch Road at a saddle at about 4 miles.

Shortly after, the trail crosses over the drainage and enters the trees, traveling downhill and dropping about 200 feet in 0.25 mile, following the road for approximately 0.25 mile to an intersection with the Colorado Trail. The road continues to the right; turn sharply left onto the Colorado Trail as it starts to go back to the east and north. You then cross the stream again, and another trail goes off to the right; stay straight/left. The Colorado Trail then goes gradually up and then downhill 2 miles to the pass.

## --70--

# Twin Lakes

**Round trip:** 12 miles
**Difficulty:** Easy
**Skill level:** Novice
**High point:** 9,400 feet
**Elevation gain:** 200 feet
**Avalanche danger:** None
**Map:** Trails Illustrated Aspen, Independence Pass
**Contact:** Leadville Ranger District, San Isabel National Forest

This route along the road that leads to Independence Pass is surrounded by superb views of Mount Elbert (highest in the state), Parry Peak, 13,000-foot Rinker and Twin Peaks, and 13,461-foot Quail Mountain. It is an easy out and back, or a suitable one way with a vehicle shuttle, in a great setting that is ideal for families or for a quick workout. It is not a good place for snowshoeing early or late in the season because of unpredictable snow.

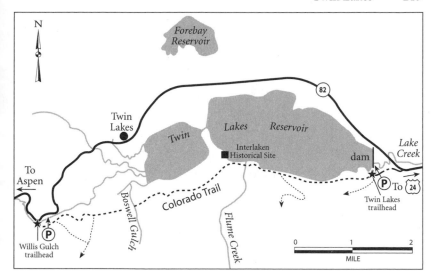

From Leadville take US 24 south 14 or so miles to State Highway 82 and turn right (west) toward Aspen. In a few miles you reach the eastern edge of Twin Lakes Reservoir. After about 3 miles from US 24, just before a bridge over Lake Creek, watch for a gravel road to the left that goes south below the dam. Take the gravel road around a wetlands area about 0.5 mile to the Twin Lakes trailhead. (For a vehicle shuttle, go back out to the highway, turn left, and drive west about 8 miles through the town of Twin Lakes to the Willis Gulch trailhead on the left/south.)

From the Twin Lakes trailhead, take the Colorado Trail to the left (south, then west). The rolling trail takes you around the southern edge of Twin Lakes Reservoir. At about 1.7 miles the Main Range Trail comes in from the left; stay straight. Cross Flume Creek at about 2.3 miles; shortly after, you can enjoy the ruins of the ghost town of Interlaken Historical Site, between the Twin Lakes. It is spectacular setting with views of the southern flank of the Mount Elbert massif and Mount Hope to the north; west and south are Twin Peaks and Quail Mountain. If you choose to go only as far as the ghost town, it is around a 5-mile out and back.

Continuing farther on the trail, you pass a wetlands area and then climb 200 feet to the 3-mile point. The trail now stays on the hillside above the second of the Twin Lakes, going southwest toward the western end of the lake. At about 4.4 miles cross Boswell Gulch, past the western end of the upper Twin Lake. There's a trail intersection at 5 miles; stay straight, and then cross another stream. In another mile reach the Willis Gulch trailhead on State Highway 82.

*Chapter 16*

# COLORADO SPRINGS AREA

Colorado Springs provides a jumping off point for numerous snowshoe routes. Rampart Reservoir in Pike National Forest (Route 71) is perfect for beginners, and the Mueller State Park and Wildlife Area (Routes 72 through 74) and the nearby Crags in the Pikes Peak foothills (Route 75) are real jewels

Just 26 miles from Colorado Springs, Mueller State Park looks out on the western slopes of the Pikes Peak massif from its east-oriented trails, and the snowcapped Sangre de Cristo Mountains are the majestic backdrop for its westerly trails. Views from park trails are 360 degrees because the park is essentially draped over the top of a 10,000-foot mountain, with all trails going downhill from the top. There is enough tree cover—a colorful tapestry of aspen, pine, fir, and spruce trees—to protect the snow, but most of the trails open up for good views and sunshine. A look at the map for this state park and wildlife area will show you that there are a seemingly infinite number of possibilities for combining trails. It simply depends on the conditions and your ambitions. Note that the large number of intersecting trails can make routefinding a bit tricky because some of the trails are not well marked. The park's campground makes a good starting point because it is on the highest point along the access road. The campground has a limited number of RV and tent sites available throughout the winter, though the showers and flush toilets are not open; vault toilets are available. In winter the visitors center is open only on weekends. There is a self-service entry station near the campground. A short distance across the highway is The Crags, northwest of the long Pikes Peak ridge.

For Rampart Reservoir, take US 24 from Colorado Springs (I-25 exit 141, Manitou Springs and Pikes Peak) west 17 miles to the town of Woodland Park. Stay on US 24 for 0.3 mile and turn right on Loy Creek Road (FR 393) when you see the sign for Rampart Reservoir.

For Mueller State Park, take US 24 From Colorado Springs west 25 miles to the town of Divide. Go west through Divide until you reach the intersection with State Highway 67 and then turn left to take it south 4 miles. The entrance to Mueller State Park is on the right (west) side of the road. The signed turnoff for The Crags Campground/Rocky Mountain Camp is in another 0.5 mile, on the left (east).

## --71--

# Rampart Reservoir

**Round trip:** 3 miles to reservoir; 11.6-mile loop around reservoir
**Difficulty:** Easy to moderate
**Skill level:** Novice
**High point:** 9,160 feet
**Elevation gain:** 160 feet
**Avalanche danger:** None
**Map:** Trails Illustrated Pikes Peak, Cañon City
**Contact:** Pikes Peak Ranger District, Pike National Forest

Easy access from Colorado Springs is the primary benefit of this recreational area. The reservoir is in a beautiful setting of foothills and mountains with giant granite boulders; aspen, fir, and spruce trees; sun-drenched hillsides; and good views

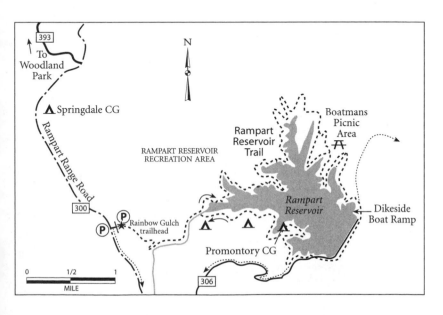

of Pikes Peak in the distance. The trail is great for beginners because it rolls gently and has no challenging terrain but snow can be spotty until midwinter.

From the turn off of US 24 in Woodland Park, follow the Rampart Reservoir signs on FR 393 north, then east, and then south 3.5 miles to Rampart Range Road and turn right. Take it 2.5 miles south to the Rainbow Gulch access road. This is the best winter access point. The access road is closed during winter but there are places to park so you can use the Rainbow Gulch Trail to the reservoir.

The trail slopes gently toward the shoreline of the reservoir, starting off in a nice ponderosa pine forest and at 0.5 mile encountering the Rainbow Gulch stream. It then opens up into a nice meadow and at a little less than 1.5 miles intersects the trail around the lake. From here you can return as you came for a short out and back or continue for a longer trek on the trail around the reservoir. To the right the Rampart Reservoir Trail goes due east on the south side of the reservoir; to the left it goes northeast on the north side of the reservoir. The north side generally has better snow conditions.

The route described here turns left to follow the north shore; at 2 miles you reach a deep inlet. The next 1.5 miles follow the shore of a long peninsula, reaching its bay at about 3.5 miles. At 4 miles the trail begins to switchback around fingers of land, then goes inland for 0.5 mile to go around a long finger of shoreline. At about 5.25 miles you return to the shore and at 5.6 or so miles reach Boatmans Picnic Area. The trail goes around this and the next peninsula in another mile and goes inland a ways, returning to the shore at 7 miles. At 7.5 miles the trail intersects the Stanley Rim Trail at the boat ramp on the north end of the dam; stay on the shore.

*Pikes Peak at Mueller State Park*

The Rampart Reservoir Trail follows a road for the next 0.75 mile, crossing the 0.5-mile-long spillway and returning to a footpath at 8.25 miles. At 9.25 miles you reach one of the three campgrounds, out on a promontory of land. As you continue to follow the shoreline, now heading west, at 10.75 miles you return to the Rainbow Gulch Trail. Turn left and in another short mile you return to the trailhead.

## --72--

# School Pond and Preachers Hollow Loops

**School Pond Loop:** 1.75 miles

**Preachers Hollow Loop:** 1.6 miles

**Difficulty:** Easy
**Skill level:** Novice
**High point:** 9,500 feet at trailhead
**Elevation gain:** 100 feet
**Avalanche danger:** None to low
**Map:** Mueller State Park and Wildlife Area
**Contact:** Mueller State Park

These two loop trails originate near the Mueller State Park Visitors Center, located just south of the Revenuers Ridge trailhead (the visitors center is open only on weekends during the winter). Both loops stay on the ridge line and don't descend as steeply as some of the other trails; they drop down to ponds at their far ends. They can be done singly, or together for a 3.2-mile combined loop.

From the Mueller State Park entrance, drive Wapiti Road (the park road) west/southwest about 1.25 miles. Find the trailhead on the south side of the road.

The School Pond Loop Trail heads south through heavy tree cover of aspen and pines that preserve snow when other trails have thinned. In 0.25 mile at a trail junction, the other leg of the loop is to the left and Stoner Mill Trail is to the right; continue straight. At 0.5 mile when the other end of the Stoner Mill Trail comes in from the right, stay straight/left. Just before 0.75 mile, School Pond itself is to the right; the trail then curves left (north). A little before 1 mile reach a T-intersection. To the right is the Aspen Trail; go left to continue the loop, now heading west. At about 1.3 miles the other end of the Aspen Trail comes in from the right; continue straight/left. In a short distance close the loop at 1.5 miles; turn right to return to the trailhead.

From the trailhead, the Preachers Hollow Loop Trail is a short distance west of the School Pond Loop Trail; there is a nice overlook at the beginning of the Preachers Hollow Loop Trail. Go to the left to do this loop clockwise, heading south. In 0.3 mile the trail forks, with the Ranger Trail to the left; stay straight/right as the Preachers Hollow Loop Trail curves west and then south again. Just before 0.5 mile the trail passes Never/Never Pond and curves west, then northwest in a short ways. At about 0.9 mile you intersect the Rock Pond Trail; go hard to the right to continue the loop, now heading northeast. At about 1.25 mile the trail goes north to curve a couple of times in the last 0.4 mile. The Revenuers Ridge Trail is on the left shortly before you close the loop.

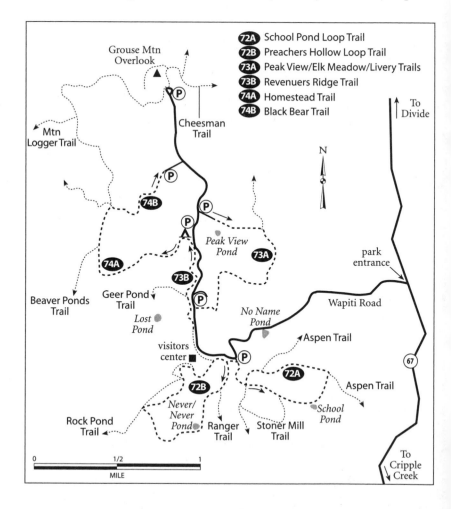

--乃--

# Peak View, Elk Meadow, Livery, and Revenuers Ridge Trails

**Loop:** 2.2 miles
**Difficulty:** Easy to moderate
**Skill level:** Novice
**High point:** 9,600 feet at trailhead
**Elevation gain:** 300 feet
**Avalanche danger:** None to low
**Map:** Mueller State Park and Wildlife Area
**Contact:** Mueller State Park

This route consists of a partial loop on the east side of the road connected by a one-way stretch alongside the road combining four different trails.

From the Mueller State Park entrance, drive Wapiti Road (the park road) west and then north 2.25 miles to the campground area. Peak View Trail is near a campground that is popular because of the great views of the western slopes of Pikes Peak. The well-marked trailhead on the right, about 0.25 mile past the campground entry station, is easy to locate.

The Peak View Trail heads southeast on a nice, open trail; Peak View Pond is on the right as you descend through the colorful mixture of aspen and pine trees. It is worth a short detour to get some closeup shots of the pond. Take the ridge down the gentle slope to a T-intersection with the Elk Meadow Trail in a little past 0.25 mile. (For an easy out and back, return to the trailhead.)

For the loop, turn right onto the Elk Meadow Trail heading the south. It rolls gently along the ridge, with good views to the east. At about 0.75 mile the trail curves west and eventually climbs back uphill toward the road, intersecting with the Livery Loop Trail at about 1 mile. Stay left on the Livery Loop Trail as it meanders across the ridge to the Livery Loop trailhead at approximately 1.4 miles.

Directly across the road from the Livery Loop trailhead is the Geer Pond trailhead; cross to this entrypoint to the Revenuers Ridge Trail, and take it to the right (north). This trail parallels the road and the ridge line, dipping down the ridge somewhat along the way. It features nice views to the west all along the way. This is one of the few trails that isn't a trail that goes downhill on the way out and uphill on the way back, so it is ideal for families with small children or group members who are less ambitious. At 1.5 miles the Geer Pond Trail comes in from the left; stay straight/right. Reach the Homestead Loop trailhead in 0.4 mile, at 1.9 miles from the start. Continue north on the road about 0.3 mile back to the Peak View trailhead to close the loop.

## --74--

# Homestead and Black Bear Loop

**Loop:** 2.2 miles
**Difficulty:** Easy to moderate
**Skill level:** Novice
**High point:** 9,650 feet at trailhead
**Elevation gain:** 300 feet
**Avalanche danger:** None to low
**Map:** Mueller State Park and Wildlife Area
**Contact:** Mueller State Park

This route offers expansive views of the Sangre de Cristo Mountains and is an ideal family excursion.

From the Mueller State Park entrance, drive Wapiti Road (the park road) west and then north 2.25 miles to the campground area. Homestead Trail is near the campground entry station, on the left (west) side of the road.

Begin the Homestead Trail near the campground entry station. The trailhead is well marked, with the statistics listed for more than one trail. You start off on a gradual downhill and immediately you will see the Revenuers Ridge Trail to the left. It looks like a hiking trail, whereas the Homestead Loop Trail is as wide as a service road. After 100 yards or so you can see the Sangre de Cristo Mountains in the distance between the trees.

The trail then plunges more steeply to the wetland valley through a mixture of stately pine and aspen trees. You cross the wetlands and go downhill for a bit and then climb up to the top of a short ridge. The trail then goes downhill again, curving right (north), and intersects with the Beaver Ponds Trail on the left at just past 0.75 mile; stay right on the Homestead Trail. It travels through a delightful aspen grove and tops out on a flat spot that is a good place for a snack or lunch. You then enter another aspen-lined valley and at just past 1 mile intersect the Black Bear Trail. The Homestead Trail continues straight ahead; instead, go right onto the Black Bear Trail.

This is a fairly hilly trail that rolls and goes uphill on the return. The last 0.5 mile or so climbs back up to Wapiti Road at about 1.6 miles. Walk south alongside the road for about 0.6 mile to connect the loop (or use a vehicle shuttle).

## OTHER TRAILS TO EXPLORE

From the intersection of the Homestead and Black Bear Trails at about 1 mile, you could continue straight on the Homestead Trail to intersect the Mountain Logger Trail in a short 0.7 mile, and then follow the Homestead Trail's pine-tree tunnel to get close to Grouse Mountain in another 0.75 mile. Then it is a somewhat steep uphill to the end of the campground road and the Cheesman trailhead.

## --75--

# The Crags

**Round trip:** 3 miles
**Difficulty:** Easy to moderate
**Skill level:** Novice to intermediate
**High point:** 10,900 feet
**Elevation gain/loss:** 800 feet
**Avalanche danger:** Low to moderate
**Map:** Trails Illustrated Pikes Peak, Cañon City
**Contact:** Pikes Peak Ranger District, Pike National Forest

The view from the top of The Crags is worth the effort, and the trail through the pretty valley is also worthwhile even if you don't want to summit. You can see the Sangre de Cristo Mountains in the distance, as well as the back side of Pikes Peak and the interesting landscape of Mueller State Park and Wildlife Area (see Routes 72 through 74).

From the turnoff 0.5 mile south of the Mueller State Park entrance, follow Forest Service Road 383, a narrow, slippery dirt or snowpacked road in winter that can be challenging because it is only plowed sporadically; four-wheel drive is recommended. At the minimum you need good snow tires. The road curves north and around to the south to The Crags Campground in about 3 miles.

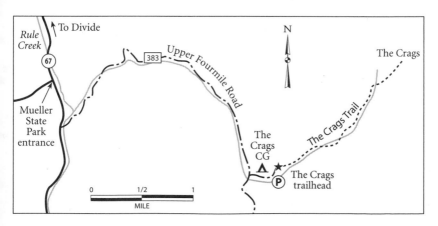

You might have to park outside of the campground and begin your trek from there. Go to the end of the campground road and you will see the trailhead.

Follow the creek drainage to the east and then northeast. There are trails on both sides of the stream and both will take you to The Crags. The right fork is a bit more tree sheltered, so it's a better choice if the snow cover is thin. However, it does have a short stretch of boulders that might require you to remove your snowshoes. The left branch is a bit more open and not as rocky. You could go up on one branch and back on the other for variety. Just achieving the ridge line in 1 mile is a rewarding experience because you'll get some views there. Use your own judgment of snow and ice conditions whether to go the additional 0.5 mile to the summit.

*Trail to The Crags*

# Appendix: Who to Call

--------------------------------------------------------

## AVALANCHE INFORMATION
American Avalanche Institute
P.O. Box 308
Wilson, WY 83014
(307) 733-3315
Email: *aai@wyoming.com*
Offers certificate courses in Colorado and Wyoming.

Colorado Avalanche Information Center
Aspen: (970) 920-1664
Colorado Springs: (719) 520-0020
Denver/Boulder: (303) 275-5360
Durango: (970) 247-8187
Fort Collins: (970) 482-0457
Summit County: (970) 668-0600
*www.caic.state.co.us*
Ultimate authority on statewide avalanche conditions and hazard ratings.

## ROAD CONDITIONS
Colorado (statewide)
(877) 315-7623

Colorado Springs
(719) 520-0020

Denver
(303) 639-1111

Rocky Mountain National Park
(970) 586-1333

## STATEWIDE WEATHER FORECAST

Colorado Springs
(719) 520-0020

Denver/Boulder Area
(303) 499-9650, (303) 275-5360, (303) 371-1080

Fort Collins
(970) 482-0457

Rocky Mountain National Park
(970) 586-1206

Roosevelt National Forest/Fort Collins
(970) 498-2770

Roosevelt National Forest/Summit County
(970) 686-0600

U.S. Forest Service/Aspen
(970) 920-1664

## CONTACT INFORMATION

### State Parks and Forests

Colorado State Parks
1313 Sherman
Denver, CO 80203
(303) 866-3437

Colorado State Forest
Star Route, Box 91
Walden, CO 90480
(970) 723-8366

Mueller State Park
P.O Box 39
Divide, CO 80814
(719) 687-2366
Email: *mueller.park@state.co.us*
*www.parks.state.co.us/mueller*

## National Forests and Parks
**Arapaho National Forest**
Clear Creek Ranger District
101 Chicago Creek, Box 3307
Idaho Springs, CO 80452
(303) 567-2901
*www.fs.fed.us/r2/arnf*

**Pike National Forest**
Pikes Peak Ranger District
601 South Weber Street
Colorado Springs, CO 80903
(719) 636-1602

South Park Ranger District
P.O. Box 219
Fairplay, CO 80440
(719) 836-2031

**Rocky Mountain National Park**
Estes Park, CO 80517
(970) 586-1206
(970) 586-1242 backcountry office
(970) 586-1319 hearing impaired/TTY
(800) 816-7662 Rocky Mountain Nature Association

**Roosevelt National Forest**
Boulder Ranger District
2995 Baseline Road 10
Boulder, CO 80303
(303) 541-2500
*www.fs.fed.us/r2/arnf/brd/vvc.htm*

Canyon Lakes Ranger District
1311 South College Road
Fort Collins, CO 80524
(970) 498-1100
(970) 498-2733 volunteer programs/Nordic Rangers
*www.fs.fed.us/r2/arnf/clrd/vvc.htm*

Estes Park Office
161 Second Street, P.O. Box 2747
Estes Park, CO 80517
(970) 586-3440

**Routt National Forest**
Hahns Peak Ranger District
57 Tenth Street, P.O. Box 771212
Steamboat Springs, CO 80477
(970) 879-1870
*www.fs.fed.us/mrnf*

Yampa Ranger District
300 Roselawn Avenue, P.O. Box 7
Yampa, CO 80483
(970) 638-4516
*www.fs.fed.us/mrnf*

**San Isabel National Forest**
Leadville Ranger District
2015 North Poplar
Leadville, CO 80461
(719) 486-0749
*www.fs.fed.us/r2/psicc/leadvile*

**White River National Forest**
Holy Cross Ranger District
401 Main, P.O. Box 190
Minturn, CO 81645
(970) 925-3445
*www.fs.fed.us/r2/whiteriver*

### *Private Organizations*
Beaver Meadows Resort Ranch
100 Marmot Drive, Unit #1
Red Feather Lakes, CO 80545
(970) 881-2450
*www.beavermeadows.com*

Never Summer Nordic, Inc.
Box 1983
Fort Collins, CO 80522
(970) 482-9411
*www.neversummernordic.com*

Tenth Mountain Division Huts Association
(970) 925-5775
*www.huts.org*

# Bibliography

Brower, David. *Let the Mountains Talk, Let the Rivers Run*. Gabriola Island, B.C.: New Society Publishers, 2000 (reprint).

Carline, Jan, Martha Lentz, and Steven MacDonald. *Mountaineering First Aid*. Seattle, Wash.: The Mountaineers Books, 1996.

Caughey, Bruce and Dean Winstanley. *The Colorado Guide*. 5th ed. Golden, Colo.: Fulcrum Publishing, 2001.

Daffern, Tony. *Avalanche Safety for Skiers, Climbers, and Snowboarders*. 2d ed. Seattle, Wash.: The Mountaineers Books, 1999.

Evans, Lisa Gollin. *Rocky Mountain National Park: A Family Guide*. Seattle, Wash.: The Mountaineers Books, 1991.

Ferranti, Philip. *Colorado State Parks: A Complete Recreation Guide*. Seattle, Wash.: The Mountaineers Books, 1996.

Fielder, John and Mark Pearson. *The Complete Guide to Colorado Wilderness Areas*. Englewood, Colo.: Westcliffe Publishers, 1994.

Graydon, Don, and Kurt Hanson, eds. *Mountaineering: The Freedom of the Hills*. 6th ed. Seattle, Wash.: The Mountaineers Books, 1997.

Hagan, Mary. *Hiking Trails of Northern Colorado*. Fort Collins, Colo.: Azure Publishing, 1994.

———*Poudre Canyon Cross-Country Ski and Snowshoe Trails*. Fort Collins, Colo.: Azure Publishing, 1996.

Jacobs, Randy and Robert Ormes. *Guide to the Colorado Mountains*. Golden, Colo.: Colorado Mountain Club Press, 2000.

Litz, Brian. *Colorado Hut to Hut*. 2 vols. Englewood, Colo.: Westcliffe Publishers, 2000.

McClung, David, and Peter Schaerer. *The Avalanche Handbook*. Seattle, Wash.: The Mountaineers Books, 1993.

Malocsay, Zoltan. *Trails Guide to Front Range Colorado*. Colorado Springs, Colo.: Squeezy Press, 1999.

Muir, John. *John Muir: The Eight Wilderness Discovery Books.* Seattle, Wash.: The Mountaineers Books, 1995.

Musnick, David, and Mark Pierce. *Conditioning for Outdoor Fitness.* Seattle, Wash.: The Mountaineers Books, 1999.

Prater, Gene, and Dave Felkley. *Snowshoeing.* 4th ed. Seattle, Wash.: The Mountaineers Books, 1997.

Roach, Gerry. *Rocky Mountain National Park: Classic Hikes and Climbs.* Golden, Colo.: Fulcrum Publishing, 1988.

Tremper, Bruce. *Staying Alive in Avalanche Terrain.* Seattle, Wash.: The Mountaineers Books, 2001.

Twight, Mark. *Extreme Alpinism.* Seattle, Wash.: The Mountaineers Books, 1999.

Walter, Claire. *Snowshoeing Colorado.* 2d ed. Golden, Colo.: Fulcrum Publishing, 2000.

Warren, Scott. *100 Classic Hikes in Colorado.* 2d ed. Seattle, Wash.: The Mountaineers Books, 2001.

# Index

**A**

Alberta Falls 130
Allenspark Trail 155
American Lakes 85
Arapaho Glacier 182
Arapaho Peaks Area 180–184
avalanche hazard ratings 28
avalanche safety 27–31

**B**

Bear Lake Loop 136
Beaver Meadows Entrance 120–145
Beaver Meadows Resort Trails 44
Big South Trail 64
Black Bear Loop 220
Black Lake 134
Blue Lake (Route 12) 68
Blue Lake (Route 54) 176
boots 17
Boreas Pass Road 200
Brainard Lake 171
Brainard Lake Recreation Area
     165–179
Buchanan Pass Trail 159

**C**

cabins 24
Calypso Cascades 152
Cameron Connection 81
Central Colorado 185–194

Chapman/Bench Trails 109
Chasm Lake 148
Cirque Meadows 62
clothing 19
Colorado Springs Area 214–223
Colorado State Forest 84–96
Colorado Trail West 197
Como Area 196–204
Coney Flats Trail 161
Copeland Falls 152
Crags, The 221
Crosier Mountain 114
Crown Point Road 53
Cub Lake 123

**D**

Deadman Road 48
Deer Mountain 121
Dream Lake 138
Dunkley Pass 97, 109–112

**E**

Elk Meadow Trail 219
Emerald Lake 138
Emmaline Lake 62
Estes Cone 147

**F**

Fern Lake 125
Finch Lake 155

Flattop Mountain Trail   140
Fox Curve Loop 2B   104
Friends of the Forest   35

**G**
gaiters   17
Glen Haven Area   113–118
Gold Dust Trail North   203
Gold Dust Trail South   202
Green Ridge Road   65
Guanella Pass Area   190–194

**H**
Halfway Gulch   200
Hogan Park Trail   98
Hollowell Park   126
Homestead Trail   220
huts   24
hypothermia   26

**I**
I-70 Corridor   186–189
Indian Peaks Area   157–184

**J**
James Peak   186
Jewel Lake   134
Jones Pass Trail   188

**K**
Kenosha Pass   197

**L**
Lake Agnes   88
Lake Isabelle   178
Leadville Area   205–213
Little Beaver Creek Trail   55
Livery Loop Trail   219
Loch, The   130
Long Draw Road   72

Long Lake   178
Longs Peak Trailhead   146–150

**M**
Meadows Trail   76
Michigan Ditch   85
Middle Saint Vrain Creek   159
Mill Creek Basin   126
Mills Lake   134
Mineral Spring Gulch   52
Mitchell Creek Loop   210
Mitchell Lake   176
Montgomery Pass   79
Mount Bierstadt   192
Mount Mahler   89
Mount Margaret   41
mountain sickness   31

**N**
Niwot Mountain and Ridge   169
Nordic Rangers   35
North Fork Trail   115
North Lone Pine Trail   48
North Longs Peak Trail   132
North Sourdough Trail   162
North Twin Cone Peak   199
North Walton Peak Trail 3C   100
Northern Colorado   39–118
Nymph Lake   138

**O**
Odessa Lake   143
Ouzel Falls   152

**P**
Peaceful Valley Area   158–164
Peak View Trail   219
poles   18, 23
Poudre Canyon   51–83
Preachers Hollow Loop   217

**R**
Rabbit Ears Pass   97–108
Rainbow Lakes   181
Rampart Reservoir   215
Ranger Lakes   93
Red Feather Lakes Area   40
Red Rock Lake   171
Revenuers Ridge Trail   219
Rocky Mountain National Park   119–156

**S**
safety gear   19
safe winter recreation   26–33
Saint Marys Glacier   186
Sawmill Creek   70
School Pond Loop   217
Seven Utes Mountain   89
Signal Mountain   57
Silver Creek   93
Silver Dollar Lake   191
skill level   37
snowshoes   13–17, 22
South Sourdough Trail   166
Southern Colorado   195–223
Sprague Lake Trails   127
Spronks Creek   109
Steamboat Springs Area   97
Stormy Peaks Trail   59

**T**
Taylor Hill   208
Ten Essentials, the   19
Thunder Pass Trail   85
Trap Park   75
Trappers Pass   44
Twin Lakes   212

**V**
Vances Hut   206

**W**
Walton Creek Loop 3A   100
West Summit Loop 1A   106
West Summit Loop 1B   107
Wild Basin Entrance   151–156
wilderness ethics   33
winter camping   23

**Y**
yurts   24

**Z**
Zimmerman Lake   76

# About the Author

Alan Apt has snowshoed, skied, hiked, climbed, and backpacked in Colorado for over thirty years. He is a reformed peak bagger who has climbed fifty of Colorado's highest 13,000- and 14,000-foot mountains. Apt is a former columnist for the *Fort Collins Coloradoan* and he served on the Fort Collins City Council for four years, working to make the wind power program available and to open the Poudre River Gateway Park. He is a member of the Nordic Rangers USFS volunteer program, Friends of the Poudre, the Colorado Mountain Club, the Sierra Club, and is currently on the board of Citizen Planners. He resides in Fort Collins with his family.

*Author in Rocky Mountain National Park*

THE MOUNTAINEERS, founded in 1906, is a nonprofit outdoor activity and conservation club, whose mission is "to explore, study, preserve, and enjoy the natural beauty of the outdoors. . . . " Based in Seattle, Washington, the club is now the third-largest such organization in the United States, with 15,000 members and five branches throughout Washington State.

The Mountaineers sponsors both classes and year-round outdoor activities in the Pacific Northwest, which include hiking, mountain climbing, ski-touring, snowshoeing, bicycling, camping, kayaking and canoeing, nature study, sailing, and adventure travel. The club's conservation division supports environmental causes through educational activities, sponsoring legislation, and presenting informational programs. All club activities are led by skilled, experienced volunteers, who are dedicated to promoting safe and responsible enjoyment and preservation of the outdoors.

If you would like to participate in these organized outdoor activities or the club's programs, consider a membership in The Mountaineers. For information and an application, write or call The Mountaineers, Club Headquarters, 300 Third Avenue West, Seattle, WA 98119; 206-284-6310.

The Mountaineers Books, an active, nonprofit publishing program of the club, produces guidebooks, instructional texts, historical works, natural history guides, and works on environmental conservation. All books produced by The Mountaineers Books fulfill the club's mission.

*Send or call for our catalog of more than 500 outdoor titles:*

The Mountaineers Books
1001 SW Klickitat Way, Suite 201
Seattle, WA 98134
800-553-4453
mbooks@mountaineersbooks.org
www.mountaineersbooks.org

The Mountaineers Books is proud to be a corporate sponsor of Leave No Trace, whose mission is to promote and inspire responsible outdoor recreation through education, research, and partnerships. The Leave No Trace program is focused specifically on human-powered (nonmotorized) recreation.

Leave No Trace strives to educate visitors about the nature of their recreational impacts, as well as offer techniques to prevent and minimize such impacts. Leave No Trace is best understood as an educational and ethical program, not as a set of rules and regulations.

For more information, visit *www.LNT.org*, or call 800-332-4100.

*Other titles you might enjoy from The Mountaineers Books:*

**100 CLASSIC HIKES IN™ COLORADO,** *Scott Warren*
The best of the best hiking trails in the most mountainous state in the lower 48. Thorough trail descriptions are illustrated with color maps and photos.

**BEST HIKES WITH CHILDREN® IN COLORADO, Second Edition,**
*Maureen Keilty*
Although the seventy-five trails in this guide were chosen with shorter legs in mind, they are also for anyone looking for a less strenuous but still rewarding hike.

**COLORADO STATE PARKS: A Complete Recreation Guide,** *Philip Ferranti*
All forty parks in this picturesque state are organized by region to help hikers, campers, white-water rafters, cross-country skiers, and other outdoor lovers explore the parks all year round.

**HIKING COLORADO'S GEOLOGY,**
*Ralph Lee Hopkins and Lindy Birkel Hopkins*
In fifty hikes, you'll explore the traces of the rise and fall of Colorado's mountains, volcanic eruptions, shifting seas, dinosaur haunts, and more.

**THE COLORADO TRAIL: The Official Guidebook, Fifth Edition,**
*The Colorado Trail Foundation*
Completely revised guide to the 471-mile trail, written for through-hikers of the entire trail or those doing a section at a time.

**SNOWSHOE ROUTES—WASHINGTON,** *Dan A. Nelson*
The most comprehensive guide to prime winter hiking in Washington, written by an editor with the Washington Trails Association.

**SNOWSHOEING, Fourth Edition,** *Gene Prater, edited by Dave Felkley*
How-to guide covering the latest in equipment and technique, plus tips on navigation and routefinding, gauging snow conditions, avoiding avalanche hazards, winter camping, and more.

**FREE-HEEL SKIING: Telemark and Parallel Techniques for All Conditions, Third Edition,** *Paul Parker*
A veteran instructor offers professional tips and tricks for all levels of expertise and for all snow conditions. Includes tips on buying equipment and physical training.

**BACKCOUNTRY SNOWBOARDING,** *Christopher Van Tilburg*
Introduction to the essential skills and techniques of the sport, fully illustrated with color photography throughout.

**AVALANCHE SAFETY FOR SKIERS, CLIMBERS, & SNOWBOARDERS, Second Edition,** *Tony Daffern*
Thoroughly illustrated manual on avoidance of avalanche hazards by skilled routefinding and recognition of dangerous slopes.

**GPS MADE EASY: Using Global Positioning Systems in the Outdoors, Third Edition,** *Lawrence Letham*
Updated for today's more precise GPS receivers ("Selective Availability" removed), this popular guide covers how GPS works, features of common receivers, and practical examples of GPS use in the outdoors.